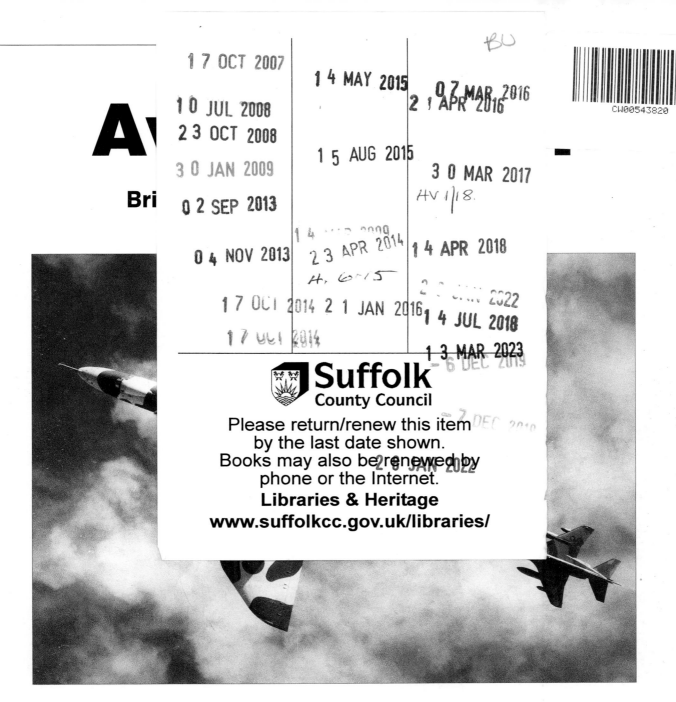

# A

## Bri

Phil Butler and Tony Buttler

**AeroFax**
An imprint of

**Avro Vulcan**
© 2007 Tony Buttler and Phil Butler

ISBN (10) 1 85780 256 X
ISBN (13) 1 85780 256 6

Published by Midland Publishing
4 Watling Drive, Hinckley, LE10 3EY, England
Tel: 01455 254 490   Fax: 01455 254 495
E-mail: midlandbooks@compuserve.com

Midland Publishing and Aerofax are imprints of
Ian Allan Publishing Ltd

*Worldwide distribution (except North America):*
Midland Counties Publications
4 Watling Drive, Hinckley, LE10 3EY, England
Telephone: 01455 254 450   Fax: 01455 233 737
E-mail: midlandbooks@compuserve.com
www.midlandcountiessuperstore.com

*North American trade distribution:*
Specialty Press Publishers & Wholesalers Inc.
39966 Grand Avenue, North Branch, MN 55056
Tel: 651 277 1400   Fax: 651 277 1203
Toll free telephone: 800 895 4585
www.specialtypress.com

Design and concept
© 2007 Midland Publishing and
Stephen Thompson Associates
Layout by Midland Publishing

Printed in England by
Ian Allan Printing Ltd
Riverdene Business Park, Molesey Road,
Hersham, Surrey, KT12 4RG

Visit the Ian Allan Publishing website at:
www.ianallanpublishing.com

# Contents

Title page: **The Vulcan K Mk.2 XM571 is seen refuelling an RAF Jaguar strike aircraft during the tanker's 'type trials' at A&AEE Boscombe Down.**

Below: **Vulcan B Mk.2 XH533 gets moving down the Farnborough runway during an SBAC Show. The four Olympus engines have left a thick blanket of smoke in its wake.**

# Introduction

**Vulcan B.1 XA891 photographed over the Mersey Estuary while on a test flight from A V Roe's Woodford factory airfield.**
via Tony Buttler

For well over two decades following its service retirement, and more than a decade since an example left the ground, the Avro Vulcan remains one of the most popular of British military aircraft. Just mentioning the name still brings plenty of interest and excitement (perhaps passion and emotion might be more accurate), yet this aircraft was actually designed to be the ultimate killing machine, a nuclear bomber. What really left its mark on the public however, was that fabulous wing shape and the tremendous noise and aerobatics the Vulcan generated during its display flying – remember that incredible rate-of-climb on take off! It had charisma in bucketfuls, but the type also proved to be very successful in service. It was operated by the Royal Air Force for nearly thirty years and, at the time of writing, it is hoped that an example will re-appear on the air show circuit during this coming year.

Vulcan has been well served over the years by books and magazine articles but here the opportunity has been taken to produce a new work, in part to mark the Vulcan's return to the public eye. It has also given the authors the chance to include a good quantity of previously unpublished documentary information plus an excellent selection of high quality photographs and illustrations, many in colour. The book does not claim to be the ultimate narrative for the type but should be seen as a complementary work to those that have gone before. In addition there is much here that will interest the modeller, including information on unbuilt variants, plus detailed histories for each aircraft built – in fact it is unlikely that such accurate airframe histories have been published before. Finally, documents held by the National Archives and in the hands of the Avro Heritage Centre have allowed a particularly detailed account to be given for the early design and development period.

Once again it has been a pleasure for the two of us to work together on a book describing such a superb aeroplane, and there are plans for future Aerofax titles covering more British military aircraft. To conclude, we must thank the following for their vital contributions – Air Vice-Marshal Nigel Baldwin CBE, Peter Berry, David Birch (Rolls-Royce Heritage Trust), Sir George Cox, Squadron Leader Joe L'Estrange, Flight Lieutenant John Farley OBE, Chris Gibson, Mike Gould, Graham Hopkin, David Howley, George Jenks and the staff of the Avro Heritage Centre, Barry Jones, Richard King, Gerry Manning, Flight Lieutenant Tim Mason, Group Captain Ted Mellor, the late Eric Morgan, Terry Panopalis, Cyril Richardson, Phil Spencer, Mike Stroud, and finally the staff of the National Archives.

The creation of the V-Force – the Vulcan, Valiant and Victor – was a huge achievement and displayed in full the creative talents of the British Aircraft Industry. For several years it formed the spearhead of the UK's nuclear deterrent. Almost certainly we will not see its like again.

Phil Butler and Tony Buttler
March 2007

# Glossary

A&AEE — Aeroplane & Armament Experimental Establishment, Boscombe Down.

AAM — Air-to-air missile.

AFB — Air Force Base (US Air Force).

AIEU — Armament & Instrument Experimental Unit, based at Martlesham Heath.

AoA — Angle of attack, the angle at which the wing is inclined relative to the airflow.

ARI — Airborne Radio Installation.

ASM — Air-to-surface missile.

aspect ratio — Ratio of wingspan to mean chord, calculated by dividing the square of the span by the wing area.

AVM — Air Vice Marshal.

AWA — Armstrong Whitworth Aviation.

BAC — British Aircraft Corporation.

BBC — British Broadcasting Corporation.

BCDU — Bomber Command Development Unit.

BOAC — British Overseas Airways Corporation.

C(A) — Controller of Aircraft (UK – MoS post).

CAS — Chief of the Air Staff (Air Ministry post).

CENTO — Central Treaty Organisation.

CFB — Canadian Forces Base.

CFE — Central Fighter Establishment.

CinC — Commander in Chief.

chord — Distance between centres of curvature of wing leading and trailing edges when measured parallel to the longitudinal axis.

CofG — Centre of gravity.

Critical Mach Number — Mach number at which an aircraft's controllability is first affected by compressibility: that is, the point at which shock waves first appear.

DMARD — Director of Military Aircraft Research and Development (MoS post).

EAS — Equivalent airspeed (a rectified figure incorporating a compressibility correction).

ECM — Electronic countermeasures.

EMC — Electro-Magnetic Compatibility.

ETPS — Empire Test Pilots School.

F/H — Flight Hours.

GPI — Ground Position Indicator.

HC — High capacity bomb.

HE — High explosive.

HP — Handley Page.

HRS — Heading Reference System.

HSAL — Hawker Siddeley Aviation Ltd. Avro became part of HSAL in 1963.

HTP — High Test Peroxide.

IAS — Indicated Airspeed.

IFR — In-Flight Refuelling.

ILS — Instrument Landing System.

IMN — Indicated Mach Number.

incidence — Angle at which the wing (or tail) is set relative to the fuselage.

IR — Infra-red.

JSTU — Joint Services Trial Unit.

LORAN — Long Range Aid to Navigation.

MC — Medium capacity bomb.

MoD — Ministry of Defence – created in the late 1940s to co-ordinate the policy of the three Armed Services. In April 1964 the MoD was reconstituted to absorb the functions of the Air Ministry, Admiralty and War Office, the Air Ministry (the civilian body that had governed the RAF) ceasing to exist.

MoS — Ministry of Supply – provided stores for the RAF from 1946 onwards. Disbanded and reconstituted as the Ministry of Aviation in 1959.

MRR — Maritime Reconnaissance Role.

MU — Maintenance Unit.

NAE — National Aeronautical Establishment.

NAS — Naval Air Station (US Navy).

NATO — North Atlantic Treaty Organisation.

NBC — Navigation and Bombing Computer.

NBS — Navigation and Bombing System.

NEAF — Near East Air Force.

NGTE — National Gas Turbine Establishment (merged with RAE, 1983).

nm — Nautical mile.

OC — Officer Commanding.

OCU — Operational Conversion Unit.

ODM — Operating Data Manual.

OR — Operational Requirement.

ORP — Operational Readiness Platform.

PDTD(A) — Principal Director of Technical Development (Air) (MoS post).

QRA — Quick Reaction Alert.

RAAF — Royal Australian Air Force.

RAE — Royal Aircraft Establishment, Farnborough.

rpm — Revolutions per minute.

RRE — Royal Radar Establishment.

SACEUR — Supreme Allied Commander Europe (NATO Force Commander)

SBAC — Society of British Aircraft Constructors (now Society of British Aerospace Companies).

SHAPE — Supreme Headquarters Allied Powers Europe (NATO Operational Headquarters)

SIOP — Single Integrated Operational Plan

SoTT — School of Technical Training.

TACAN — Tactical Aid to Navigation.

TACEVAL — Tactical Evaluation.

TAS — True airspeed (Actual velocity relative to the surrounding air mass).

t/c — Thickness/chord ratio.

TI — Trial Installation.

TMB — Target Marker Bomb.

TOD — Take Off Director.

TRE — Telecommunications Research Establishment, Malvern (became RRE).

**Vulcan B.2 XM597 seen landing at Waddington.**

# Chapter One

# Origins

For a period during the late 1950s and into the 1960s the Royal Air Force's V-Bomber fleet formed a very powerful and impressive weapon. Made of up three outstanding aircraft, the Avro Vulcan, Handley Page Victor and Vickers Valiant, its creation gave the UK a nuclear deterrent capability. In addition, during difficult times the ability of these bombers to deliver conventional weapons in large quantities gave politicians a tool for negotiation. The creation of the V-Force was also a huge achievement for the creative talents of the British Aircraft Industry and we will probably never see its like again. Such is the pace of progress however, that the Force's frontline role was soon cut back by the Soviet Union's acquisition of more effective defensive equipment. New fighters and surface-to-air missiles made the subsonic V-Bombers very vulnerable and in 1969 the country's nuclear deterrent passed into the hands of the Royal Navy with its Polaris submarines. The Valiants had to be retired prematurely in 1964 due to structural fatigue problems but the other two bombers soldiered on, the Vulcan serving into the 1980s and the Victor right through into

the 1990s, their duties now embracing other roles such as in-flight refuelling.

Which V-Bomber was the best is an argument that can probably never be settled. However, it seems fair to suggest that the Vulcan was certainly, to the general public, the most well-known of the three. In part this may be due to its long service career, although as noted the Victor actually enjoyed an even longer career. Vulcan however, appears to have been more active on the air show front (or maybe is remembered as such) and certainly hit the headlines in 1982 with its contribution to the Falklands War. People remember too that the type had enormous presence and its popularity was the reason why an example (initially XL426 and then XH558) was kept serviceable by the Ministry of Defence until 1993 as the Vulcan Display Flight, purely for air display purposes.

So how did the Vulcan and its sisters come into existence? In fact they formed just part of a huge RAF modernisation programme that got going in the second half of the 1940s to supply new aircraft in all categories. The initial stimu-

**The first Avro 698 Vulcan prototype, VX770, seen undergoing ground testing at Woodford, possibly before its first flight. Note the Hawker Siddeley Group logo on the nose.**

lus for the V-Bombers however, was the development of the jet engine, which made the RAF's piston-powered Avro Lancaster and Lincoln bomber fleet obsolete; faster jet-powered bombers were needed to replace them. Next, the development of Britain's atom bomb also required a suitable aircraft to carry it; in fact the arrival of the atomic bomb would actually prove to be the biggest driving force behind the development of all of the country's future bomber programmes. Finally, the ever-growing threat from the Soviet Union during the late 1940s added more urgency to these plans. In these circumstances were the Vulcan and its V-Bomber partners born.

In February 1945 the Air Ministry asked Short Brothers to study the possibilities for a long-range bomber powered by jet engines and capable of a range of 5,000 miles (8,045km). These studies continued throughout the year

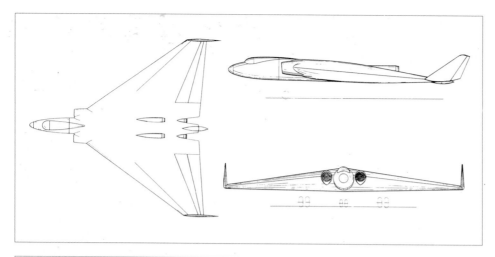

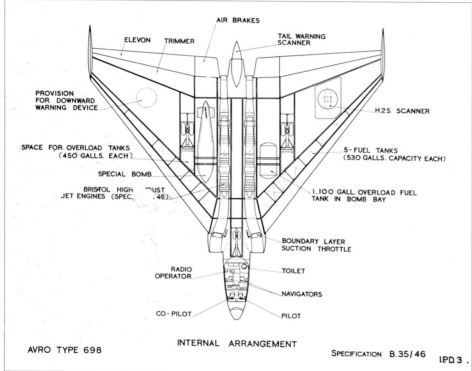

under the company's S.A.4 project number and in the summer of 1946 the Air Staff put together a fairly detailed outline for this type of aircraft. A long-range (4,350nm [8,060km]) bomber was what the Service really desired and it was covered by Operational Requirement (OR) 230. Alongside Shorts' offering, designs were also forthcoming from Bristol with its Type 172 and Handley Page with the HP.72A, and all three were assessed by the Royal Aircraft Establishment (RAE) at Farnborough. None of them were ordered and by December 1946, following advice from the Ministry of Supply (MoS), the Air Staff had changed its plans. It was now likely that the long-range bomber would result in plenty of design difficulties and, fully laden with fuel and weapons, it would be a huge aeroplane with a gross weight in the region of 200,000 lb (90,720kg). The size of such machines, coupled with the other major technical advances that they would introduce (such as swept wings), made it very clear that an OR.230 type of bomber would be extremely expensive to develop. In addition financial limitations would ensure that, at most, only a few squadrons could be equipped with this bomber.

**Medium Bomber Requirement**

However, studies also showed that an aerodynamically advanced design of bomber having around 75% of the range of the long-range aircraft could still hit most of the bigger type's targets. This was the direction in which the Air Staff chose to move forward and Operational Requirement OR.229 and Specification B.35/46 were therefore issued in December 1946 and put to industry for tender in January 1947. These documents described an aeroplane intended to hit a target at distances up to 1,500nm (2,778km) away while cruising at a continuous 500 knots (576mph/ 926km/h) and an altitude of between 35,000ft (10,668m) and 50,000ft (15,240m). The bomber's all-up-weight was not to exceed 100,000 lb (45,360kg) and, with a 10,000 lb (4,536kg) bomb on board, its still air range had to be 3,350nm (6,208kg).

The maximum weapon load was 20,000 lb (9,072kg), made up of either two 10,000 lb concrete piercing, two 10,000 lb HC (High Capacity), four 5,000 lb (2,268kg) HC or twenty 1,000 lb (454kg) MC (Medium Capacity) bombs, twenty 1,000 lb incendiary and fragmentation clusters or one Special (nuclear) gravity bomb. This last weapon, created against OR.1001, was later called Blue Danube. There would be no defensive armament, just warning devices, and two pilots, two navigator/bomb aimer/radar operators and

**Three-view drawing of the original Avro 698 proposal of May 1947, completed to B.35/46.**

**Internal detail of the May 1947 version of the Avro 698.**

**Drawing from the Avro 698 brochure showing the arrangement of radio and radar aerials.**

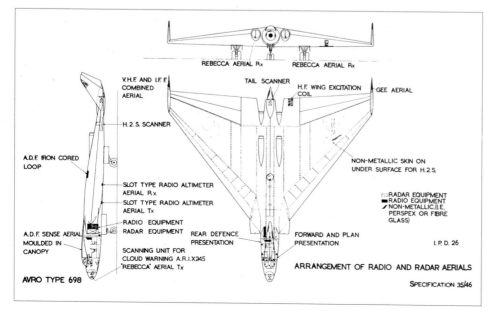

one wireless/warning and protective device operator would form the crew. The cruise ceiling (50,000ft) had to be reached inside two and a half hours after leaving the ground and the ultimate aim was maximum performance, which was not to be sacrificed unduly for ease of maintenance. However, the Air Staff still hoped that this medium bomber type, in the overload condition, might actually achieve the longed-for long range of 4,000nm (7,412km). The basic design of a medium bomber proposed to these requirements had to be an aircraft free from impediments such as blisters and external fuel tanks.

At this time the new problems faced by the designers were many and considerable. An A V Roe & Company (Avro) report from April 1951 noted that at speeds approaching the speed of sound it was necessary to sweep the wings back at a very pronounced angle to keep down drag and permit flight without burning an unacceptably high rate of fuel. Low wing thickness was also important while flight as far and as fast as possible with an economical fuel load required the pilot to take the aircraft as high as possible into air that was not so dense. Advanced aerodynamic shapes were bound to feature and the result was a major design competition between six proposals. This and detailed descriptions of the competing designs are available in another Midland book written by Tony Buttler and published in 2003 called *British Secret Projects: Jet Bombers Since 1949*. Suffice to say here that the rivals were the AW.56 project from Armstrong Whitworth, the Type 698 from Avro at Manchester, Handley Page HP.80, Short S.B.1 and designs from English Electric and Vickers. The salient points of Avro's May 1947 brochure for the very advanced 698 were as follows.

## Avro Type 698

Avro had established that it would be near impossible to meet B.35/46 with a conventional aeroplane, but the designers felt that a delta wing would provide the solution. Fitting such a surface to an aircraft was still largely in the realm of the unknown but Avro felt it would be easier to create such a type, aerodynamically and structurally, rather than adopting the possible alternatives of a swept wing and tail or a tailless swept wing. Designs featuring both of these alternatives had been studied closely and had indicated that, whereas the delta offered a gross weight at just over 100,000 lb (45,360kg), a tailless design could be as heavy as 137,500 lb (62,370kg) while it seemed impossible to meet the specification with a conventional swept wing plus tail aeroplane at any gross weight. In fact Avro claimed that the conventional aeroplane was no longer a sound

basis for planning new examples of such types of military aircraft. The desired high speeds would require input from recent and future research in aerodynamics while much more powerful jet engines than those currently available would also be needed.

In terms of control and stability the delta would be no more difficult to develop than the alternative wing forms, while structurally it offered great advantages. The depth of wing section inherent in a delta would take care of the various in-flight loads it would experience while, almost as a by-product, it automatically provided a great amount of internal space for powerplant, equipment, fuel and bombs, plus a low structure weight. The speed requirement of 500 knots (576mph/926km/h) at heights between 36,000ft (10,973m) and 50,000ft (15,240m), when the speed of sound was 574 knots (661mph/1,064km/h), implied that the critical Mach number (the start of rapid increase in drag with speed) had to be greater than Mach 0.872. This automatically made it

necessary to have a thin wing of high-speed section coupled with a large amount of sweep back. Avro concluded that a delta design was the only one which would meet the speed, range, load and weight limitations as laid down; it would also give the lowest possible percentage structure weight of any form of aeroplane.

The only excrescences on the 698 were the air intakes, jet pipes and a nose extension to hold the crew nacelle. The latter was designed to comply with the requirement that the crew should be able to parachute down in the section of the aircraft which they normally occupied. Pilot view was good and the inside of the nacelle was expected to be exceptionally quiet because heavy lagging was to be provided while the engines themselves were placed well behind. Power came from four 9,140 lb (40.6kN) Bristol 'High Thrust Jet Engines' (which later became the BE.10 Olympus), stacked superimposed in two pairs and buried in the wing. In the tropics the rated thrust for these engines was somewhat lower at 7,140 lb

(31.7kN). They were placed very close to the centre line so that if an engine did fail the offset thrust was very low and easily kept under control. The upper 'forward' pair of power units exhausted above the centre wing upper surface, the lower 'rear' pair through a cut-back section of the trailing edge. Two massive circular air intakes completed the powerplant.

Longitudinal control and trimming would be effected by means of trimmer surfaces controlled by irreversible screw jacks with electric actuation, and by differentially operated elevons which were both aerodynamically and statically balanced. This double elevon arrangement along the trailing edge was based on a system used by the Armstrong Whitworth AW.52 flying wing research aircraft flown in November 1947. (Armstrong Whitworth and Avro were sister companies within the Hawker Siddeley Group.) There were no landing flaps because the aircraft's low wing loading made them unnecessary and their presence would also have required a tailplane to counter pitching moments. Directional control was forthcoming from wingtip fins and rudders while boundary layer suction control (from a large valve in the air intake) was available for take-off and landing only. Wing thickness/chord ratio was 12% throughout and the fuel, 5,030gal (22,871 litres) in all, was housed inside the wing in ten equal-size tanks placed in the leading edge. With no proper fuselage available to them, the designers had split the bomb bay into two, one to each side of the engines. Both bays could hold eight 1,000 lb (454kg) conventional bombs but the standard nuclear load had the Blue Danube in the port bay with extra fuel in the starboard side.

The 698 would have an all-metal structure and a tricycle undercarriage with twin wheels on each leg. There was a full set of the specified radio and radar equipment including the latest H2S blind bombing aid with NBC (Navigation and Bomb Computer). The Avro 698's span was 91ft 6in (27.9m), length 92ft 0in (28.0m), minimum height 16ft 6in (5.0m), gross wing area 3,364ft² (313m²) and estimated all-up-weight 104,000 lb (47,174kg). At 50,000ft (15,240m) the estimated maximum cruise speed was 576mph (927km/h). This figure gradually increased as the altitude was reduced – at 36,000ft (10,973m) it reached 607mph (976km/h) and at 20,000ft (6,096m) 632mph (1,017km/h) (the bomber's highest speed); at sea level the 698 could cruise at 591mph (950km/h). At maximum weight the aircraft's sea level rate of climb was 5,900ft/min (1,798m/min), reducing to 2,911ft/min (887m/min) at 30,000ft (9,144m). The 698 met all of the performance requirements except for its gross weight (which was a fraction high) while the predicted altitude over the target would be slightly down at 49,000ft (14,935m).

The six proposals varied greatly in conception. Four of them, from Armstrong Whitworth, Avro, Handley Page and Shorts, were classed as being very advanced in design. The other pair were more conventional and in fact the assessors described these as semi-conventional. At this stage the Air Staff realised that its knowledge of aerodynamics, and to some extent of powerplants, was not sufficient to enable any of the advanced types to be constructed with any degree of confidence. However, it seemed probable that one of the more advanced designs was likely to meet the objective when neither of the less advanced efforts from English Electric or Vickers actually met the specification in full.

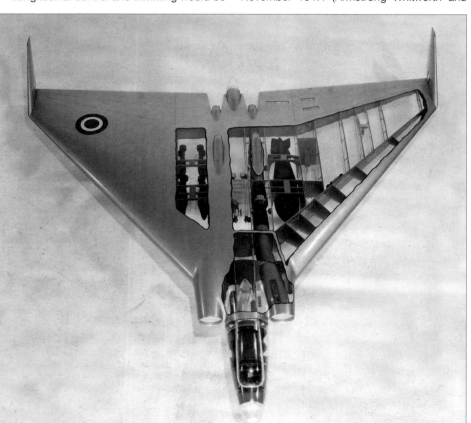

**This cutaway display model built by Avro shows the 698's internal detail including the air intake ducting, bomb bays and wing structure.**
Avro Heritage

## Four Medium Bombers

The B.35/46 Tender Design Conference was held on 28th July 1947 and eventually resulted in an agreement that an order should be placed for Avro's Type 698, together with a flying model to be designed and built in parallel to further study the delta's aerodynamics. The Conference felt that the 698 was clearly the most promising design with the HP.80 next and Armstrong Whitworth's AW.56 third. A meeting held at the Ministry of Supply on 27th November chaired by the Principal Director of Technical Development (Air), or PDTD[A], discussed the technical position on Avro's B.35/46 project. It was here that Avro proposed that flying models should be built to give preliminary information on the high and low-speed characteristics of the 698's design. This proposal was agreed and it was recommended that an Instruction to Proceed should be given.

RAE Farnborough was instructed to investigate the aerodynamics of Handley Page's crescent wing project, a totally untried wing planform, and in due course this too was ordered together with a flying scale model. The need for such flying models came from the fact that both delta and crescent wings brought with them a technical risk that could not be removed entirely by tunnel testing. The HP.80 was eventually named Victor and the first prototype flew in December 1952. For a short period it was expected that Armstrong Whitworth would also receive an order for a prototype and flying model, but this never materialised.

Because of the fact that both the Avro and Handley Page designs were very advanced, bringing with them many unknowns, in September 1947 the Air Staff and MoS agreed that it might be desirable to order a third type to the same specification but with certain relaxations on performance. This would allow a less advanced design to be employed, but such an aircraft would still have a better performance than a straight wing 'insurance' type already under development at Short Brothers (and discussed below). It would also require less prolonged development and testing than the Avro 698 or HP.80 and could therefore enter service ahead of the two more complex types. Thanks to the threat posed by the Soviet Union, a rather pessimistic view was currently being taken in war planning discussions and so an accelerated programme like this would be welcome.

Consequently, a further competition was held between Armstrong Whitworth, English Electric and Vickers which resulted in two prototypes of the Vickers Type 660 design being ordered to Specification B.9/48 (although still under OR.229). The first 660 flew in May 1951 and the type entered service in January 1955 as the Valiant, the first of the V-Class of bombers to join the RAF. (This aircraft is described thoroughly by Eric Morgan in another Aerofax title, *Vickers Valiant: The First of the V-Bombers*, published in 2002.)

A fourth medium bomber design would also reach prototype form: an aircraft built by Shorts

**The 'best of the rest' in the B.35/46 medium bomber competition was the handsome Armstrong Whitworth AW.56 flying wing design. This image shows a manufacturer's display model.** Ray Williams

in Belfast and later called the Sperrin. Short Brothers' proposal to B.35/46 had been a swept flying wing design called the S.B.1 (not to be confused with the company's S.B.1 research glider first flown in 1951), but earlier in this chapter it was noted how in 1945 Shorts had been asked to study a long-range bomber. The resulting design from that work was called the S.A.4 and was powered by six Rolls-Royce Avon jet engines. However, by April 1946 this design had been superseded by a smaller four-engine job fitted with moderate wing sweep which was also called S.A.4. In the following November the project was chosen to serve as an interim insurance bomber. Agreement was reached in February 1947 to order two prototypes, although the order itself was not placed until January 1948 (but still ahead of the prototype orders for the other three designs). Later the S.A.4 Sperrin was modified with a near straight wing and the first example flew in August 1951. The type was covered by Specification B.14/46 and Operational Requirement OR.239, but any plans for production aircraft were killed by the arrival of the Vickers 660. Only the two Sperrins were built.

Many books and articles have criticised the plans to build four different types of medium bomber at the same time. However, the development of each of these aircraft was a quantum leap forward over what had gone before. The RAF's then current Avro Lincoln heavy bomber used piston engines and had an unpressurised cockpit, so its speed and altitude were limited whereas the new jets flew much faster, much higher, had pressurised cockpits and advanced aerodynamics. Such progress alone was a big technical risk but there was also the need to introduce a nuclear delivery system as soon as possible – one of the advanced designs had to be ready, and working properly, very quickly.

In the event all four jet bombers flew well and suffered relatively few development problems. However, readers must remember that three contemporary British jet fighters produced during the same period, the de Havilland DH.110, Gloster Javelin, and Supermarine Swift, each suffered from structural or aerodynamic weaknesses. Some of their flaws were never cured and one or more of the medium bombers could quite easily have suffered major development problems as well, maybe even to the point of bringing cancellation to an entire project. In the author's view that situation justified the concurrent development of four different bombers. Aircraft design at any time, but particularly during the post-war period, has always been to some degree a matter of luck.

The man leading Avro's design team when the delta wing was adopted for the new bomber was Roy Chadwick. Chadwick had joined A V Roe & Company as a draughtsman way back in 1911 and designed his first bomber, the

Picture showing an unidentified Handley Page Victor B Mk.1.

XD823 was a production Vickers Valiant.

One of the Short S.A.4 Sperrin prototypes, possibly VX158 but the serial is unreadable.

Type 523 Pike, in 1916. His greatest and most famous creation was the wartime Lancaster and he rounded off his war efforts with the updated and enlarged Lincoln. After the conflict was over Avro looked closely at the anticipated boom in air transport, coming up with the all-new Tudor airliner for the North Atlantic route. The arrival of B.35/46 switched some of the emphasis back to military aircraft and here Chadwick favoured the all-wing type. During 1947, before and after a period of illness with shingles, he was either heavily employed on modifications to the Tudor or campaigning with the Ministry to get the delta wing bomber accepted. His workload was huge and then, on 23rd August, he was killed when the Tudor 2 in which he was flying crashed. It was an awful blow to the company because Roy Chadwick was considered to be the complete designer, personally supervising each detail of a new aircraft's design from paper drawing through to manufacturing line. His death threatened the jet bomber's future.

Although Avro had sadly lost its champion, fortunately the design of the Vulcan was still in good hands, namely one Stuart Davies. Davis had joined Avro in 1938 as assistant designer and by the end of the war he was the manager of the company's Projects Department. In late 1946 Chadwick was made technical director and Davies was promoted to the position of chief designer, with Robert Lindley moving up as head of the Projects Office. After his death, Chadwick was succeeded as technical director by William Farren who had previously been a director of RAE Farnborough. Farren's reputation within the aviation world was formidable and this gave Avro's standing a huge boost, but it was Davies and his team who brought the delta to the stage where it could be taken on as an acceptable configuration. As noted above, his team realised that its studies into conventional designs gave aeroplanes that were far too large, but by reducing the span and filling the wing out into a delta the aircraft could still have a large enough wing area. Dispensing with the tailplane also brought the weight down to an acceptable level.

## Design Evolution and Scale Models

Detail design of the Avro 698 Delta bomber commenced in January 1948. Since the issue of the tender brochure for the 698 however, many problems had arisen, a considerable number of which had been solved by alterations to the aircraft's layout. On 6th April 1948 Avro completed a 'Recent Design Development' brochure, which served as a current situation document for the Ministry. To begin with development work in RAE Farnborough's high-speed tunnel had shown a general need to introduce a way of retaining adequate control at air speeds somewhat above the critical Mach number. The solution suggested by RAE had been to add all-moving pointed wingtips outside the tip fins and these had been applied by Avro. However, their addition had also produced a substantial aft movement of the required centre of gravity which forced the designers to rearrange the 698's equipment completely. An advantage from adding these wingtips was an increase in wing aspect ratio from 2.5 to 3.0, which was in line with RAE's advice for obtaining a greater height over the target.

RAE's high-speed tunnel had also revealed that two changes to the original wing section were desirable to increase the critical Mach number to 0.88 and reduce the low-speed profile drag. The first was to reduce the wing's thickness/chord ratio from 12% down to 10% and the second was to move the chordwise position for maximum thickness forward from 40% to 30%. Avro felt confident that, with these two alterations, the 698 could now attain this critical Mach number, which the designers had chosen for normal cruise. Once the engines had been rearranged to line abreast and the wing thickness reduced, it was found preferable to use a single bomb bay on the aircraft's centre line instead of the two bomb bays shown in the tender brochure.

In its new form the Avro 698's span was 99ft 0in (30.2m), length 86ft 9in (26.4m), height 18ft

**Avro 698 as at 6th April 1948 with new additional wing sections outside the fins and side-by-side engines.**

0in (5.5m) and all-up weight 101,764 lb (46,160kg). Power would be supplied by four Bristol TE.1/46 (Olympus) engines, the estimated sea level rate of climb was 6,900ft/min (2,103m/min), rate of climb at 40,000ft (12,192m) 2,600ft/min (792m/min) and the time needed to get to that height was 3.4 minutes. Gradually the 698 was being turned into the Vulcan as we know it but the 'Design Development' document also noted that, despite many of the design problems met so far having been solved, it was clear that a large number of outstanding points would require much more research and development to find satisfactory solutions. This would be reflected by further changes in the 698's appearance.

This brochure also gave the first details and drawings of the planned flying scale models. To investigate the problems at comparatively low speeds and low altitudes, it was proposed to construct a one-third-scale aircraft called the Avro 707. This would be easy to produce, involving, as it did, wooden construction for the most part together with the adoption of existing standard items such as main undercarriage units, nosewheel, controls, seat, sliding hood installation, and the like. In general the performance of the 707, powered by a Rolls-Royce Derwent V jet engine, would be 400mph (644km/h) EAS up to 10,000ft (3,048m). This would enable all of the preliminary aerodynamic investigations to be undertaken in flight, particularly the problems concerning the landing of the delta aircraft. As proposed the 707 had a span of 33ft 0in (10.1m), length 30ft 0in (9.1m) and an all-up weight of 7,972 lb (3,616kg).

To investigate the problems surrounding flying the Delta aircraft at the Mach numbers and

operating altitude used by the bomber, it was proposed to construct a half-scale model called the Avro 710. Unlike the one-third 707, this aeroplane would simulate the full-scale machine much more closely and would enable a check to be made on performance, control and stability. Using the maximum continuous cruise power of its twin Rolls-Royce Avon engines, the 710 was expected to be capable of cruising at the bomber's specified speed of 575mph (925km/h) at heights up to 60,000ft (18,288m) if required. The 710's span was 49ft 0in (14.9m), length 44ft 9in (13.6m) and all-up weight 19,651 lb (8,914kg). Predicted rate of climb at sea level was 8,250ft/min (2,515m/min) when flying at a constant EAS of 224mph (360km/h), but much higher climb rates, particularly near sea level, would be possible when using higher speeds. Rate of climb at 40,000ft (12,192m) was 3,200ft/min (975m/min) and reaching that height would take 7.4 minutes. The 710 would carry 820gal (3,728 litres) of fuel in the wings and both scale models had the all-moving pointed wingtips outside the fins. The brochure's covering letter indicated that the 707 could fly in about twelve months and the bigger 710 in twenty-one months.

On 10th May the Ministry's R W Symmons responded to Avro's proposals because he felt that the brochure did not demonstrate conclusively the need for both scale models. Symmons wanted to highlight the real technical need for the provision of each type. He noted that the 'Avro design to the B.35/46 specification, though showing good prospects at meeting the requirements, does however mark a definite departure in general form. This form is chosen in order to reduce the drag at very high speeds to such a level that the fuel consump-

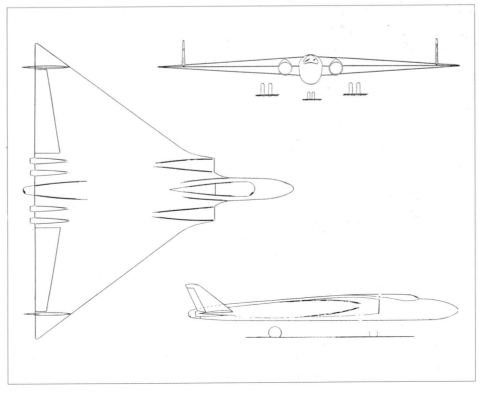

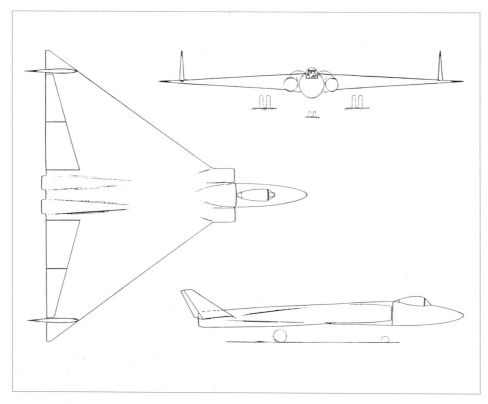

Avro 707 scale model design as first drawn, 6th April 1948.

Avro 710 scale model design, 6th April 1948.

and speed up its design and construction and it was not practicable to increase the performance of these machines enough to equal that of the full scale aircraft. However, nothing but experiments at the specified speed and height, 500 knots (926km/h) and 50,000ft (15,240m), could settle certain vital points. These could be achieved by the larger half-scale machine and Symmons declared that 'if as expected it solves the remaining problems of drag reduction at high speed, and the problem of control at high speed, it would be possible for us to accept a demonstration by this model as justification for placing a production order without waiting for manufacture of the full scale prototype'. The current political and world situation indicated that production of these new bombers might become a matter of urgency.

Symmons admitted that the 710 would not solve the structural problems of the full-scale 698 but, although difficult, these did not involve so many unknowns as the aircraft's aerodynamic features. It was thought that the structure problems would be soluble by normal development processes. This lengthy programme of development with flying models was therefore justified because it would allow knowledge to be obtained as quickly as possible, and which itself could not be acquired in any other way. Symmons concluded by stating that this programme might cut down the total development time of the bomber by nearly a year. Today the characteristics of the delta wing are well known, but in late-1940s Britain this shape represented a very revolutionary design and it was the desire to get things right that brought the need for a model programme.

## Refined Programme

An Instruction to Proceed for both models was given on 8th June 1948 with serials VX799 and VX808 allocated to the 710s and VX784 and VX790 to the 707s; design work on the 707s had commenced in May. On 19th July however, W G Perring, director of RAE Farnborough, wrote to J E Serby, Director of Military Aircraft Research and Development (DMARD) at the MoS. Perring explained that, while the RAE had always had doubts about the wisdom of building a large number of scale models of projected aircraft, they had hesitated to condemn the proposal to have two different models for this particular project because of its importance and novel features. However, after a full discussion, they had now concluded that the best programme would be to build a third-scale model as cheaply as possible, to omit the half-scale 710, and to build a full-scale flying shell. The justification in the 707 lay with its cheapness and in the increased facilities over and above present ongoing experimental delta projects (the Boulton Paul P.111 and Fairey

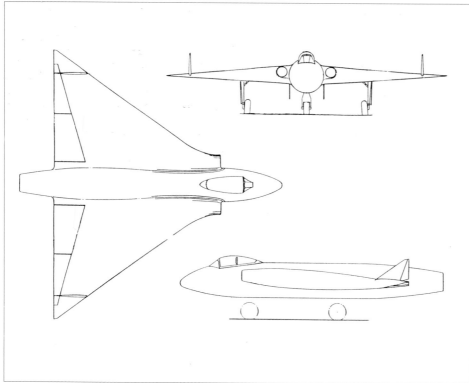

tion at the long range required will not exceed the capacity of the aircraft. The development of this new form will involve many very difficult problems, some of which may very well lead to danger in the experimental stages'. Symmons added that, as far as possible, problems would be solved in the wind tunnel but there was no equipment available in the UK or elsewhere that was capable of solving all of these problems. 'Some could only be solved in flight and this

could be done at less expense and more quickly by the use of flying models.'

The purpose behind Avro's one-third-scale model was primarily to investigate problems of control and stability and response at relatively low speeds and altitude, including that of landing. Unless these problems were overcome, the high-speed qualities of the delta were of no practical significance. Limiting this aircraft to a maximum of 400mph (644km/h) would simplify

Delta I) that it offered for low-speed work. It would also give Avro experience in working with delta wings and Perring noted that the 707 had a different aerofoil section to the other current experimental delta wing projects.

The reasons for suggesting the deletion of the 710 and building a 'flying shell' were:

1. The half-scale model would be a major design job and the difference in time spent in designing and building this or the full-scale shell was likely to be small.
2. There was reasonable hope that the general ongoing research work would enable the designers to avoid important troubles on this project at high Mach numbers.
3. If trouble, now unforeseen, did arise it might actually be of a character which would condemn the whole project. The 710 model would merely bring it to light a little earlier.
4. If little or no trouble was experienced then the building of the 710 would have delayed the design and building of the operational aircraft.
5. Both models, 707 and 710, were useless from a structural point of view.
6. It was important to bear in mind, in conjunction with these points, that there was some insurance against complete failure of Avro's project by the presence of the other high-speed bombers now being designed.

On the 26th Serby told Avro that it would be wiser and faster to do just the one size of scale model and Farren gave his support on 14th September, but he also suggested the addition of a third 707 modified for high-speed work. This would have a different intake and a stiffer structure. Farren also suggested a single flying shell 698 with no service equipment on board and the simplest possible fuselage, but otherwise having the same structure as a full prototype. He acknowledged that Avro did not have enough staff to handle the 698, 707 and 710 together, but noted that a certain additional risk would be involved when the full-size machine approached very high Mach numbers for the first time. He added however, that 'I do not now consider this as serious'. Farren thought this would bring a definite saving in time, advancing the fully equipped prototype by a year.

Farren's plans were accepted at an MoS meeting held at Thames House on 30th September, although in fact the 710 was not officially cancelled until 15th February 1949. The meeting was chaired by H M Garner, the Ministry of Supply's Principal Director of Scientific Research (Air) (PDSR[Air]), and involved Serby, Farren, Avro project designer J G Willis, Morien Morgan and Handel Davis from Farnborough's Aero Department, and the Ministry's H F Vessey and H G Jones. On 26th October Willis reported that the 707 seemed quite strong enough to operate to the same Mach number limits as the full-size bomber – 478mph (769km/h) EAS or Mach 0.95, whichever was

the lesser. It would be Willis and his team of engineers who would turn the 698 and 707 from paper concepts into metal aeroplanes. Avro was anxious to have the 707 flying as soon as possible and to this end was not in favour of fitting an ejection seat. This was agreed by the Ministry but with the stipulation that, due to the lack of such a seat, the speed should be limited to 300 knots (345mph/556km/h) EAS.

## Contract and a Single Fin

A development contract for the two 698 prototypes was awarded on 22nd June 1948. The delay between the Tender Design Conference and the placement of this contract came about because the MoS needed to be satisfied that the technical strength of Avro's team was sufficient to handle the project, a result of course of Roy Chadwick's tragic loss. Specification E.15/48 of 22nd October 1948 was raised for the original pair of 707s while E.10/49 (8th July 1949) covered the third machine (plus another two that were ordered later). E.11/49 was allocated to the 698 'flying shell' but in the event this aircraft was also dropped, its specification was cancelled and two 'full' 698 prototypes, VX770 and VX777, were built to Issue 2 of B.35/46 (dated 1st June 1948). These serials (and those for the 707s and 710s) were allocated on 22nd June with the development contract. The specified 20,000 lb (9,072kg) bomb load now included the Blue Danube, two 10,000 lb (4,536kg) HC or two 10,000 lb Blue Boar weapons, or eighteen 1,000 lb (454kg) stores. Blue Boar was a TV-guided glide bomb developed by Vickers for the V-Bombers and was to be built in 5,000 lb (2,268kg) and 10,000 lb versions; it was cancelled in 1954. While E.15/48 actually requested a maximum level speed of 350 knots (403mph/648km/h) at

altitudes up to 10,000ft (3,048m), E.10/49 marked the difference in the third 707 stating a maximum of 500 knots (576mph/926km/h) at 36,000ft (10,973m).

The next update design brochure from Avro was completed on 15th October 1948 and for the first time a large single central fin was in place instead of the tip fins. The massive round intakes had also gone, to be replaced by deep slit intakes that could feed two engines mounted side-by-side in the wing roots. The shape of these intakes however, was still different to final form and there were other subtle differences to the prototypes. Wing span was 99ft 0in (30.2m), length 95ft 1in (29.0m) and with four Olympus engines and a 10,000 lb (4,536kg) bomb on board, plus 40,900 lb (18,552kg) of fuel, the estimated all-up weight was now 109,806 lb (49,808kg). The drawing shows twenty-six different fuel cells, although some of these held overload fuel.

Although all along B.35/46 had requested two pilots, up to this point the possibility of actually having either one or two pilots had never been decided. In February 1949 a firm decision was finally made confirming that two were definitely required. The first edition of the Operational Requirements had also called for a jettisonable cabin for the crew, but by April 1949 the technical problems that this presented had still to be solved and so it was agreed that the prototypes should be fitted with pilots' ejector seats. A Preliminary Mock-Up Conference for the full size bomber was held at Manchester in July 1949 but so many changes were required within the crew and instrument layout that a second Conference had to be held on 30th September 1950. In fact there was also a third which followed in November of that year.

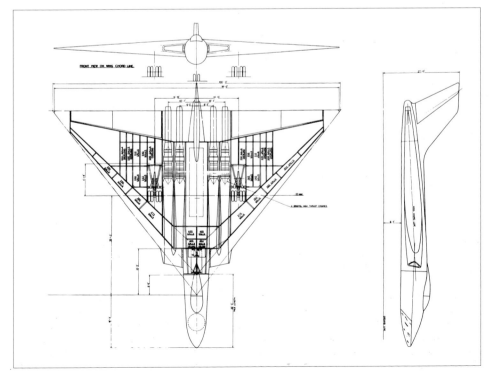

**Full-size Avro 698 bomber as at 15th October 1948 – now fitted with a single fin.**

## Nuclear Weapons and Engines

This is not the place for an exhaustive account of the development of Britain's nuclear deterrent but a brief summary is important to help explain some of the urgency behind the medium bomber programme. When atomic bombs were detonated over Japan in August 1945 they brought in their wake a strong shift in strategic thinking. These new weapons were so powerful and destructive that they would change the nature of war. Many now felt that conflicts in the future would be fought with these weapons right from the start, their delivery being achieved over vast distances, and so the possession of a nuclear arsenal became one of the key elements of a great power's status.

After the end of the Second World War Britain committed itself to maintaining its position as a major power and the development of an independent atomic capability was authorised at government level in January 1947. This

followed a decision made in October 1945 by the Joint Chiefs of Staff that the country should now design and produce her own weapons. In November 1946 America banned all overseas access to its own atomic secrets, a decision which brought with it an end to co-operation between Britain and America in this field. This provided a spur to opening the UK's independent programme and, despite the loss of the American partnership, Britain still had a supply of uranium available from Canada. The development of Britain's first atomic weapons was undertaken by a team controlled by Dr William Penney who was the MoS's Chief Superintendent of Armament Research. In the meantime the Air Staff drafted an Operational Requirement for an atomic bomb and this eventually became Blue Danube. The RAF's first Blue Danubes were delivered to the Bomber Command Armament School at RAF Wittering in November 1953. The weapon had a nominal

yield of 20 kilotons and was contained inside a casing derived from the wartime Tallboy conventional bomb.

To go with this weapon, the development of new bombers capable of carrying them over long ranges at high speeds and altitudes was approved and this brought forth the B.35/36 design competition and the programmes outlined above. After extensive trials the RAF revealed to the rest of the world that it now had a credible deterrent when a Vickers Valiant dropped a live Blue Danube at Maralinga in Australia on 11th October 1956. In their heyday Britain's V-Bombers operated as strategic weapons systems having been designed specifically to deliver nuclear stores after a high-level penetration to a target. Before the country's nuclear deterrent role passed into the hands of the Navy on 31st May 1969, the V-Bomber's alternative conventional weapon capability always came second to their nuclear duties. Blue Danube itself was withdrawn from service in 1962 to be replaced by more capable weapons.

Work on Britain's first hydrogen or H-Bomb, a weapon more powerful than an atom bomb because it employs the fusion rather than fission of atomic nuclei, got moving during the 1950s. During 1957 and 1958 the *Grapple* series of tests, with test rounds again delivered by Vickers Valiants, helped to clear these new devices for service. Britain's first operational megaton-range thermonuclear weapon was

**Clean Prototype. VX770 performs a gentle climb for the publicity camera.** Mike Stroud

**Clean Scale Model. The first Avro 707, VX784.**
Barry Jones collection via Terry Panopalis

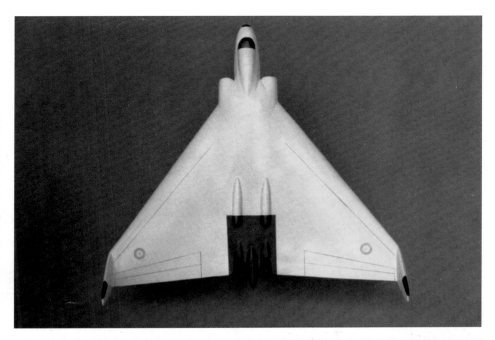

Three models showing the design process for the 698 Vulcan wing. The first is the original 698 as first proposed in May 1947, the second shows the wing as fitted to the 698 prototypes, and the third is the much larger form used on B Mk.2 production aircraft. George Cox

called Yellow Sun and during the 1960s it formed the backbone of the RAF's free-fall nuclear arsenal. Weighing around 7,000 lb (3,175kg), Yellow Sun Mk.1 gave a yield of 0.5 megatons and from 1960 it was carried by the Mk.1 versions of both Vulcan and Handley Page Victor. Other air-delivered nuclear weapons carried by the Vulcan included a selection of American stores, weighing up to 7,500 lb (3,402kg), which from 1958 were made available to Bomber Command under the codename Project 'E', although they stayed under US Air Force control. Their carriage by Vulcan and Victor was brought to an end in 1962.

The nuclear store that took their place, and the one with which the Vulcan is most associated during its nuclear career, was the Blue Steel stand-off missile developed against specification UB.198. Blue Steel was designed to be carried under the fuselage of both Vulcan and Victor, it was a substantial size and weighed more than 15,000 lb (6,804kg); length was 34ft 11in (10.64m) and span 12ft 10¾in (3.93m). Vulcan launched Blue Steel as a cruise missile and, if flown to its target at around Mach 0.9, the weapon had a maximum range of about 200 miles (322km). More typically, a launch at high altitude, around 50,000ft (15,240m), would give a 100-mile (161-km) range if the weapon completed its journey at high supersonic speed. Power came from a liquid-fuelled 20,000 lb (88.9kN) thrust Bristol Siddeley Stentor rocket motor and Blue Steel was guided by an Elliott-designed built-in automatic inertial navigation system.

The weapon's acceptance into service meant that, for a period, the Vulcan no longer had to try to penetrate a target's defences. The RAF's first Vulcan/Blue Steel unit was 617 Squadron, which achieved an emergency operational capability in September 1962 before becoming fully operational during February 1953. However, during the early 1960s the development of more advanced Soviet defensive systems made it clear that Blue Steel's stand-off range would soon be insufficient to guarantee that the V-Bombers could reach their launch positions at high level before being intercepted. Therefore, in 1964 the Blue Steel force was switched from high to low level and, in this attack profile, their missile was to be released 25 to 30 miles (40km to 48km) from the target a height of just 250ft (76m), zoom climbing to an altitude of 17,000ft (5,182m) before diving down onto its objective. Blue Steel was withdrawn in 1970.

The engines specified for the V-Bombers made their appearance at around the same time as the new airframes. The choice for

Vulcan was a Bristol engine eventually named Olympus and when the project design for this power unit was completed in 1949 the intention was to make it more powerful than any axial turbojet previously produced in Britain. In fact it became the world's first real two-spool engine, that is having a low-pressure axial compressor followed by a high-pressure axial compressor in series, each driven by its own turbine. This offered the advantage that the overall compression ratio could be higher than anything possible using a single-spool unit and this high ratio would be available over a wide range of running speeds. It also offered a low fuel consumption.

Design work on the Olympus began in 1946 and it was first run on the bench at Patchway on 6th May 1950, but for some time this new engine was kept just as secret as the bomber it was intended to fly with. The fact that the Olympus was to power production versions of the Vulcan was not made known to the public until the week ending 6th February 1953; even then the only data given out was the initial thrust rating, which was 9,750 lb (43.3kN). On 23rd December 1954 the Engine Division of the Bristol Aeroplane Company completed the Olympus's first official 150-hour type-test at a rating of 11,000 lb (48.9kN). This was the version to be installed in the Vulcan and indeed, at the time, it was the highest figure so far attained by a British turbojet, and possibly in the world. Prior to this, however, six production engines had been released at a reduced rating of 10,000 lb (44.4kN) to enable installation work on the first production aircraft to proceed. Failure in creep of the high-pressure turbine blades had been the main reason behind this temporary reduction, but in due course the problem was overcome. Uprating the Mk.101 to 13,000 lb (57.8kN) static thrust was planned by

adding an extra stage at the front end of the compressor, together with re-designed blading in the existing first four stages.

In 1956 the Vulcan engine was type-tested to 12,000 lb (53.3kN), by which time Bristol was working on the more powerful Olympus B.Ol.6 that would go on to be developed into the versions powering the B Mk.2. The ultimate Vulcan power unit was the 20,000 lb (88.9kN) thrust B.Ol.21, which in due course became the Mk.301. Throughout the 1950s the Olympus's great rival was the Rolls-Royce RB.80 Conway, which powered the B Mk.2 version of the Handley Page Victor (Victor B Mk.1s were powered by four Armstrong Siddeley Sapphire engines).

The Avro 698's delta wing shape was indeed a novel design and one outcome of this was that Avro put together a comprehensive set of ground testing rigs. These included an engine and wing test rig, something which at the time was unique, and the facility was built after experience had highlighted the difficulties of getting suitable and satisfactory conditions for an engine to run on the ground. The rig comprised a replica port-side engine installation together with a half-fuselage, the latter projecting some 10ft (3.0m) ahead of the air intake, and duplicated accurately the aircraft's equipment and ventilation. Each of the 698's intakes would feed two engines and it was predicted that disturbances from one Olympus might influence the intake conditions experienced by the unit next to it, which indeed proved to be the case.

Over six hundred hours of engine running in the rig proved most valuable in dealing with problems like this, and sorting out the arrangements for cooling and other important aspects. When Olympus units were first installed in the second prototype, VX777, the amount of engine running required on the ground had already been much reduced by work com-

pleted in the rig. Airworthy Olympus engines however, would not be ready for the first 698 prototype and in December 1949 it was agreed that Rolls-Royce Avon power units could be used on this machine to get it flying. The Avon was already in use on the English Electric Canberra tactical bomber, the first example of which had flown in May 1949.

**Avro Long-Range Bomber**

We began this chapter noting the RAF's wish to have a long-range bomber and a recently discovered document shows that Avro actually looked quite closely at the OR.230 requirements. This report was completed in July 1947 just two months after the original 698 brochure had been submitted. Avro's designers found that the OR.229/B.35/46 project could achieve the range called for in OR.230 at 20% overload. However, the 698 would have a gross weight of 124,000 lb (56,246kg) and fly at a lower altitude over the target, but with the same speed of Mach 0.88, 500 knots (576mph/926km/h). It was of interest to Avro to know what size of delta wing aircraft would be required to meet OR.230 in full, that is to raise the operating altitude over the target from 46,500ft (14,173m) to 50,000ft (15,240m).

In fact the answer was somewhat startling because the gross weight actually rose to 190,000 lb (86,184kg) – a heavy price to pay for an increase in altitude of just 3,500ft (1,067m) at the target. Also the OR.230 aeroplane would require four jet engines of 15,000 lb (66.7kN) static thrust each compared with the B.35/46's four 9,140 lb (40.6kN) units. One advantage of Avro's OR.230 however, would be its ability to carry 30,000 lb (13,608kg) of bombs as against 20,000 lb (9,072kg) on the smaller shorter range type, there being three bomb bays of the same capacity as the 698's two. The unnumbered OR.230 study appears to have been a scaled-up 698 (no 3-view drawing is currently available) with a span of 129ft (39.3m), length 120ft (36.6m) and wing area 5,940ft$^2$ (552.4m$^2$). Fuel load was 10,550gal (47,970 litres), all of it housed in wing leading edge tanks.

This chapter has concentrated entirely on the initial competition, discussions and ground work behind creating the Avro Vulcan and its scale model sisters. Perhaps what it shows most of all is the effort and thinking that had to go into the design and planning of these aircraft before any fabrication of such a highly important new bomber could begin. We have pretty well reached the end of the theory behind the delta wing, Avro's designs and all of the other items associated with them. Metal bashing was by now under way and it was time to get some flight experience.

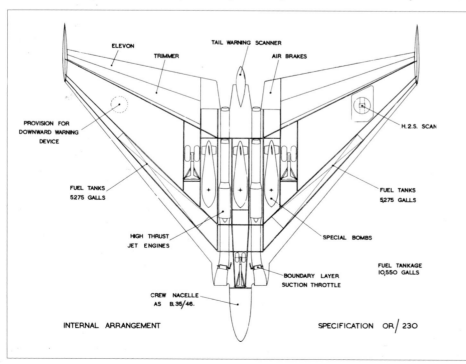

INTERNAL ARRANGEMENT

SPECIFICATION OR/230

**Planview of Avro's OR.230 study. Note the three bomb bays, flight control surfaces on the trailing edge of the wing and four engines stacked in two pairs. In most respects the shape of this aircraft appears to have been very similar to the Avro 698 to OR.229 and B.35/46.** Avro Heritage

# Chapter Two

# Scale Models and Prototypes

The previous chapter highlighted how the RAF's V-Bombers presented a massive step forward for the British Aircraft Industry in terms of capability and technology. Consequently the flight test programme for the new types, and their scale model test aircraft, were critical elements in the development process. Since the first 707 was the first of Avro's delta family to get airborne, we will take a look at all five of these machines in the opening part of this chapter. The 698 Vulcan prototype testing comes next, the whole lot of course embracing both manufacturer's and customer's trials. Much of the government and RAF testing took place at the Aircraft & Armament Experimental Establishment (A&AEE) at Boscombe Down, the centre for acceptance trials of new aeroplanes destined for service with the RAF.

### The First Avro 707

The drawing in Chapter One showed that, when first drawn and like the 698 at that time, the one-third-scale 707 had circular wing root intakes and fins very close to the wingtips. However, like the full-size bomber the 707 soon acquired a single fin on the rear fuselage, but it also had a dorsal air intake placed ahead of this fin. To begin with it was planned that the 707 would have a predominantly wooden structure and make use of numerous existing items of equipment. However, the structure was soon switched to all-metal although it was kept very simple with a fuselage of steel tubing covered in light alloy panels and a two-spar wing. To illustrate how savings were made the first machine employed a standard Gloster Meteor F Mk.3 fighter cockpit canopy and nosewheel plus the main undercarriage from an Avro Athena trainer. Thanks to the extremely short nosecone of the first 707, the pilot had a superb view. Powerplant was a single 3,500 lb (15.6kN) Rolls-Royce Derwent 5 engine and one 205gal (932 litres) fuel tank was housed mid-fuselage. There were four control surfaces on the wing trailing edge, the inboard pair were the elevators with the outer pair acting as ailerons. The first 707 was unpainted.

Specification E.15/48 required the low-speed Avro 707s to take enough fuel with them to allow a take-off and climb to 30,000ft (9,144m), flight at full throttle for fifteen minutes followed by cruising at that height for another thirty minutes. As noted in Chapter One, when this document was first released an ejection seat was not required unless the aircraft's maximum permissible flying speed exceeded

345mph (556km/h), but an amendment issued in April 1950 made one compulsory. A critical role for this aircraft would be the examination in flight of the high angles of incidence that a delta wing needed at take-off and landing. By September 1948 work was under way on the first 707, serial VX784, and after its completion in August 1949 it was soon carrying out some brief taxying trials at Avro's Woodford airfield. However, on 3rd August William Farren had written to J E Serby stating that, although the 707 had been assembled at Woodford, the Avro design team would prefer it to make its first take-off from Boscombe Down because of the long runway there. Serby was perfectly happy with this and told him to fix it directly with A&AEE.

As a result on the 26th VX784 was dismantled and carried by road to Boscombe, from where it completed a successful maiden sortie on Sunday 4th September (having made an unplanned hop the day before). In the cockpit was Avro's deputy chief test pilot Flt Lt S E Esler and, due to a strong crosswind, the flight was unable to go ahead until around 7.30 in the evening. How-

**Thrilling sight of two white Avro 698 Vulcan prototypes and four Avro 707s seen during their flypast over the Farnborough Show in September 1953. The second Vulcan prototype VX777 leads having just flown for the first time a few days earlier on 3rd September, the first VX770 brings up the rear and they are flanked by (clockwise from top) WZ736 (orange), VX790 (blue), WZ744 (silver) and WD280 (red).** Eric Morgan

ever, that was just in time to allow VX784 to make an appearance at the SBAC Show at Farnborough. After three more flights from Boscombe to ensure the type had enough 'on the clock' (a stipulated two hours in all plus three take-offs and landings), Esler flew the aeroplane to RAE on 6th September. The agreement that VX784 could be displayed at Farnborough, provided that it had completed sufficient flying, had been a spur for Avro to get the machine ready. To bring the CofG sufficiently far forward, it had been necessary to add 545 lb (247kg) of ballast in the nose. It was found that the little craft handled well and in a similar manner to a jet-powered aircraft of conventional configuration, although it did require a long take-off run. It was

agreed that after the show VX784 could continue its flight trials programme from RAE. However, it would not it fact see the month out.

On 30th September, on its first flight from RAE following modifications to the main flying controls, VX784 crashed into a plantation close to Blackbushe Aerodrome just seven or eight minutes after leaving the ground. Eric Esler was again the pilot and he had planned to perform some handling checks. He was tragically killed and the cause has never been accurately traced. At the time of loss, the machine was flying at low speed and low level. It completed its fall in a near-flat attitude with very little forward speed and the circular clearing made in the plantation was no greater in diameter than the wing span of the machine, there being no path or run through the trees. It appeared that, although flat, the machine contacted the ground in a slightly tail down attitude, but there was no penetration into the ground and the aircraft was pretty complete. The nose and centre fuselage were burnt out. Wind tunnel tests in the RAE's 11ft 6in (3.5m) and 24ft (7.3m) tunnels were immediately put in hand to check the control hinge moments and the effect of the dive brakes on these.

The accident meeting was held on 10th February 1950. It was considered that the wing air brakes had been fully lowered without operation by the pilot following a circuit failure in the electrical part of the brakes control system. It was not possible to identify the failure in the wreckage but it seems likely that this was a contributory cause of the accident. The pilot was probably also worried by light or overbalanced ailerons. During flight the fuselage airbrakes were also opened about one third of their range. These were in fact classified as braking flaps and when retracted they rested on top of the skin rather than flush with it. When operating they gave considerable drag and, at low speed and with the aircraft's already low thrust/drag ratio, high rates of descent. It is thought that this combination could have resulted in a flat spin with insufficient time to recover. As noted previously the pilot had no ejection seat. On later 707s the aft fuselage airbrakes were deleted and a set of retractable air brakes was placed on both top and bottom wing surfaces. Fortunately the delta wing had not been at fault but, following its first flight, VX784 had lasted for just three weeks and five days.

## Second 707

E.15/48 also covered the second aircraft, VX790, which became known as the 707B. As a result of VX784's crash Avro put in hand several changes to this airframe. Although already under construction, VX790 was redesigned with a 12ft (3.66m) longer 'custom-built' front end. The move was designed to improve the aerodynamics and push the centre of gravity forward, and it also made room for a Martin-Baker ejection seat. The cockpit itself was redesigned and a 12in (30.5cm) extension was made to the top of the fin. Instead of VX784's structure of welded steel tube, VX790 also introduced monocoque construction throughout. This aircraft made use of a nose leg from a Royal Navy Hawker Sea Hawk fighter, although later the fitting was modified by the addition of a 9in (22.9cm) extension to give a better angle of incidence at take-off. The first 707's long take-off run had been caused by a lack of incidence, which meant that the elevators had remained ineffective until VX784's ground speed was approaching its unstick speed. The most important changes from the accident were, however, a modified air brake and the installation of that ejection seat.

The introduction of such substantial modifications slowed things down and prevented VX790 from making its first flight until 6th September 1950, although a short hop had been

In contrast to VX784, there are plenty of photographs of the next scale model aircraft, Avro 707B VX790, shown in these two views. The nose-on angle gives an idea of the streamlined form offered by the delta configuration and the reduction in wing thickness from root to tip. Note the original air intake arrangement. Lower view: Barry Jones via Terry Panopalis

Close up revealing good rear fuselage and wing detail of VX790 in its early form.

achieved the previous day. Boscombe was again the venue and the pilot was Wg Cdr Roland J Falk. 'Roly' Falk had joined Avro in June 1950 to work under chief test pilot Capt J H 'Jimmy' Orrell, having served with the RAF right through the war. In 1943 he had become chief test pilot at RAE Farnborough and with Avro would forever be associated with testing the 707s and, especially, the Vulcan. In fact after Eric Esler's death the 707 test programme passed almost entirely into Falk's hands.

VX790 was displayed statically at that year's Farnborough Show, arriving two days after the event had opened. It then went to Boscombe to begin a full 707 flight test programme for the first time, completing over one hundred hours of research flying over the next twelve months operating out of both Boscombe and Dunsfold. The tests included the investigation of two different landing techniques – in one the nose was held right up to reduce the landing speed, in the other use was made of a small anti-spin parachute. On the 21st September 1951 VX790 suffered a landing accident but full repairs were completed at Woodford and the aircraft returned to the air in 1952. Its demonstration at

the Farnborough Show in September 1952 was flown by 'Jimmy' Orrell and afterwards VX790 stayed with RAE where it was used on general delta wing and other research work.

The nose leg extension made to VX790 also had to be made to the Vulcan undercarriage. A January 1951 brochure noted how it had been found on the 707B that, due to the abnormally far forward position of the CofG relative to the rear wheels of the aircraft, the pilot was unable to raise the nosewheel until after the normal take-off speed was reached. The take-off therefore needed careful judgement and required a greater distance than should have been expected. As a result the larger vertical strut was fitted, which automatically gave a higher ground incidence, and this did reduce the take-off run.

By January 1951 VX790 had flown for some thirty-seven hours at speeds between 438mph (704km/h) EAS and the stall at 94mph (152km/h), and some 177 landings had been completed. A considerable body of flight test evidence had been accumulated which showed that, over the conditions tested, a tailless aircraft could exhibit entirely satisfactory

flying qualities. An Avro report noted that the following had been examined and confirmed, all of which were applicable to the 698: neutral point and static margin, dynamic longitudinal stability, effectiveness and power of all three controls, behaviour in sideslips and at high rates of roll, dynamic lateral stability, stalling behaviour, approach and landing including crosswind, and air brake size.

The 707B was a very docile aeroplane. Its flight characteristics were examined across the full speed range between about 94mph (152km/h) and 400mph (644km/h), but disturbed airflow produced by the cockpit canopy at higher speeds was found to impede that entering the intake, resulting in partial starvation. Consequently, to allow the higher speed work to be completed, some structural modifications had to be made to the intake geometry. These comprised a deeper guide channel and also extra depth to the intake itself, which between them produced a pronounced 'hump' to the back of the aircraft. The alterations were made in February 1951 and gave a much-improved airflow to the engine in all regimes, particularly at high angles of attack. This was fine for the little 707B but irrelevant to the Vulcan itself and thus affected the timing of the whole programme.

One discovery that did benefit the full-sized bomber, however, was that angling the 707's jet exhaust could reduce the need for changes of trim. Consequently, the designers arranged for the 698's jet nozzles to be angled slightly outwards and downwards which improved the Vulcan's stability, while also permitting a reduction in the size of its fin.

Trials with VX790 showed that the delta configuration was fine and Falk rolled and looped the aircraft without trouble. Lateral control

**Air-to-air view of VX790 in its original form without the raised intake lip.** Mike Stroud

**VX790 seen early in its career preparing to land.**

Views of VX790 made by Avro after the air intake had been modified in February 1951. Sadly these images are in black and white preventing us from seeing the aircraft's bright blue colour scheme. However, what is visible are the prototype 'P' marking and Hawker Siddeley logo on the extended nose, and a small edition of the Avro logo on the forward part of the fin.

## High-Speed Machines

Specification E.10/49 covered the high-speed Avro 707, still built at one-third scale of course, and the document requested the same flight profile and fuel requirement as the slow-speed machines, except that the quoted height was now 40,000ft (12,192m). One Rolls-Royce Derwent 5 engine was to be fitted and the aircraft had to be capable of aerobatics. An ejection seat was required, the air intakes would be in the wing leading edges and dive recovery flaps were to be provided. An amendment dated 17th December 1951 added that a pressure cabin should be provided but in fact no 707 ever received a pressurised cockpit. As a result 'Roly' Falk had to be hyperventilated with oxygen for an hour prior to undertaking any high-altitude flying. The aircraft covered by this specification, whose serial WD280 was granted on 6th May 1949, was known as the 707A.

WD280's construction was undertaken at Woodford and the machine's forward fuselage was identical to the 707B, but there was a new wing complete with bifurcated root intakes; this made it very representative of the Vulcan except of course for the back end. Avro's initial proposal had suggested that the dorsal intake used on the earlier machines should be retained, but this idea was not received with any favour by the MoS and so Avro had to agree to fit wing root intakes. The wing itself, like the 707B, used a two-spar structure but the rear spar had been repositioned. Apart from a small inboard section that was straight, the wing trailing edge was now swept very slightly. The inboard straight section's new and separate control acted as the dive recovery flap and there were new ailerons and elevators that, with the wing root intakes, were all fully to scale. From the fuselage side outboard the wing was to be an exact aerodynamic replica of the 698 wing but, since the body diameter of the 707 was more than one third of the 698, the span would of course be slightly larger than a correct one-third scale. The removal of the dorsal intake and an extended fin fairing made for a more balanced and handsome aeroplane. On the level WD280 could never be supersonic but, instead of the specified Derwent V, it did get a more powerful Derwent 8 of 3,600 lb (16.0kN) thrust to help it achieve higher speeds.

could be maintained right down to 115mph (185km/h), at which point the nose would drop, while a 30° angle of attack could be held without stalling when a conventional-wing aircraft would have struggled to go above 15° without losing its lift. It is believed VX790 was also used for a trial carrying underwing stores on a pylon placed a little outboard of the underside air-brakes. The aeroplane passed into the hands of the Empire Test Pilots' School at Farnborough on 26th January 1956 but suffered another landing accident on 25th September. This time it was seriously damaged, to the point that repairs would not be worth the cost, and so VX790's flying career came to an end. In October 1957 it was transferred by road to RAE's facility at Bedford and on 8th November VX790 was struck off charge to be used as a spares supply for the other 707s. The airframe was later scrapped.

**Panned-camera view of VX790 about to touch down.**

**VX790 was similar to VX784 but had a lengthened nosewheel to assist take-off, a longer nose and different canopy. All of these features are clearly seen in this view, as is the 'hump' of the revised air intake. Venue unknown (possibly Boscombe) but the picture is dated 8th July 1955.** Eric Morgan

**VX790 photographed on display at Thorney Island on 15th September 1956. The nose writing says 'Empire Test Pilot's School', the aircraft having joined ETPS the previous January 26th in order to give future test pilots some experience with delta wings.** Eric Morgan

WD280 took off on its maiden flight from Boscombe Down on 14th June 1951 with Falk in the cockpit. To begin with this aircraft had manual controls but some stability problems were encountered, the principal difficulty being oscillation in pitch caused by an out-of-phase movement of the elevators. After more than a year WD280 was fitted with powered controls that cured the trouble completely, but once again this problem had nothing to do with the Vulcan itself. In fact by now the relevance of the 707 programme to the Vulcan was reducing all the time. Progress on the bomber's development had in many areas rather left the models behind and so these later 707s made little direct contribution to the Vulcan's progress. In fact the first Vulcan flew in August 1952, just after Avro had received its first production contract for the type, and this meant that by mid-1951 much of the full-size design had been frozen and the manufacture of components was well under way. Test flights on the first 707A did however affect one important area.

During flight at maximum altitude and speed to explore buffet boundaries, a pronounced wing 'buzz' (high-frequency vibration) was experienced when WD280 began to pull 'G'. This had to be rectified because the bomber would reach such speeds and heights quite easily. Wing fences failed to achieve a desirable result and the eventual solution introduced compound sweepback and a kink to the outer portion of the leading edge. The inner

**This Avro photograph of 707A WD280 revealing plenty of underside detail.**

**Although designed to undertake the high-speed end of the 707 flight test programme, WD280 is here given the chance to show its slow-speed performance as it formates on a biplane camera aircraft.**

**In contrast, a 'high-speed' air-to-air shot of WD280.** Barry Jones via Terry Panopalis

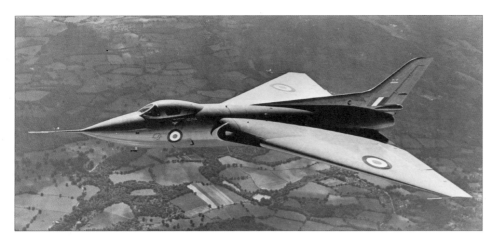

Two Avro air-to-air images of WD280.
Terry Panopalis

**Print made from a small snapshot showing one of the Avro 707As on display at an air show.**
Eric Morgan

**Manufacturer's view of the second Avro 707A WZ736 showing the wing root intakes and extended vertical fin fairing.**

part of the outer wing had its sweep angle reduced but the outermost section was swept even more. This new wing form was test flown on WD280, the aircraft being modified at Bracebridge Heath, and proved a success. Unfortunately, several production Vulcans had already been completed with the original wing so the switch to what was called the Phase 2 Wing made necessary a rather expensive modification programme. This discovery highlights perfectly the value of flying scale model aeroplanes and almost all Mk.1 Vulcans would be fitted with the kinked wing.

In 1953 WD280 attended the Paris Air Show, taking part in the weekend displays at Le Bourget on the 4th and 5th of July. After completing some general research work with RAE, which included an assessment of handling with powered controls, in the spring of 1956 this aircraft left England for further service in Australia. The possibility of Australia acquiring one of the 707s for research came through a recommendation made in early 1955 by the Commonwealth Aeronautical Advisory Research Council. Discussions between the two governments began at senior level in March with a meeting at Woodford. The idea was accepted and in November WD280 was selected as the airframe to be supplied. There were a number of plus points for choosing this particular aeroplane, not least the fact that Gloster Meteor fighters flown by the Royal Australian Air Force (RAAF) also used Derwent 8 power units, so plenty of spare parts would be available. The acquisition of a 707 by the Australians brought with it much speculation in the press that Australia might buy the Vulcan.

WD280 departed RAF ownership on 3rd March 1956 and arrived in Australia aboard the aircraft carrier HMAS *Melbourne* on 11th May. It made its first flight on 13th July and, to begin with, its tasks included buffet research and then flow separation studies, the aircraft being based at RAAF Laverton. During the establishment of drag curves it had been found that two different conditions of drag existed and these were investigated more thoroughly in another test programme. Carborundum dust or grit of varying coarseness was glued to the wing undersurface and it was found that at low speeds the rougher finish gave much improved control and more aileron and elevator effectiveness.

From July 1959 onwards this research was extended to include the pouring of kerosene over the port wing when in flight, the objective being to trace the path of the boundary layer. The wing itself was coated in black shellac and had a fine layer of white china clay on top. The clay was very porous and the kerosene made it translucent, thereby revealing the black undercoat and thus the flow pattern of the boundary layer. Next came some tests at very low speeds to determine the delta's dynamic stability characteristics. In fact most of WD280's work in Australia was undertaken at low speeds when of course this machine had been built as a high-speed test aircraft. WD280 made its last flight in 1963 and then went into store. It was struck off charge on 10th February 1967.

Returning to events in Britain, at the request of RAE two more 707As had been ordered for more general research as part of a contract issued on 13th November 1951. These aircraft, WZ736 and WZ739, were ordered along with an example of a two-seat 707C, WZ744, for pilot training. WZ739 was later cancelled. RAE wished to use the second 707A for basic research, taking the testing of its delta wing a stage further than Avro, measuring the various possible derivatives and comparing this with other data in an attempt to predict the characteristics of future types. At this time Avro had a long programme of work planned for the first 707A so the company was unlikely to be in a position where it could release that aircraft to RAE.

The three serials were allocated on the same day under E.10/49 and WZ736 followed WD280 into the air on 20th February 1953. This aeroplane, together with 707C WZ744 (below), was built at Bracebridge Heath near Lincoln which

**Head-on shot of WZ736. The elevators are deployed thus revealing the three control surfaces along each trailing edge; starting inboard the narrow surface was the dive recovery flap, next came the elevator and, furthest out, the aileron.** Eric Morgan

**An Avro 707A pictured, most probably, at one of the SBAC Shows at Farnborough. This is almost certainly WZ736.**

**WZ736 photographed at Cottesmore, still in service and painted in a yellow colour scheme with black trim.**

**This air-to-air picture presents the last in the series of Avro 707 prototypes, the solitary 707C WZ744. Later a TV camera was fitted to the leading edge of the fin.**
Mike Stroud

**Another air-to-air image of WZ744 which shows beautifully the small cockpit canopy for the two side-by-side seated crew, the wing root intakes and both sets of airbrakes fully deployed. Note also the matt black anti-glare panel in front of the canopy.**

**WZ744's flat windscreen is seen to advantage in this view.**
Terry Panopalis

was the home of Avro's repair and overhaul organisation. Both aeroplanes had to be towed by road to RAF Waddington for their first flights and RAE Farnborough used WZ736 for many tasks including the development of automatic throttles. This was important because the huge rise in drag created by a delta wing at high incidence when the aircraft was on the approach to land had to be compensated for, and a facility that could do this automatically was very helpful. WZ736 was struck off charge in May 1962 to act as a spares source for WZ744 below.

## Two Seater

On 22nd November 1951 Issue 2 of E.10/49 was released to cover a two-seat dual-control version of the 707 to be used for delta training within the RAF (a role which in the end was never required). The powerplant was to be a Derwent 8, fed again from wing leading edge intakes, and in fact the only difference to the second 707A was the new two-seat cockpit. Because no increase in fuselage width had been provided, this was a very cramped affair and the shortage of space prevented the installation of ejection seats. Circular side windows fitted into the metal canopy also offered poor lateral vision.

As noted above, two machines were ordered as 707Cs but the first, WZ739, was never built. The second, WZ744, was flown for the first time on 1st July 1953 by Sqn Ldr T B Wales before going to Woodford for its manufacturer's trials. From 1958 WZ744 was used by RAE on some of the earliest research into fly-by-wire control systems, a feature that is today commonplace on many types of aircraft. The benefit of using the two-seat WZ744, however, was that the new circuits could duplicate the normal system. One set of pilot's controls would keep their manual operation while the other received electronic control, and this provided the opportunity to make a relatively easy comparative assessment. WZ744 stayed on RAE strength until June 1966, at which point it was released for preservation.

WZ744 completed a quartet of flying 707s and at the 1953 Farnborough Show the opportunity was taken to display all four of them and both Vulcan prototypes together, flown by Avro and RAE test pilots. When the colourful little 707s performed a flypast in formation with the two white Vulcans they left an enormous impression on the public. *Flight* described the event thus. 'Towards the airfield from Laffan's Plain came a new type of formation – a delta formed by deltas. In the lead was the large white Olympus-Vulcan, in an impeccable vee formation were poised the attendant silver, red, blue and orange 707s, and in the box was the Sapphire-Vulcan that by itself had stolen the show just one year ago. Again the show had been stolen – this time by six of the dart-like shapes.'

In fact the 707 family is well remembered for its paint schemes, which followed a theme of non-standard brilliant colours. The original

**Mood silhouette picture of one of the Vulcan prototypes and the four 707s flying in formation in 1953. The black outline of the Vulcan is quite intimidating.**

VX784 had an unpainted metal finish but the 707B (VX790) set the trend when it appeared in a glossy bright blue livery. WD280 was initially salmon pink but this (thankfully?) was quickly changed to a bright red scheme; WZ736's glossy orange completed the A-series. The two-seater must have seemed a touch demure because it was painted silver with a matt black anti-glare panel in front of the canopy.

The Avro 707 has been particularly fortunate in the preservation field because three out of the five airframes built still survive. After its withdrawal, the Australia-based WD280 was bought privately and put on display in its new owner's back garden in Williamstown, Melbourne, where it was kept in superb condition for over thirty years. In May 1999 it joined the RAAF Museum at Point Cook. On retirement, both WZ736 and WZ744 went to the RAF Museum's Reserve Collection at Finningley as ground instruction airframes. Today the former is housed in the Manchester Museum of Science and Industry and the 707C is held by the Aerospace Museum at Cosford.

The benefits of the Avro 707s to the full-size bomber programme were mixed. The compound sweep wing and modifications to the powerplant exhaust arrangement were a big help, but the first of these still necessitated an expensive modification to completed Vulcan wings. One weakness of the 707 programme was that delays were caused by solving problems relevant only to the scale model aeroplanes and not the full-size bomber. For example the 707B was fitted with manual controls that produced a pitching oscillation (although in many respects manual controls were also beneficial, as Roly Falk reveals in a moment). The consequent investigation of out-of-phase movements of the manual elevators consumed time and effort when the bomber would use powered controls anyway; when powered controls were applied to the 707A, the

**This 1953 publicity shot of both Vulcan prototypes and the four 707s all flying together is well known, but still impressive.** Eric Morgan

oscillation disappeared. As a result some of the synchronisation in the overall programme of Vulcan and 707 was lost, a fact that is usually criticised in published works. With hindsight it is easy to make such criticisms, yet the fact that the first prototype was lost right at the start of the programme is often forgotten. That crash prevented any test flying for over a year and modifications had to be introduced to the second 707.

It must also be said that the family of Avro 707s did prove extremely useful in providing data for the aircraft industry in general, a point that cannot be made against several of the plentiful supply of British experimental jet aircraft built and flown during the 1950s. One might say that this was one of the most successful groups of research aeroplanes to be produced and they also fully vindicated the concept of the delta wing in the eyes of Government, RAF and manufacturer. In fact throughout the first half of the 1950s Avro promoted the delta wing as 'The Shape of the Future'. When the 707 was first proposed as a one-third-scale model of the Vulcan, it is very doubtful if anyone at Avro could have predicted that members of the family would still be operating in the mid-1960s.

## A Delight to Fly

Test pilot Roly Falk recorded some of his thoughts and memories from flying the 707B in a report written in April 1951. For the sake of simplicity, to begin with it was decided that the 707B should fly without power operation of the controls. This paid very good dividends in serviceability and Avro was able to concentrate entirely on developing the aeroplane. On the evening of 5th September 1950, a year and a day after VX784's first flight, VX790 was complete and ready to fly at Boscombe Down. However, it was too late in the day to leave the airfield so Falk made some fast taxi runs plus a 100-yard (91m) hop up to 10ft (3m) off the ground. Fortunately conditions on the following morning were fine and the maiden flight was completed.

From the start Falk was delighted with the feel of the controls and after just a couple of flights he had great confidence in the 707B. In fact he was able to say, without hesitation even at this early stage, that if a pilot flew it without knowing it was a tailless delta, he would not be able to tell from the controls that it was anything but an orthodox aeroplane. In normal flight there was no difference in response from a standard aircraft of comparable size. Though classified as a low-speed aircraft, Falk was soon flying at quite high speeds and Mach numbers and in rate of roll the 707B handled like a fighter. When flying at maximum speed,

any sudden and violent disturbance of the controls would never prevent the 707B, at all times, from remaining under complete control. Once the handling characteristics had been established, the next stage was the development of the new take-off and landing techniques that were required for a delta-wing aircraft. Here it was found that a strong cross wind had little effect on the aeroplane.

## First Bomber Prototype

By January 1951 it was possible for Avro to report that the detailed design of the 698 had progressed to the point at which considerable reliance could be placed on the weight estimate. In the year since January 1950 some changes had been made to the external layout of the aircraft, notably an increase of 2ft (0.61m) to the span, alterations to the wingtip and the addition of a bomb-aimer's cupola. Along with the two prototypes, a static test airframe had also been ordered together with a flight simulator.

Construction of the first Avro 698, VX770, began in the spring of 1951. The wings were built at Woodford and the rest of the airframe at Chadderton, the latter in due course having to be moved by road through Manchester to be mated with its wings. The movement of the large and well-wrapped centre section by lorry to Woodford caused much speculation because no-one outside Avro appears to have known what it was. The *Aeroplane* for 25th April 1952 published a photograph which was captioned 'Mystery Parcel' and added that it 'seems to be part of an aeroplane'. However, one imagines that anyone 'in the know' would have worked it out. As completed, VX770 was actually little more than the 'flying shell' that had previously been abandoned and it was only fitted with one pilot's seat; the second was added later. The planned Olympus engines were also unavailable, so for its early flights VX770 would have four 6,500 lb (28.9kN) thrust Rolls-Royce Avon R.A.3 units installed. These provided a lot less power than the aircraft needed but would allow at least some of the flight characteristics to be explored.

VX770 was completed in early August 1952 and began its first flight at 09.45 on the 30th of the month; Roly Falk was the pilot. This first sortie would comprise a steady climb to 10,000ft (3,048m) with the undercarriage raised, a series of gentle manoeuvres, and then a descent. However, there were some concerns when both rear undercarriage fairings were seen to fall off, but Falk was able to complete a safe landing. The fairings were later strengthened while the first flight itself, which lasted thirty-six minutes, had proved a success. Between 30th August and 9th September the aircraft completed eleven flights, but most of these early sorties were made chiefly as transit and demonstration flights at the SBAC Farnborough Show. For this purpose the aircraft operated out of Boscombe Down but involve-

ment in the Show meant that few specific tests could be made during this period.

Despite having a brand-new, full-size and near-untested aircraft in his hands, Falk performed a phenomenal display with the 698, throwing it about the sky with what *The Aeroplane* magazine thought might be described as abandon. In fact some commentators were staggered, saying that Falk's handling was so sure and certain that it was difficult to realise that the prototype had flown for the first time only a few days previously. The 698 made its debut late on the Tuesday afternoon, on just its fourth flight, sweeping in low and fast in formation with the red 707A on one side and the blue 707B on the other, before splitting away to perform solo. The all-white colour scheme also did much to enhance the spectacle but the aeroplane was not allowed to land at Farnborough. Falk commented that 'it set an entirely new standard of manoeuvrability for an aircraft of this size'. For the pilot this was helped by having a fighter-type stick rather than the old spectacle style of control column used in the past by piston bombers. In fact Falk had been heavily involved with the 698's cockpit design, which included this particular feature.

At this stage Avro's bomber was still unnamed and the media in particular stoked up the interest in regard to what title would be selected. The discussions were brought to a close by Sir John Slessor, the Chief of the Air Staff (CAS), when he ruled that the aircraft would receive a name beginning with 'V' to fol-

low the practice already established with the Valiant. The choice, Vulcan, was revealed to the public during the week ending 24th October and referred to the ancient Roman god of fire and destruction. Valiant and Vulcan also brought to an end the long-used custom of naming British bombers after towns or cities.

Total airborne time at the end of Flight Eleven was seven hours and forty minutes but VX770 did not fly again until 24th November. That trip was followed by eleven flights made during December that pushed the total up to twenty-three, embracing twenty-seven take-off and landings and twenty-one hours and five minutes in the air. Gradually more features and equipment were added to VX770, such as a permanent fuel system to replace the temporary affair in the bomb bay fitted at the start of the aircraft's career.

By April 1953 VX770 had been re-engined with four 8,000 lb (35.6kN) Armstrong Siddeley Sapphire engines which made the prototype capable of achieving higher maximum speeds and altitudes. On 15th July it performed a display as part of the RAF's parade held at Odiham to mark the Coronation of the new Queen Elizabeth, following both the Victor prototype and then a Valiant in the programme. Falk flew VX770 and for the first time was able to display

**The centre-section of the first Avro 698 prototype seen in the spring of 1952 during a slow journey to Woodford to be mated with its wings.** Avro Heritage

**Avro 698 Vulcan prototype VX770 showing the full-size bomber's original wing.**

**Similar view of the second prototype VX777 modified as the B Mk.2 aerodynamic prototype, in which form the aircraft was first flown in August 1957.** Mike Stroud

the bomber to the public at speed. It arrived at roughly 460mph (740km/h), which was a higher speed than that achieved by the other V-Bombers. Few people who saw VX770 flying that day realised that it was now powered by Sapphires. Despite appalling weather conditions, VX770 also put in an appearance at the display held at Royal Naval Air Station Stretton on 25th July, on which occasion it was flown from Woodford by Sqn Ldr Jack Wales, another Avro test pilot.

In June 1956 VX770 was allocated to receive 15,000 lb (66.7kN) Rolls-Royce Conway engines and during August it went to Avro's Langar facility to be fitted with them. On 24th August 1957 it was delivered to the Rolls-Royce test airfield at Hucknall to begin a career as an engine test bed and in this form took part in both the 1957 and 1958 Farnborough Shows. The Conway was to be fitted in both the Victor bomber and examples of the Boeing 707 airliner acquired by British Overseas Airways. Some-

what ironic then that Avro's prototype bomber would help clear the engines that were to serve its great rival. However, for a period the Conway was also considered as an interim Vulcan engine. In fact, in 1955/56, each of the two V-Bomber engines, Olympus and Conway, was seen as an insurance against the failure of the other, and a meeting held at the Ministry on 9th February 1956 stated that a Vulcan flight test bed for the Conway 'was essential'.

This choice also spilt over into the decision-making process for the engines chosen to power the Vulcan B Mk.2. Originally, Avro wished for the Olympus 6 to be adopted, but then in the spring of 1956 Sir Roy Dobson, Avro's managing director, intervened in favour of the Conway. In fact he went so far as to refuse to proceed with work on a Vulcan flying test bed for the Conway without an assurance that the Conway would be the engine for the Vulcan B.2. By July 1956 however, Dobson had reversed his attitude and was pressing very strongly for the Olympus 6.

Tragically, on 20th September 1958 VX770 suffered a structural failure while taking part in a display at RAF Syerston in Northamptonshire.

The aircraft was flying at about 250ft (76m) when the starboard wing began to disintegrate, it reared up and then dived into the ground. All four crew were killed, as were three RAF ground staff. On board were K R Sturt of Rolls-Royce who was the pilot, R W Ford from Fairey Aviation (co-pilot), W E Hopkins (Rolls-Royce flight observer) and the navigator Flt Lt R M Parrott. Although VX770 was not flying at a high Mach number, the display routine took the aeroplane beyond its combined speed and 'G' limits. VX770 was replaced as a Conway test bed by early production Mk.1 XA902 (see Chapter Five).

Back in June 1951 the Air Staff was advised by Avro and Handley Page that both of the B.35/46 bombers (at this time still called B.35s by officials and not Vulcan and Victor) could be developed to carry much greater bomb loads. This would be at the expense of about 1,500 lb (680kg) of additional structure in the Avro and 500 lb (227kg) in Handley Page's aircraft. The Air Staff accepted these proposals, acknowledging that there would be a small cost in performance. Similarly, in August 1951 the Air Staff agreed to the development of the B.35/46 aircraft for greater ranges by the carriage of extra fuel under the wings. This would allow both bombers to travel an approximate 5,000nm (9,260km) still air range with a 10,000 lb (4,536kg) bomb on board.

However, early in 1952 the Air Staff qualified these previous decisions by saying that it did not want the B.35 aircraft to be developed to carry great loads of bombs, or go for great distances, at the expense of performance in the aircraft's basic role. It did finally agree that any structure weight penalty to achieve these increased bomb loads or ranges would be accepted, provided that the performance penalty in the basic role did not exceed 400ft (122m) of height at the target. The events described in these two paragraphs alone reveal very clearly the give and take that was necessary in an aircraft's design and development process, and the 'balancing act' that was usually needed to meet the various requirements.

## Second Bomber Prototype

VX777, the second 698 prototype, made its maiden flight on 3rd September 1953 powered by 9,750 lb (43.3kN) Olympus 100 engines. As such it came rather closer to the production standard than VX770. This machine was intended to undertake high-altitude navigation and bombing trials and so was provided with observer's seats and equipment, a visual bomb-aiming blister beneath the nose, and a full H2S Mk.9A radar coupled with its NBC Mk.1 computer. VX777 also had the extended nose leg and a 16in (40.6cm) extension to the nose section to accommodate it (VX770 had used a more complicated nose leg that could be shortened by telescoping before retraction).

Afterwards VX777 began some high-speed and high-altitude trials out of Boscombe Down. For ten minutes of a one-hour test flight made on 13th March 1954 VX777's controls were

**This nose angle of one of the 698 prototypes, taken at Woodford, shows quite beautifully the aircraft's massive air intakes and wing.**

taken by Minister of Supply Duncan Sandys. He subsequently commented 'it was like sitting in an armchair' and added that, for a large aircraft, it was also proving itself exceedingly manoeuvrable at high altitude and speed. On 27th July 1954 VX777 suffered substantial airframe damage when it swung off the runway on landing at Farnborough. A spring link in the rudder control circuit had jammed causing the rudder to be permanently displaced 12.5° to starboard with the rudder pedals central. The pilot found it necessary to attempt a landing from an unusually high approach speed, the brake parachute failed, the wheel brakes proved inadequate to stop the aircraft and the undercarriage collapsed. VX777 had been prepared for bomb-dropping trials and was expected to be out of action until at least November. In fact the aircraft did not fly again for six months which severely hampered the flight test programme because the first prototype was so limited in what it could achieve by its lack of available thrust. However, while VX777 was out of action the opportunity was taken to fit it with Olympus 101 units.

By August 1954 the two prototypes had between them completed a total of two hundred hours of flying. However, since both the proper pressurising and fuel system had been installed only recently, most of the flying up to

capabilities of this particular airframe. However, due to the July 1954 accident, it was not until the early weeks of 1955 that VX777 could begin to look into the type's high Mach number, high-altitude performance and associated buffet limits.

Between 7th and 25th May 1955 VX777 underwent a brief preliminary assessment in the hands of the test pilots at Boscombe Down. The primary objective was to assess the aircraft's flying qualities and operational potential for the bomber role and this was made on the evidence of seventeen sorties totalling twenty-seven hours of flying. The tests were made at an intermediate centre of gravity position but, in respect of some planned wing geometry modifications and additional engine thrust, VX777 was not as yet representative of forthcoming production machines. For example it lacked a drooped leading edge or some vortex generators that would subsequently be fitted to the outer wings. In addition, each Olympus 101 had been derated from 11,000 lb (48.9kN) to

this point had been done at low and medium altitude. The most important of the outstanding work on the basic aircraft was to check and develop the high-altitude and high-speed characteristics and the lift boundaries. As indicated already, this was best done on the second aircraft because VX777's Olympus units offered so much more thrust than VX770's Sapphires. In fact the first prototype could only explore the high speed part of the flight envelope when it was taken into a shallow dive and testing at the required high altitudes was beyond the current

**This time VX770 has landed – on the runway after a covering of light snow. Note that the airbrakes and the aircraft's huge drag chute have both been deployed.**

10,000 lb (44.4kN) thrust for take-off, and by 200 lb (0.89kN) for cruising conditions.

Another factor in the equation was that, at the time of the test, the runway length at Boscombe Down had been reduced to 2,000 yards (1,829m) by resurfacing work. Consequently, it was not feasible to fly the aircraft at the representative operational weight to which it had been cleared (165,000 lb/74,844kg). The flights were therefore made at medium take-off weights – actually 119,000 lb (53,978kg) and 130,000 lb (58,968kg). Because of these factors the final report stated that a full assessment of the type's flying qualities and operational potential could not be made – the non-representative state of VX777 limiting the scope of the assessment. For example, it was not possible to investigate the characteristics in flight with asymmetric thrust, extreme sideslip or reduced power control output, but it was still possible to make a number of important observations.

Although the Vulcan prototype showed certain outstanding features, serious deficiencies were present, particularly in and above the cruising Mach number range, and until these could be rectified the bomber could not be considered satisfactory for Service use.

The six features requiring most serious attention were:

a) Inadequate buffet boundary at high Mach number and serious associated aileron oscillation.

b) Longitudinal instability and poor damping in pitch at high Mach number.
   The expected cruising Mach number was 0.87M (500 knots/576mph/926km/h TAS) and the design Mach number was 0.95M. Above 0.86M a nose-down change of trim occurred, which became pronounced with increase of Mach number towards the limit, and this made the aircraft difficult to fly accurately and required great care on the part of the pilot to avoid exceeding the maximum permitted Mach number. This characteristic was unacceptable and Avro proposed to eliminate it in production aeroplanes by introducing an artificial stability device. In addition, with increase in Mach number above 0.89M the damping in pitch decreased to an unacceptably low level, particularly near the maximum permitted Mach number, and VX777 was difficult to fly steadily. Here, Avro proposed to install a pitch damper in production aircraft. As tested the Mach number/buffet characteristics were unacceptable for a high-altitude bomber, but considerable improvement was hoped for with the drooped leading edge and vortex generators.

c) A tendency to yaw uncontrollably near the 'stall'. While the stall had no operational significance on V-class aircraft, this tendency to yaw uncontrollably at high incidence and develop large angles of sideslip was unacceptable for Service use.

d) Serious external reflections in the windscreen panels during night landings. Judgement of take-off attitude by night was not easy and if the aircraft was pulled off at a steep angle the acceleration and climb away would be very slow. At full load this would be dangerous and further investigations were required to determine a take-off technique for Service use at high weights. Fair weather landings by day were straightforward, but in poor visibility, rain or by night, the view was very poor. By night there were also dangerously confusing and unacceptable multiple reflections on the approach lights in the windscreen.

e) Inadequate high-altitude performance. Making due allowance for the current engine situation, the performance in terms of attainable altitude was not outstanding. The likely target height with a 10,000 lb (4,536kg) bomb on board would only be about 43,000ft (13,106m) with the 11,000 lb (48.9kN) thrust engines in place, and the high-altitude turning performance would be poor. In fact this level of performance was considered to be inadequate for an unarmed subsonic bomber, even under cover of darkness and using radio countermeasures (RCM). It was recommended that the projected more powerful engines should be introduced as soon as possible to raise the cruising altitude band.

f) The engine handling characteristics experienced during the trials were also unsatisfactory.

There were good points too. The general handling qualities under conditions other than those mentioned were very pleasant. The airbrake characteristics were unpleasant, but development action was proceeding with a view to improving the transient trim changes experienced when the brakes were operating, and the buffet produced by the brakes in the 'high drag' setting. The cockpit was generally well laid out and the best yet seen in this class of aircraft. Clearly much needed to be done but the report concluded that 'providing the action already in hand to rectify these deficiencies is successful, and making allowances for changes in weight and thrust, it is believed that the Vulcan will be a satisfactory high-altitude bombing platform subject to functional clearance of the bombing and associated installations'.

At this stage both prototypes had flown with the original wing but the presence of buffet at high altitude when 'G' was applied (the 'buzz' experienced on the 707A) would soon give problems of fatigue and possible failure. The buffet, which was above the minimum acceptable standard, appeared when airflow broke away from the upper wing surfaces and the variable loads thus applied to the wing could reduce its fatigue life quite rapidly. There had been little evidence of buffet when flying with the low engine power available to VX770, but the extra thrust now on tap to VX777 took the bomber into this regime. Therefore, from July 1955 VX777 was fitted with the kinked Phase 2 wing and the prototype first flew with it on 5th October. The Phase 2 featured a reduced leading edge sweep up to half span, but with a higher sweep angle further out – just like the modifications made to 707A WD280. The kinked wing was introduced onto the production line on the ninth aircraft, and retrospectively on most of the previous eight. The relevant 'envelope jigging' had to be modified of course and up to sixteen examples of the Vulcan's original leading edge had to be scrapped. This was a major alteration and the refit work brought a delay in the overall programme.

On 10th July 1956 VX777 was selected for another conversion to allow it to serve as an aerodynamic prototype for the B Mk.2 and it made its maiden flight in this form on 31st August 1957. As such it was fitted with more powerful 12,000 lb (53.3kN) thrust Olympus Mk.102 engines and a much larger wing. VX777's flying career came to an end in 1960 but at Farnborough its working life continued for a further two years through to the autumn of 1962. Here RAE used the airframe for ground-based armament and equipment vibration trials before it was withdrawn in October of that year and subsequently scrapped. Long before then the first production Vulcans had been making their contribution to the test programme, in readiness to join the RAF.

Throughout the period covered by this chapter, Avro pressed ahead with the Vulcan programme with enormous energy and urgency and had its workforce working flat out. This was in part because the company wished to stay ahead of its rival from Handley Page. In the end the effort proved very worthwhile, not least because the first 698 prototype made it into the air ahead of the first HP.80 Victor prototype.

Top: **The first Avro 698 prototype takes off for another test flight.**

Left: **VX777 seen at Farnborough after its retirement from flight testing.**

Opposite page:

Top: **Beautiful air-to-air view of VX777, complete with modified wing.** Barry Jones

Centre and bottom: **Views of VX777 being scrapped in 1963. A sad end, but this is the way that the great majority of aeroplanes go.**

# Chapter Three

# Real Vulcans and Proposed Versions

During the latter part of 1951 and into early 1952 the Air Staff and Air Ministry were led to believe that the Ministry of Supply was preparing an appreciation to show which of the two B.35/46 bombers should be bought for the RAF. According to an Air Staff document, at the end of this period it seemed that no-one was prepared to commit themselves in favour of one type or another and many reasons, political or otherwise, were put forward to justify a production order for both the Avro and Handley Page designs. As a result, in July 1952 a production order was placed for twenty-five examples of each series aircraft, although no prototypes had yet flown. Avro was in a position to start a production programme rather earlier than Handley Page. One reason for this was the development flying that had been carried out on the 707 series, the data provided enabling the company to finalise some aspects of the Vulcan's design (Handley Page's solitary HP.88 scale model aircraft was lost in August 1951 just a couple of months after its maiden flight). A second point was the set of jigs that Avro used for the prototype 698s – these were built from the start as production jigs and as they stood could be used for a production pro-

gramme of one aircraft for every two months. Avro had agreed with the Ministry that its production programme for the first twenty-five aircraft should begin in July 1954, allowing four aircraft to be built in the remainder of that year.

## Avro Vulcan B Mk.1

The first production version of Avro's delta bomber was designated B Mk.1, and specification B.129P was raised on 25th September 1952 and issued on 21st November to cover it (B.128P covered the Handley Page Victor B Mk.1). Despite additional requirements at that stage for tail armament and jettisonable cabins, it was agreed in August that the first twenty-five production aeroplanes should be based substantially on the second prototype. By January 1953 the jettisonable cabin had been dropped and, of course, most production Mk.1s actually got the modified Phase 2 wing. A further twenty B Mk.1s were ordered in September 1954, but this second contract also included another seventeen that were to be manufactured to B Mk.2 standard. More Mk.2 orders followed, in February 1956 and December 1957, which brought the total B.2 run to eighty-nine aircraft. XA889, the first production

**Lovely picture of Vulcan B Mk.1 XA891 after it had been fitted with the Phase 2 kinked wing.**
Mike Stroud

B Mk.1, made its maiden flight on 4th February 1955, by which time a Vulcan flight simulator had been ordered for training purposes.

In fact simulators were ordered for all three V-Bombers. The modern V-Bomber was a complex machine and a trend towards more specialised pilot training, the need to operate aircraft to the limits of their capability, and the lack of sufficient aircraft specifically for training, had made training crews more difficult. As a result the schedules had grown longer and the RAF was forced to look at the flight simulator as a solution. It was a success and the Vulcan simulator, designed and built by Air Trainers Link Ltd of Aylesbury, was put into service at Waddington.

With the prototypes the number of Vulcans completed was 136, and all of them were built at Woodford. However, there was some subcontracting. Towards the end of 1955, following the completion of contracts to build Hawker Sea Hawk and Hunter jet fighters, the employees at the Coventry plant of Sir W G Armstrong

**The first production Vulcan B Mk.1 to fly was XA889, which is seen here very early in its life with the original wing.**

**This shot of XA889 was taken during Olympus trials with Bristol Engines at Filton.** Mike Stroud

Whitworth Aircraft Ltd were facing extensive redundancies. Fortunately a contract was then received to manufacture Vulcan sub-assemblies for Avro and this eased the situation somewhat (during the following year the Sea Hawk production line was also re-opened to fulfil three overseas orders, which helped even more). Some Vulcan pieces were also manufactured by Hawker Aircraft at Kingston. As regards the parent company, at the time Vulcan production began to gain momentum a batch of English Electric Canberra bombers built by the Manchester firm was nearing completion, which then made it free to concentrate on its own bomber. Vulcan won no export orders, but in 1956 Australia did express an interest in buy-ing either twenty-nine Vulcans or Victors; France also enquired about prices and delivery dates.

To begin with the existence of production Vulcans was kept secret. On 11th February 1955 *Flight* magazine reported that a Vulcan with serial XA889, and in silver finish with black lower 'mandible' (radome), 'was seen flying from Woodford on 4th February. Although the makers have nothing to say on the matter, it may confidently be assumed that XA889 is the first production Vulcan'. The reporter was of course spot on.

Between 26th March and 17th April 1956 XA889 was used by A&AEE Boscombe Down for a programme of trials to release to type for use by the RAF in the high-altitude medium bomber role. During this period the aircraft was flown twenty-six times for a total of forty-eight hours and fifteen minutes flying. In all respects XA889 was representative of the Service aircraft, save for operational equipment, and it was flown to a maximum weight of 165,220 lb (74,944kg). Overall the test pilots concluded that 'the modifications which have been incorporated in production Vulcan aircraft have successfully overcome the unacceptable flying characteristics exhibited by the second prototype in the preliminary assessment carried out at A&AEE in May 1955, and when all the stability aids are functioning the Vulcan has safe and adequate flying qualities for its primary role as a medium bomber'. The aircraft was described as 'an adequate bombing platform' and was released to the Service, but at a maximum weight limit of 167,000 lb (75,751kg) and a maximum speed of 438mph (705km/h) IAS between sea level and 30,000ft (9,144m) and 0.98 IMN above that height.

However, the report requested 'more powerful engines and aerodynamic refinement where possible to improve the altitude performance'. With Olympus 101 engines the aircraft had an inadequate high-altitude cruising performance, still reaching only 43,000ft (13,106m) over the

**XA891 had a flying life of less than four years, all of it spent on testing. It was also one of the most photographed of the early Vulcans, completing several publicity flights. This gorgeous shot with a splendid cloudscape shows XA891 with the original delta wing.** Mike Stroud

**Another early picture of XA891 revealing underfuselage detail.** Mike Stroud

**XA891 landing at the Farnborough Air Show in 1958.** Mike Stroud

**XA891 seen on publicity duty once again, in silver finish. Note the elevator and aileron arrangement on the wing trailing edge.**

This page:

After the three V-Bombers had all entered production, a series of photographs was taken by A&AEE Boscombe Down of one of each flying together. This pair of images was part of the result and show Vulcan B.1 XA892, Vickers Valiant B Mk.1 WZ373 and Handley Page Victor B Mk.1 XA919, all in silver finish. A&AEE via Terry Panopalis

Opposite page:

Vulcan B.1 XA894 leads a V-Bomber line-up on the apron at A&AEE Boscombe Down.
A&AEE via Terry Panopalis

Vulcan B.1 XA900 shows the white colour scheme introduced as a replacement for the silver livery.
Mike Stroud

target at the selected cruising speed of Mach 0.85. By contemporary standards this was too low for an unarmed bomber and had to be improved as soon as possible. Efforts were in hand to increase the maximum continuous engine rating; if successful this would raise the target height by some 1,500ft (457m). The radius of action with full fuel and a 10,000 lb (4,536kg) bomb load, assuming a 20% fuel reserve, was 1,500nm (2,780km). Although released for service subject to certain conditions, further extensive trials were still necessary to clear the operational installations. XA889 later became one of the test aircraft for various marks of Olympus (see Chapter Five).

Other early Mk.1s used for release work were XA892 on armaments and XA894 on autopilot clearance, while XA895 was put to work clearing the bomber's electronics for service. Trials at A&AEE with XA892 during the first half of 1957 cleared the carriage and release of a 10,000 lb (4,536kg) iron bomb between 14,000ft (4,267m) and the maximum obtainable height, at 438mph (705km/h) or Mach 0.97 whichever was less. XA890 was used for radio, radar and weapons trials and never actually joined a squadron, spending the whole of its career either at Boscombe Down or Farnborough; as such it retained its pure delta wing for all of its life.

XA890 with its delta wing, and in a silver finish, also attended the 1955 Farnborough Show. As such it showed no external changes from the familiar all-white prototypes, except for the large dielectric nose radome. XA890 was described in some press accounts as a pre-production aircraft, but that didn't stop Roly Falk from performing a superb display. Quoting from 'The Aeroplane', Falk 'hoiked the massive Vulcan off the ground in a steep climbing turn, and returned over the airfield at about 1,000ft (305m) to do a beautifully smooth upward roll'. Yet again this made a big impression on the public and one is left with the feeling that Falk, from an aerobatics point of view, has been rather forgotten as a display pilot; his achievements in the Vulcan must have matched many contemporary fighter pilots. Earlier, on 18th and 19th June, XA889 had made an appearance at that year's Paris Air Show, making a fast and then a slow run, the latter 'with airbrakes out and plenty of up-elevon'. However, the aircraft did not land at Le Bourget.

Clearance for the Vulcan to carry and drop the Blue Danube nuclear bomb, a 10,000 lb (4,536kg) training store or 25 lb (11.3kg) practice bombs was completed by A&AEE in

Opposite page:

**A specially posed photograph of an unidentified Vulcan Mk.1 flying at height with undercarriage down and airbrakes deployed.**

**Three B.1 Vulcans seen flying in line astern on their way to Embakasi Airport in Nairobi on 18th September 1957. Nearest is XA907, then XA905 with the last example unidentified.** Mike Stroud

August 1957. In December A&AEE also cleared the carriage of 1,000 lb (454kg) Medium Capacity Mk.7 Star Bombs and the operation of the B.1's T.4 bombsight. Between 1959 and 1962 the remaining operational B Mk.1s were upgraded with revised electronics, including a tail warning radar similar to that fitted to the B Mk.2, and were consequently reclassified as B Mk.1As. After Avro had completed a trial installation on XA895, the remainder of the B.1A conversions were then carried out by Armstrong Whitworth.

The B Mk.1 was not by any means the complete Vulcan – more capability was soon required. By 1954 the Chiefs of Staff had accepted that the RAF's medium bombers constituted the country's only strategic striking force. They also agreed that the nuclear threat was the main deterrent to war and that, in the event of global war, the only hope of preventing the complete devastation of this country was an immediate and overwhelming counter-offensive by the Allied strategic air forces. The view was also held that the ability to wage war with the most up-to-date nuclear weapons would be the measure of military power in the future. It was, therefore, of over-riding importance that Britain had these weapons and a demonstrably effective means of delivering them. The only effective means of delivery, for at least the next ten years, would be the medium bomber force. Consequently, some modifications and improvements, at least, would be required.

For these reasons the Air Staff became increasingly concerned about the vulnerability of the V-Bombers. Studies suggested that by 1960 it would be excessively dangerous for them to fly over their target, or even within about 50 miles (80km) of it. Consequently, both Avro and Handley Page were asked to study seriously to what extent the aircraft could be developed. Little improvement was likely from a speed point of view, so their effort was concentrated on improving height performance. The response from Avro was to extend and add camber to the wing leading edge, make the outer wing thinner and increase both the chord and span. This enabled local airflow velocities to be kept subsonic up to a higher aircraft Mach number, thus delaying the separation and consequent buffeting as lift was increased. These changes would allow engine thrusts up to 17,500 lb (77.8kN) to be fully absorbed by the aerodynamics and the modified wing was known as the Phase 2C. It was first proposed in August 1955 and during December instructions to proceed were given by the Ministry. This was also the period when the carriage of the Blue Steel cruise missile was first considered, which is discussed shortly.

However, perhaps it is time to explain the various Vulcan wing developments produced by Avro during the mid-1950s. The altitude that could be obtained at high subsonic Mach number was limited by one of two factors. The first was the maximum thrust that could be obtained from the engines, and the second was the

product of the lift-co-efficient at which airflow breakdown over the wing caused buffeting. Given engines of sufficient power, it was necessary to avoid buffeting in level flight and in gentle manoeuvres. The Vulcan had originally been designed for a cruising lift coefficient of 0.2 at the cruising Mach number and it was found that the first measurable onset of buffeting came at a slightly greater lift coefficient. To utilise the increase of altitude made possible by more powerful engines, it became necessary to raise the lift coefficient where buffeting began. On the Vulcan's delta wing the maximum local lift coefficient occurred near the wingtip, which in this region was up to 9% thick. By 1955 Avro had learnt that a thickness:chord ratio of 4% to 5% was more suitable for Mach numbers of 0.87 to 0.9.

Buffeting was caused by flow separation from the wing, which might occur either at the leading edge or further back on the wing section. The leading edge separation was fundamentally a function of the nose shape and camber of the section and could only be postponed to higher lift coefficients by modifications to these parameters. Its effects were most pronounced in the region of Mach 0.7 to 0.85. If the wing section was much thicker than about 5%, shock-induced rear separation occurred at higher Mach numbers, but this separation could be alleviated by fitting vortex generators to the wing.

The first modification, known as Phase 2 and described in Chapters Two and Six, gave the maximum improvement for the minimum structural alteration; this being confined to the outer wing ahead of the front spar. The wing chord near the tip was extended by 20%, some droop was incorporated and this showed good increases in lift coefficient on both the Avro 707A and the Vulcan. Above Mach 0.86 the gain dropped off rapidly but the addition of vortex generators maintained the buffet threshold on the Vulcan at a lift coefficient of at least 0.32, at Mach numbers up to 0.89. This would enable engines of 12,000 lb (53.3kN) and 13,000 lb (57.8kN) thrust to be accommodated (which they were), but as more powerful engines became available a more extensive modification would be needed.

As new information was obtained on buffeting phenomena, it became possible to consider more extensive modifications; the results were the Phase 2A and Phase 2B wings. Phase 2A was similar in principle to the Phase 2, but the structural changes were taken back to the maximum thickness of the sections. The span was increased and a stronger undercarriage fitted to allow operation at take-off weights up to 190,000 lb (86,184kg). In fact, with a 15,500 lb (7,031kg) stand-off bomb on board, overload fuel for a 5,000nm (9,265km) range, and Olympus 6 engines, the estimated all-up weight for a Vulcan with the 2A wing was 189,698 lb (86,047kg) and target height 53,400ft (16,276m). The main restriction of this modification was that the rear portion of the wing

section was unaltered and, therefore, any flow separation dependent upon the surface slopes aft of the maximum thickness would as a result be unchanged. Phase 2B was an interim development of 2A but was never officially submitted to the Ministry. In due course both were superseded by Phase 2C, which endeavoured to obtain the highest possible buffet threshold by a combination of chordwise and spanwise extensions of the outer wing and the use of very thin (5%) cambered wing sections in the critical region.

There was also the Phase 3 proposed by Avro in February 1955, where the outer wing was replaced by a new unit of reduced thickness and increased span and area. With this modification the flow separation from the rear of the aerofoil sections was eliminated but it involved a complete redesign of all the control surfaces, the undercarriage and fuel system. Advantage was taken of using metal honeycomb sandwich construction (little of which was to be found on the Vulcan itself, despite Avro's pioneering work in this area) to increase the internal fuel capacity, thus bringing considerable benefits in terms of range when using the same engines. The Phase 3 wing would have been capable of accepting any engine up to the Olympus 6 rating of 16,000 lb (71.1kN), and the ability to use the thrust of these engines would have given big increases in altitude over the target. A new main undercarriage would allow take-off weights up to 220,000 lb (99,792kg) and, with the same parameters as the 2A (cruise missile, range, B.Ol.6), take-off weight was 184,893 lb (83,867kg) and target height 54,100ft (16,490m). However, the 3's big disadvantage was the amount of redesign that was necessary, and so an investigation was started which looked into the possibility of obtaining the same order of improvement in buffet threshold without the extensive structural modifications. That led to the Phase 2C.

Avro's brochure concluded that, in general, the 2C wing had an altitude performance that was very similar to the Phase 3 aircraft and was capable of accepting all of the engines associated with the 3, but it did not have the outstanding range characteristics. Since the Phase

2C modifications only affected the outer portion of the wing, the normal bomb-carrying capabilities of the Vulcan were unchanged. Another very important feature was that the time needed to complete the 2C modification was such that it could be introduced into the Vulcan production line at about the same time as suitable engines would be available to make use of it.

## Vulcan B Mk.2

As noted in Chapter Two, Avro turned the second prototype, VX777, into an aerodynamic test vehicle for the Phase 2C, the development in due course being labelled B Mk.2. The aircraft flew with its new wing (and new Olympus jet pipes) on 31st August 1957. The earliest Vulcan had been designed to reach Mach 0.95 in a shallow dive but Phase 2C was stressed to cover Mach 1.0. The Mk.2 Vulcan also introduced an AC electrical system and other improvements and in April 1956 consideration was given to fitting the new more powerful Olympus 6 or 7, or the Rolls-Royce Conway Stage 2 or Stage 3. The two Conway variants offered less thrust and aircraft ceiling than the Olympus, but more range.

Much of the development work to clear the features that distinguished the Mk.2 from the Mk.1 was carried out using Mk.1s as flying test beds. For example, XA893 received the revised electronics that would go into the new mark. Specification B.129P Issue 2 of 7th January 1958 was prepared to cover the production of this version and the powerplant chosen was the 16,000 lb (71.1kN) Bristol Olympus Series 200 – the Olympus 6. XA891 was used for a trial installation. A B Mk.2 Mock-Up Conference was held in October 1957 and the first production aircraft, XH533, made its maiden flight on 30th August 1958. The introduction of the B Mk.2 and its wing, with B.1 production terminated at a relatively small number, did create a bottleneck and slowed down the delivery programme. There were other delays too, not least from a strike by employees at Woodford over dissatisfaction with piecework rates for the manufacture of Vulcan mainplanes. This strike lasted for ten weeks and made the situation far worse.

In July 1959 Avro completed an assessment report that covered the development of the B Mk.2 up to the version's preview trials by A&AEE Boscombe Down (before this preview the first aircraft, XH533, had completed approximately forty hours flying). The report's focus of attention was the overall standard of the Mk.2 in its present form and it was generally considered that the flying qualities of the new mark had fulfilled design expectations. Even at the preview stage there appeared to be only minor problems still to be investigated before full C(A) Release trials. The general reliability of the aircraft could be judged from the fact that the thirty hours flying up to the first minor inspection were completed in just twenty-nine days. The general position was summarised as follows:

a) The change of wing aerodynamics had completely fulfilled the original predictions with regard to high Mach number buffet.

b) The altitude performance was naturally superior to the Mk.1 and it was interesting to record that the change of wing aerodynamics alone had yielded a dividend of 2,000ft (610m) on the aircraft's cruise ceiling. The additional engine thrust from the Olympus 200 gave a further 4,000ft (1,219m), so that the target height of the Mk.2 should be some 6,000ft (1,829m) in excess of the Mk.1 figure at comparable weights.

c) The handling qualities of the Mk.2 were improved in several respects over the Mk.1. In particular, both visibility and control on the approach were superior and the aircraft had a high degree of manoeuvrability at cruising conditions.

d) The high Mach number characteristics of the basic aircraft were similar to those of the Mk.1 and the static instability and loss of damping in pitch which occurred well above cruising Mach number were corrected by artificial stabilisation, similar to the Mk.1's equipment but of improved design. So far this equipment had functioned extremely well.

e) The AC electrical system had to date given very little trouble and this was almost certainly due to the thorough test programmes carried out in flight on Mk.1 aircraft and on ground rigs.

In July 1959 the Air Council made the decision that B Mk.2 Vulcans should receive even more powerful engines because a plan to install rocket assisted take-off gear had been abandoned (Chapter Five). Consequently production aircraft were eventually fitted with the 17,000 lb (75.6kN) Olympus Mk.201 or the 20,000 lb (88.9kN) Mk.301 – XJ784 was the first Vulcan to get the Mk.301. The first seven B.2s all became involved in development and equipment testing in readiness to put the mark into service; for example XH536 took part in radio and navigation trials and XH537 on weapons testing. The second production B Mk.2, XH534, was given an extended and bulged tail-

cone which housed new electronic and countermeasures equipment. Controller(Aircraft) Release of the B Mk.2 was issued on 31st May 1960. Full Rapid-Take-Off Release to Service for the Mk.2, with Olympus 201 and 301 in the free-fall role, was issued on 25th April 1963.

One of the key weapons in the Vulcan's armoury was Avro's Blue Steel missile and the first indication to the public that the bomber might carry an 'air-to-ground missile known as a stand-off bomb' was published in 'The Aeroplane' on 10th May 1957. This snippet also noted that the Avro company was associated with the weapon's development but no details, or even a name, were given. Blue Steel was indeed a winged, rocket-propelled inertia-controlled supersonic cruise missile or stand-off bomb. Its carriage by Vulcan B.1 aircraft was discussed in a meeting held at Avro on 29th January 1957, in reply to a request from the Resident Technical Officer (a Ministry man based at the factory) made the previous 19th November.

However, on B.1 airframes the lower boom of the centre section front spar was not cranked and so it was impossible to submerge the missile sufficiently within the fuselage. As a result the protruding store would impair the Mk.1's performance and increase its drag (profile drag would rise by over 30%). Estimates suggested that a Mk.1 with Blue Steel, plus bomb bay fuel

tanks, would weigh 190,163 lb (86,258kg) which, with the aft movement of the CofG, would then require some flight development. As a result, the weapon was only ever carried by the B Mk.2, apart that is from early production Mk.1 XA903 which became the development aircraft and flew for the first time with a dummy Blue Steel on board in late 1957. Even then, adapting the B Mk.2 to take the missile did still require some modifications to the main spar.

During the mid-1950s Blue Steel was considered vital for keeping the V-Bombers in the front line. By late 1954 plans were in place for a new supersonic reconnaissance bomber (the Avro 730) but these were eventually cancelled, so the V-Force would probably stay in the front line for longer than had been expected. The threat to a V-Bomber flying close to its target after 1960 has been noted, but the Air Staff expected the V-Force's potential to diminish only between 1965 and 1970, so the period when the flying bomb would have maximum use would be 1960 to 1965. It was considered

unlikely that there would be another relatively safe method of delivering a high-yield warhead for this period – at this time Blue Steel was the only answer.

XH539, the first B Mk.2 to be completed to Blue Steel configuration, was delivered to the RAF on 1st September 1961 and it was this aeroplane which achieved the first live Blue Steel firing at Woomera in Australia (Chapter Five). Blue Steel-equipped Vulcans were actually called B Mk.2As. The first official photo of a Vulcan (XA903) with a dummy round in place beneath the fuselage was not released until April 1958. XA903 showed this off at that year's Farnborough Show in September, but only in the air – the aircraft did not land.

However, for that particular Show the Vulcans were out in force. Their contribution began with a combined V-Bomber formation of Vulcan, Valiant and Victor (from Nos 83, 90 and 10 Squadrons respectively). Afterwards both the Vulcan and Victor demonstrated nuclear-weapon delivery tactics – Vulcan Mk.1 XA891 going into a LABS manoeuvre immediately

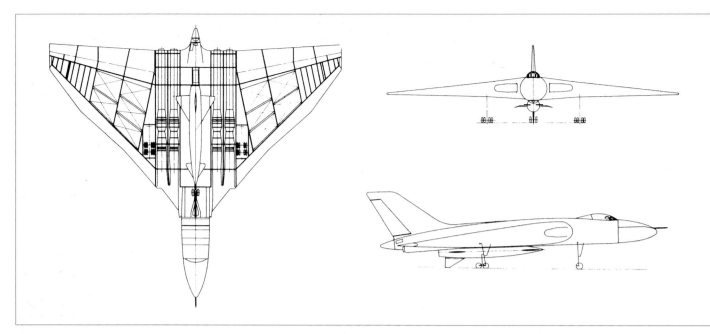

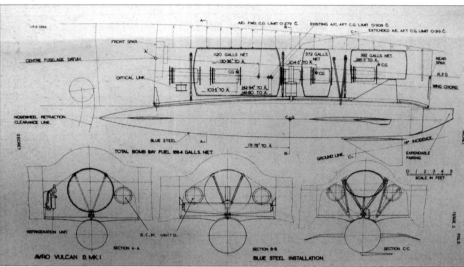

after take-off (LABS = Low Altitude Bombing System, or Toss Bombing). Also in attendance were the Mk.2 aerodynamic prototype VX777 and the first Mk.2 XH533. With examples of both versions flying, the public was able to see at first hand the benefits of the extra engine power available to the Mk.2, which performed an upward roll from the take-off as well as a casual roll in the circuit.

In 1963 Boscombe Down cleared Vulcan to carry twenty-one 1,000 lb (454kg) bombs. The trials employed a Mk.1 between November 1962 and February 1963 and the final report concluded that, after modifications to B Mk.1A standard, bomb release could be made up to the maximum permissible height and speed limits of the aircraft, but in a straight and level attitude plus or minus 5°. Clearance for the Vulcan B.2 to carry the Yellow Sun Mk.2 nuclear weapon was given in August 1961, and clearance for in-flight refuelling was issued the following month. The Green Satin Doppler navigation radar was cleared to the aircraft's maximum altitude in October 1961, having previously been limited to a degraded accuracy above 48,000ft (14,630m). In January 1962 A&AEE passed the use of 2,000 lb (907kg) Medium Capacity bombs.

Back in September 1956 the Air Staff had discussed taking either the Vulcan Mk.2 or the Victor Mk.2 out of the RAF programme, because it was realised that after April 1957 the

**Avro drawing from February 1958 showing the first proposal for carrying Blue Steel on a B Mk.1 Vulcan.**

**Detail drawing of how Blue Steel would have been carried on a Vulcan B Mk.1.**

**XA903 was the Vulcan selected to serve as the development aircraft for carrying the Blue Steel missile and is seen here with what is probably a dummy round. Note how the missile's lower fin is folded.** Mike Stroud

The third Vulcan B.2, XH535, reveals good detail of the upper wing surfaces on this later version. It has dark roundels and markings with its white livery. Note the different trailing edge arrangement to the B Mk.1, as shown by the earlier photograph of XA891. Mike Stroud

XJ781, another B Mk.2, this time displays white livery but with roundels and other markings in the paler shades used later. Mike Stroud

extra equipment fitted in Mk.2 V-Bombers would bring substantial increases in expenditure. Such a move would depend on the size of the V-Force that could be afforded after the forthcoming Defence Policy Review. The cancellation of either type would save some Research and Development expenditure but whether this would be a decisive factor was uncertain. It was also realised that, to build up the V-Force as quickly as possible, it might be necessary to find money for the development of both Mk.2s. In the end both types did survive to join the RAF in numbers.

## Vulcan B Mk.2 Developments and Low Level

To succeed Blue Steel, there were plans to have the Vulcan carry the American Douglas GAM-87A Skybolt nuclear ballistic missile as Britain's principal deterrent weapon, and this reached an advanced stage of development. The new policy was announced on 13th April 1960 but it was July before it was decided that the Vulcan would be a better carrier aircraft than the Victor. The Skybolt Vulcan was known as the Phase 6 and Avro's first project brochure was completed in May. This showed a package of modifications that were designed to be applied retrospectively to the B Mk.2. It would have reheated Olympus engines, Mk.21 or Mk.21/2, a new large outer wing, and four Skybolt missiles on underwing pylons. This wing featured new inner elevons coupled with the existing outer elevons, an integral fuel tank outboard and bag tanks inboard. There was a new dorsal fuel tank behind the canopy and to provide adequate lateral stability the area of the fin was increased by 18% and its height by 3ft (91cm). A certain amount of structural alteration and stiffening was required, with some large forgings replaced by new ones, and a new main undercarriage was to be introduced with a four-tyre bogie to meet the much higher all-up weight. Fuel capacity was more than doubled.

The idea was to give the aircraft a much longer flight endurance. As a result, by having the deterrent force continually airborne it would

be virtually indestructible by the enemy. At this stage it was quite apparent that no practical amount of dispersal could guarantee that the V-Bomber Force would not be destroyed on the ground in a single ballistic missile attack. Currently, a Vulcan's typical endurance with its present fuel capacity was seven hours. Fitted with four Olympus Mk.21/2s, the total airframe weight was increased by 22,450 lb (10,183kg). With four Skybolts and 21,940gal (99,759 litres) of fuel aboard (= 168,938 lb/kg), the bomber's estimated all-up weight would now be 339,168 lb (153,847kg). Span was 121ft 0in (36.9m), length 99ft 11in (30.4m) and wing area 4,215ft$^2$ (392m$^2$). Endurance would be around 11.1 hours and range 4,450nm (8,246km). This project, also described as the Mk.3 long endurance Vulcan, was a theoretical development – the Vulcans actually adapted to carry Skybolt showed far fewer changes.

Skybolt itself was 38ft (11.6m) long and each round weighed 12,000 lb (5,443kg). To give the Vulcan B.2 the capability to carry it on four underwing hardpoints, a Vulcan/Skybolt modification programme was put together in October 1960 and XH537 and XH538 were allocated as test airframes. The maiden flight of a Mk.2 with two captive mechanical Skybolts was successfully completed on 29th September 1961 (two days ahead of schedule), and in December this was followed by the first successful dummy drops. Another three drops were made in January 1962 and the dummy trials were completed in February. The first Skybolt Vulcan was to be delivered to the RAF in March 1963, but Britain's plans to buy Skybolt were terminated in December 1962 once development problems back in the US had forced the cancellation of the missile. All Skybolt modifications and associated trials were stopped immediately and this left the UK with no new nuclear weapon, so in December 1962 an agreement was reached with America to buy the submarine-launched Polaris system instead. In the long term this move brought an end to the RAF's control of Britain's airborne ballistic missile force, which in 1969 passed to the Royal Navy with its new fleet of Polaris submarines.

Avro's studies into Vulcan modifications for Skybolt were quite extensive. In October 1960 an addendum to the original Phase 6 proposals suggested a modified crew cabin to make the longer sorties more comfortable. The pressure cabin was re-arranged and extended by inserting a 10ft 9in (3.28m) portion of fuselage immediately forward of the rear pressure bulkhead. The nose and the forward pilot's and bomb aimer's positions were unchanged, but there were now four forward-facing crew stations, in pairs, on the starboard side of the cabin. This allowed for an extra crewman and each crewmember now had his own ejection seat. This modification extended the aircraft's fuselage to give an overall length of 110ft (33.5m); maximum take-off weight was 348,500 lb (158,080kg).

On 23rd January 1963, following the cancellation of Skybolt, the Defence Committee approved the measures that would be necessary to give the V-Bombers a low-level capability. These included some modifications to the aircraft and low-level training for aircrew. All three 'V' types were, of course, designed for high-level flight and so needed strengthening plus new or modified weapons, navigation aids, and the like. When compared to high-level operations, the buffeting normally expected at low level was also likely to induce greater crew fatigue over very long flights. An interim clearance for Vulcans to fly at low level was issued on 15th January 1964, which in February was extended to include the training version of the Blue Steel missile. In July full operational low-level carriage and pop-up release (on the level) of Yellow Sun Mk.2 was cleared, followed in August by pop-up and level release of Blue Steel.

Camouflage modifications to a batch of thirty Vulcans were begun in March 1964 by Hawker Siddeley (formerly Armstrong Whitworth) at Bitteswell, and eighty-nine production sets of camouflage modifications were produced for aircraft on the manufacturing line or just completed. The final ten Vulcan B Mk.2s were completed in camouflage configuration. In August the Mk.2 was given 'ferry' clearance to carry and use overload fuel tanks and the last brand new Vulcan to fly, XM657, made its maiden flight on 21st December 1964.

There were two more versions of Vulcan, but instead of being new developments, their designations covered adaptations and conversions that were introduced late in the Vulcan's service career. The B Mk.2[MRR], also known on occasion as the SR Mk.2, with SR standing for Strategic Reconnaissance, was a Maritime Radar Reconnaissance conversion performed in the 1970s to selected Vulcans assigned to No 27 Squadron. By this time all Vulcans operating in the low-level strike role had been fitted with a Terrain-Following Radar, but for the

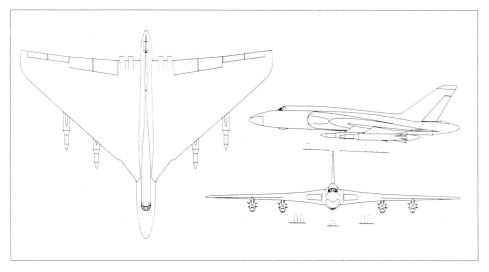

**The Vulcan Phase 6 Skybolt-carrier proposal of May 1960.** Mike Stroud

One of the Vulcan B Mk.2s selected to serve as a Skybolt test aircraft, complete with special underwing hardpoints. **Barry Jones**

The modified Phase 6 of October 1960 with a longer forward fuselage to house the revised crew cabin, and no dorsal spine. This particular design also has aft fans fitted to its Olympus 21/2 engines. **Mike Stroud**

The crew's cabin in the October 1960 version of the Vulcan 6. The forward pair of rear seats would be occupied by the two navigators, those behind by the air electronics officers (starboard) and the optional 'supernumerary crew member' (port). **Mike Stroud**

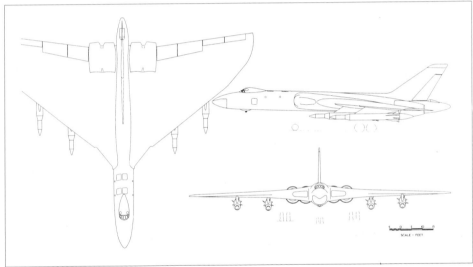

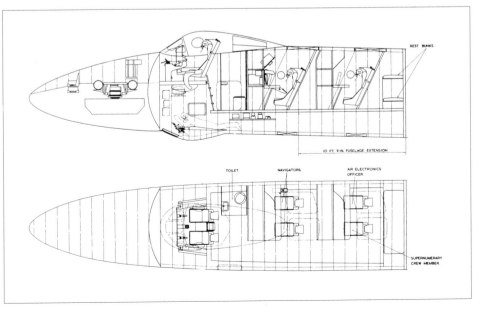

Maritime Radar Reconnaissance role this kit was taken out and replaced by LORAN C navigation equipment, although the rest of the standard Vulcan electronics were retained. Since the new role would occasionally require the B.2(MRR) to carry atmospheric-sampling pods beneath the wings, the first conversions were Vulcans that had been fitted with wing hard-points specifically for carrying Skybolt. In all, nine aircraft had been converted (XH534, XH537, XH558, XH560, XH563, XJ780, XJ823 and XJ825) but not all of them were adapted to carry these sampling pods.

The last Vulcan variant was a rush job. This was the K Mk.2 tanker conversion of the B.2, which was put together at very short notice in 1982 to supplement the RAF's tanker fleet during the Falklands Conflict. They were never ready to take part in the war itself, but these Vulcans were used to reduce the RAF's shortage in tankers. The long distances involved in getting aircraft to the Falklands, via Ascension Island, put quite a strain on the RAF's tanker aircraft for some time after the war was over and the Vulcans acted as a gap-filler. In all, six aeroplanes (XH558, XH560, XH561, XJ825, XL445 and XM571) were modified to the in-flight refuelling configuration and, although this work was done in such a short time, it proved a success. To illustrate the urgency behind this project, it was assessed on 1st May 1982, go-ahead was given three days later, the first conversion (XH561) made its maiden flight on 18th June, and when this aircraft flew to Waddington on the 23rd the modification was released to the Service.

## VULCAN DEVELOPMENT PROPOSALS

Besides the various marks of Vulcan that were put into service, and the proposed Phase 2A, 2B, 3 and 6 modifications already discussed, there were other advanced development proposals from Avro covering a wide variety of ideas. Some of these are summarised below, although none of them were built.

### Avro Type 698 with T-Tail

To compare with the original tailless Type 698 bomber concept, a study was made for an equivalent aircraft fitted with a T-tail. Chapter One in particular stressed the worries raised by the fact that the flying qualities of the delta wing remained something of an unknown when the 698 was first proposed to B.35/46 in 1947. In fact it was recognised that a tailplane might be required, as it was on a later delta wing project – the Gloster Javelin fighter flown in November 1951. The date of Avro's T-tail study is not given, but it was around mid-1951. Note that this was not an official proposal, just a comparison of the, as yet unnamed, Type 698 with and without a T-tail – and it makes interesting reading.

Model tests and flight experience on two other types of tailless aircraft (which are not identified) had shown that, under certain conditions, the longitudinal damping of such aircraft might reduce or become non-existent at high Mach numbers. Although there was no evidence that this might occur on the 698, Avro wanted to consider what action might be required should it arise. If an undamped oscillation occurred at a Mach number well above normal flight conditions, it would be reasonable to damp it using an automatic control. However, if this happened within the speed range below to slightly above the critical Mach number, it would be desirable to overcome it without recourse to such mechanisms. 'Natural' longitudinal damping could be provided by adding a tailplane and it was the purpose of this report to look at the consequences of fitting one.

Adding a tailplane of any size would, of course, increase the weight and drag and, thus, the take-off weight for a given range or, for the same weight, reduce the amount of fuel to be carried. In both cases the height over the target would also be lower. At this stage the minimum size of tail required could not be determined – that still needed the analysis of the flight data from the 707A test aircraft. Nevertheless the investigation had used a tailplane size that it was thought would be adequate; in fact the tailplane proposed was of identical size to the 707A's wings and was attached to a root fairing instead of to the fuselage. To get the most effect, it was considered essential to place the tail wholly aft of the wing trailing edge, and this also involved an extension of the fuselage and an increase in the size of the fin. The tailplane had elevators for normal control, but the complete tail surface was also all-moving to provide trimming.

At the time the present design of the 698 was considered optimum. Should fitting a tail become essential, the advantages given by the tailplane to offset the loss in performance were found not to be great. They were as follows:

1. The greater control over pitching moment provided by the all-moving tail made possible a CofG range which extended aft of the present one. This would make possible certain bomb loadings that were, at this stage, not thought to be usable.
2. The increase in longitudinal stability should improve the aircraft's flying qualities, in particular its steadiness as a bomb aiming platform. The effect of the tailplane as an end-plate to the fin would also improve the lateral stability.
3. Should the longitudinal control limit the usable Mach number, (and, hence, the ability to pull out of a dive) the trimming tailplane would improve this.
4. Since the tailplane was powerful in controlling changes of trim, and since the space on the wing presently taken by the elevators would become available, it would be possible to fit flaps on the wing in the elevators' place. Split flaps would give a valuable increase in lift at take-off and landing, with consequent reductions in the take-off and landing distances.

The report added that the loss in performance could always be overcome by an increase in engine size, but a tailed aircraft would always have less range and height over the target than the comparable tailless aircraft.

The data included a comparison of the two 'versions' at maximum range with full fuel tanks, both powered by four Olympus B.Ol.2 engines. The tailplane aircraft, shown in the drawing, does have split flaps on the wing undersurface in the position normally occupied by the elevators. These were designed for operation during take-off and landing with flap deflections set at 30° and 55° respectively. The take-off weight included a 10,000 lb (4,536kg) bomb and 8,300gal (37,739 litres) of fuel; the landing data was given for half fuel and no bombs.

| | Normal Aircraft | Tailplane Version |
|---|---|---|
| Take-Off Weight | 143,050 lb (64,887kg) | 145,230 lb (65,876kg) |
| Take-Off Distance | 3,127yds (2,859m) | 2,930yds (2,679m) |
| Height over Target | 46,570ft (14,195m) | 44,600ft (13,594m) |
| Fuel Weight | 67,230 lb (30,496kg) | 67,230 lb (30,496kg) |
| Range | 4,686nm (8,683km) | 4,250nm (7,875km) |
| Height on Return | 52,250ft (15,926m) | 50,000ft (15,240m) |
| Landing Distance | 2,006yds (1,834m) | 1,665yds (1,522m) |

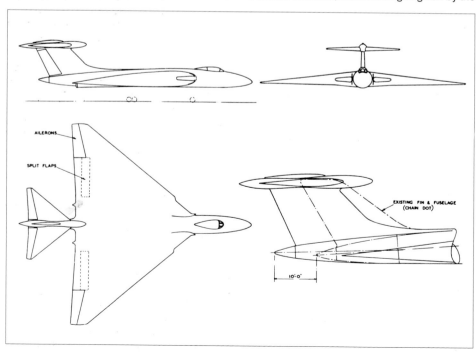

**Drawing showing the proposed tailplane for the Avro 698 (1951). This also shows a comparison of the new tail with the existing fin on the 698. With this modification the 698's span was unchanged at 99ft 0in (30.2m), but the length had increased to 111ft 7ft 6in (34.0mm). The direct weight penalty for fitting the tail and enlarging the fin was 2,180 lb (989kg), the tail itself having a span of 35ft 4in (10.8m) and a gross area of 439ft² (40.8m²). The 10ft (3.05m) of additional rear fuselage alone added 290 lb (131.5kg) of weight.** Avro Heritage

AILERONS

SPLIT FLAPS

EXISTING FIN & FUSELAGE
(CHAIN DOT)

10'-0"

**Three-view drawing showing the Avro 698 fitted with underwing pannier tanks. This also shows, pretty closely, the original Vulcan prototype's delta wing. At this stage the aircraft's length was 95ft 7in (29.1m).**

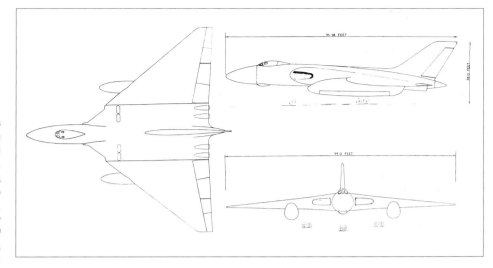

## Underwing Pannier Tanks

At about the same time as the T-tail was being examined, Avro also looked at fitting underwing nacelles or 'panniers' to the standard aircraft to allow it to carry more bombs or fuel. These were placed beneath the inner wing a little way outboard of the intakes and a nacelle could hold a single 10,000 lb (4,536kg) bomb, nine or thirteen 1,000 lb (454kg) bombs or 1,545gal (7,025 litres) of fuel. Different sizes of nacelle were envisaged for various bombs loads and this could bring the 698's maximum load to four 10,000 lb, or up to fifty-three 1,000-pounders.

## Photo-Reconnaissance and 'Pathfinder' Vulcans

Avro proposed a photo-reconnaissance version of the Vulcan in October 1952, with the bomb doors and their associated equipment removed and a camera unit installed in the bomb bay. The fitting embraced ten FX96 cameras and one F49 camera plus two 70mm (day) and two 70mm (night) cameras. The photo-reconnaissance aircraft was heavier with 1,150 lb (522kg) of extra weight in the wing/fuselage and another 450 lb (204kg) in the undercarriage. There was an extra 2,580gal (11,731 litres) fuel tank in the fuselage, and a shallow 870gal (3,956 litres) tank in the bomb bay with eleven photo-flash bombs underneath that. Estimated take-off weight was 171,900 lb (77,974kg) and range 6,520nm (12,082km). An Air Staff requirement for a photo-reconnaissance Vulcan was finally raised in June 1956, but this version was never built.

References have also been found for a Target Marker 'Pathfinder' version of the Vulcan. This seems to have been an Avro pitch to upset the Vickers bid to the B.104D specification of 1950, met by the Valiant B Mk.2, because Avro's project was stated as being designed to 'a comparable specification'. The Valiant B.2 was a one-off prototype, painted all black, which flew in September 1953. A small quantity of production aircraft were planned but these were cancelled – at one stage the aircraft was intended to carry the Blue Boar guided bomb. The bid letter for Avro's Pathfinder was dated 25th April 1951 and the project was heavier than a standard 698/Vulcan through the addition of 1,775 lb (805kg) of wing strengthening plus another 70 lb (32kg) in the fuselage, 625 lb (284kg) in the fin and 145 lb (66kg) in the undercarriage. The warload was seven Target Marker Bombs and, to ensure that the aircraft met the role requirement (time over target at lower altitude), there were two extra 1,210gal (5,502 litres) fuel tanks, one in front of and another behind the bombs.

## In-Flight Refuelling

In January 1954, long before the K Mk.2 came into existence, Avro completed a brochure for In-Flight Refuelling Tanker and Receiver conversions of the Vulcan B Mk.1. This was based on some requirements laid down in a letter from the Air Ministry dated 16th January 1954, following meetings held at Avro on 14th December 1953 and 8th January 1954. The basic requirements were:

1. A Receiver to cater for a rate of flow of 500gal/min (2,273 litres/min).
2. A Receiver to cater for a rate of flow of 1,000gal/min (4,547 litres/min).
3. A Tanker to cater for a rate of flow of 500gal/min or 1,000gal/min and a transfer capacity of at least 10,000 Imp gal (45,469 litres). This would have two massive fuel tanks in the bomb bay and the IFR package behind them.

Avro reported that the modifications required to install the fixed fittings in this version were of a relatively minor nature, involving the bomb bay only, and could be embodied retrospectively. However, calculations showed such retrospective action would involve a large increase in labour time, so the manufacturer suggested that the modifications should be made on the production line, or by the contractor during repair or overhaul. The equipment would be supplied by Flight Refuelling Ltd and the 500gal/min (2,273 litres/min) and 1,000gal/min (4,547 litres/min) receiver units were to be interchangeable. The total additional weight from the two units was 412 lb (187kg) and 583 lb (264kg) respectively, and the receiver aircraft's normal all-up weight with either fitting would be 160,000 lb (72,576kg).

The role of the 10,000gal (45,469 litres) tanker was to refuel a low-level bomber at an altitude of 10,000ft (3,048m) to 15,000ft (4,572m). Both aircraft would take off from the same base, climbing and refuelling on track. The tanker's range would be 530nm (982km) and action radius 265nm (491km), assuming maximum climb and cruising speeds up to the transfer point and economical cruising on the return. With the removal of the standard bomber's radar and other equipment, and the addition of 170 lb (77kg) of fixed and 5,168 lb (2,344kg) of removable fittings, the all-up weight of the tanker was estimated to be 181,631 lb (82,388kg). In addition Avro made calculations for another version carrying 5,000gal (22,735 litres) of fuel which, transferring at a rate of 500gal/min (2,273 litres/min), offered a range at normal all-up weight of 1,725nm (3,196km).

## Supersonic Vulcan (Avro Type 732)

A drawing has recently been discovered by Avro Heritage for the Type 732, a supersonic development of the Vulcan from 1956 which shared the latter's general delta wing shape, single fin and no tail layout; however, the fuselage was much more streamlined. Power was to be supplied by eight de Havilland Gyron Junior engines, probably with a thrust rating of about 7,000 lb (31.1kN) to 7,500 lb (33.3kN). The engine arrangement looked quite complicated with four engines laid in pairs side-by-side in the mid/rear centre fuselage and fed by what appears to be individual intakes arranged one above the other at the sides of the fuselage. The other engines were housed in pairs in underwing nacelles. A tricycle undercarriage had twin wheels on the nose leg and twin bogies and eight wheels on each main leg, the latter retracting forwards into a bay just outboard of the intakes. The underfuselage weapon is unidentified but may be a theoretical design by RAE; it appears to have two engines and its lower fins would be folded when the 732 was on the ground. Aircraft span was 94ft (28.7m), length 102ft (31.1m), wing area 3,875ft² (360.4m²), wing thickness/chord ratio 4% and leading edge sweep angle 50°. No predicted performance details are available.

## Alternative Missiles and Weapons

There were other proposals for Vulcans powered by alternative engines, or carrying different underfuselage weapons or missiles, not all of which were of a destructive nature. As early as October 1952 there were suggestions for fitting two more Olympus 3 engines in small

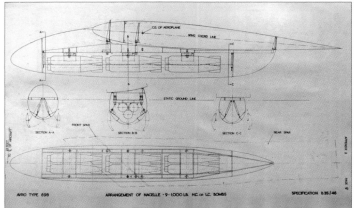

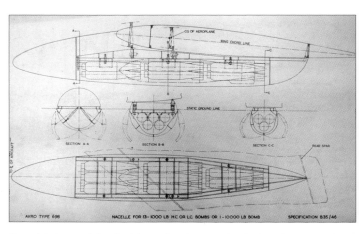

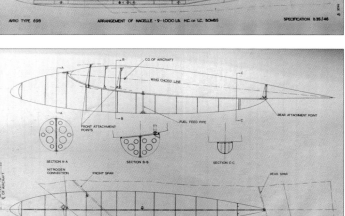

Above left: **Internal detail of the underwing pannier designed to carry nine 1,000lb (454kg) bombs.**

Above right: **Internal detail of the underwing pannier designed to carry thirteen 1,000lb (454kg) bombs.**

Left: **Detail of the underwing pannier intended to carry additional fuel.**

Below left: **Fuselage detail of the proposed photo-reconnaissance variant of the Vulcan.**

Below right: **Bomb load detail for the proposed 'Pathfinder' Vulcan of 1951.**

Bottom: **Avro Type 732 supersonic bomber (1956).** Chris Gibson via Avro Heritage

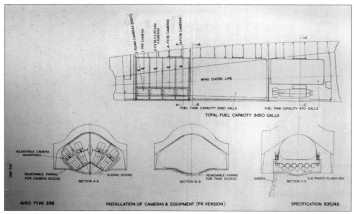

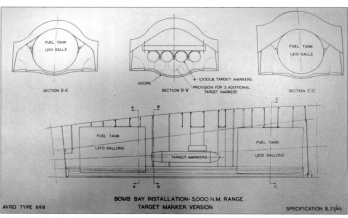

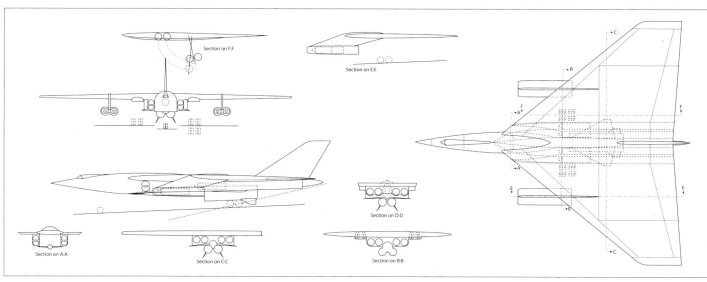

underwing nacelles two-thirds of the way out along the wing, but it was found that this would reduce the aircraft's range and increase drag. An alternative was to bury them in the fuselage behind and below the normal four engines, and also have the outer wing thinned to a thickness/chord ratio of 5%. The overall result in the second case was an estimated increase in drag rise Mach number of 0.02 from Mach 0.87.

Information is currently not available, or at least the identity is unknown, for the Vulcan Phase 4. However, the Phase 5 from November 1956 was to intended carry another Avro powered missile, the proposed W.107, which itself weighed 23,000 lb (10,433kg). With the weapon aboard, the aircraft's take-off weight powered by either the 20,290 lb (90.2kN) Olympus Ol.21 or 20,000 lb (88.9kN) Conway Co.31 was 223,535 lb (101,395kg) and 225,000 lb (102,060kg) respectively.

In October 1957 Avro produced a brochure that looked closely at maintaining Vulcan operations into the 1970s. Emphasis was placed on carrying more fuel – the basic 9,290gal (42,241 litres) load was to be supplemented by another 3,300gal (15,005 litres) in the bomb bay, 800gal (3,638 litres) in a new dorsal spine and a further 1,250gal (5,684 litres) in the wing. In fact this Mk.2 development would have two alternative sets of bomb bay fuel tanks: one tailored to the installation of Blue Danube or Yellow Sun which would hold about 1,000gal (4,547 litres), the other to Blue Steel which was the 3,300gal (15,005 litres) version. Other features included larger intakes, four-wheel undercarriage and a vertically retracting nosewheel. Flight and tunnel testing had shown that the standard Vulcan canopy actually gave an undesirable amount of drag (perhaps 3% of the lift/drag ratio), so Avro had designed a new shape. This was then extended aft and faired into the existing dorsal fin, which made additional space for more fuel but without increasing the aircraft's frontal area or reducing its critical Mach number.

The extra fuel supply, plus the new Olympus 200-series engines and larger intakes, now offered a range of 5,000nm (9,260km). Estimated take-off weight, when fitted with electronic countermeasures equipment in the rear fuselage and carrying one Blue Steel, was given as 221,047 lb (100,267kg). This variant was expected to cruise at Mach 0.873. It had the same wing as a Mk.2 – span was 111ft (33.8m) and length 105ft (32.0m).

In November 1961 Avro produced a brochure that showed a Vulcan carrying two, three or four Avro W.140 stand-off long-range

**The basic Vulcan updated in an October 1957 proposal to take its career through to the 1970s. It is shown carrying a 46ft (14.0m) long 'Stand-Off' missile designed by RAE Farnborough.**

**Vulcan shown with four Avro W.140 missiles.**

**Vulcan B Mk.2 shown as a carrier of the French Diamant booster rocket.** Chris Gibson

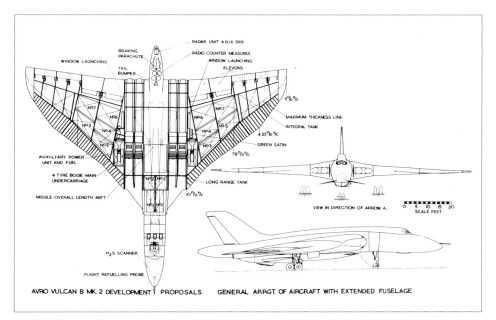

AVRO VULCAN B MK.2 DEVELOPMENT PROPOSALS    GENERAL ARRGT. OF AIRCRAFT WITH EXTENDED FUSELAGE

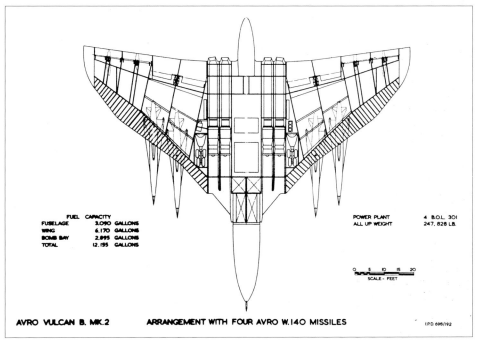

AVRO VULCAN B. MK.2    ARRANGEMENT WITH FOUR AVRO W.140 MISSILES

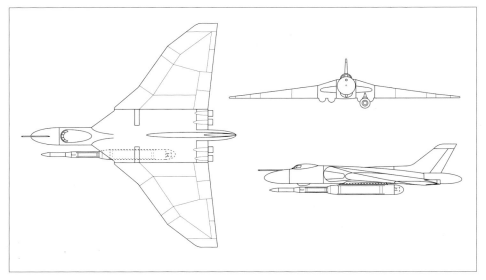

missiles, an advanced weapon that was intended to fly at Mach 3 and 70,000ft (21,336m). A year later, anticipating the end of Skybolt, the Air Staff thought about carrying a BAC Bristol ramjet-powered missile called the X-12 Pandora. This slim weapon was 50ft (15.2m) long and was designed for Mach 2.5. A drawing from January 1963 showed a Vulcan with two of these on pylons just outboard of the main wheels; however, work on Pandora was halted soon afterwards. In 1958 Vulcan was also considered as a carrier for a high-speed vehicle designed for high-altitude research. This was proposed by J E Allen of Avro's Weapons Research Division and the Vulcan would take this machine to height before release, very much like the work done in America with the X-1, X-2 and X-15 aircraft. A similar idea brought the Vulcan into the picture as a carrier of the Diamant (Diamond), a French booster rocket from the early 1960s that had the potential to launch satellites, but this idea was not taken up.

## TRANSPORT AND CIVILIAN PROPOSALS

In addition to its mainstream military development the Avro designers found time to come up with ideas for expanding the Vulcan's role.

## Avro Type 718

1951 was a busy year for Avro's advanced projects team with several proposed 698/Vulcan developments. One was the Type 718 military transport version of August 1951. Avro had been given some approximate requirements for such a type by the Director of Military Aircraft Research and Development at the MoS in a letter dated 22nd June 1951, and these were increased following discussions with an MoS Working Party on 15th August. Since the 718 was derived from the bomber, Avro had been able to make all the components directly interchangeable, with the exception of the fuselage itself of course. This naturally had a bearing on the pace with which a prototype could be built and the type put into production. With an immediate instruction to proceed, Avro estimated that the first unequipped prototype could be completed in September 1953 and the first production aeroplane a year later.

The complete wing with engines, undercarriage and control surfaces was interchangeable with the bomber. A new production joint was proposed for the 698 at the inboard engine/bomb bay rib position, so that either fuselage could be fitted to the wings. In addition the fin, rudder, nose undercarriage and the majority of the crew's cockpit would be interchangeable. It was anticipated that neither the

flight behaviour at high Mach number nor the drag rise would be affected by the new fuselage.

The 718 had a two-deck layout of the 'double-bubble' type in which the lower deck replaced the bomber's fuselage and the upper deck was superimposed. The cockpit was situated at the forward end of the top deck and was on similar lines to the 698. The main cabin on the top deck had an unrestricted length of 55ft 6in (16.9m) and an internal diameter of 9ft 8in (2.95m). It was closed at the aft end by a pressure bulkhead, which was completely removable for loading freight. On the lower deck the only portion used for passengers or freight was that between the two spars, the latter conveniently forming the ends of the pressurised region. There was a fixed stairway from upper to lower deck at the forward end of the latter, and an adjacent hatch in the floor of the lower deck that formed a second entrance from ground level. In addition there was a hatch in the floor of the upper deck for loading freight into the lower deck, and large loading doors were provided in the bottom of the aft fuselage outside the pressurised region. Forward of the front spar in the lower fuselage were tanks containing 2,770gal (12,595 litres) of fuel. No windows were fitted in the pressure cabins since the risk of failure was considered unacceptable, but having the jet pipe exits all aft of the pressurised area was expected to make the noise level extremely low throughout.

The 718 was designed to have a still air range of 4,280nm (7,931km) when carrying eighty fully equipped troops weighing 250 lb (113kg) each; that is, with a payload of 20,000 lb (9,072kg). With full civilian safety allowances for diversions and navigation, plus fuel used in taxying, take-off, climb, descent, stand-off, circuit, landing and taxi, this equated to a stage distance of 3,000nm (5,559km). The requirement determined the normal gross take-off weight, which was 164,000 lb (74,390kg), and rocket assistance was required if the aircraft needed to get off from 2,000yd (1,829m) runways. The performance was achieved from a cruising speed of 500 knots (576mph/ 927km/h) and a mean altitude of 47,000ft (14,326m). Power came from four 12,150 lb (54.0kN) Olympus Ol.3 and 66,258 lb (30,055kg) of fuel was carried. Span was 99ft (30.2m), length 124ft (37.8m) and gross wing area 3,446ft² (320.5m²). Alternative versions could carry 110 passengers with less equipment or 22,000 lb (9,979kg) of freight, or serve as an ambulance (casualty clearing) aircraft. For shorter ranges, up to 40,000 lb (18,144kg) of freight could be carried on the two decks. The 718's seats faced rearwards and a galley was provided in the 80-90-seater; the 110-seater had no galley.

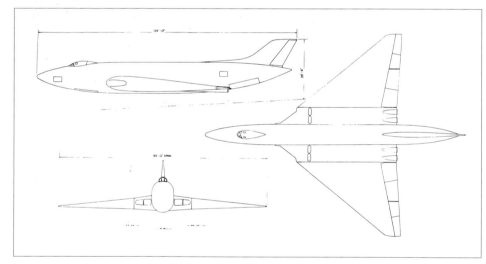

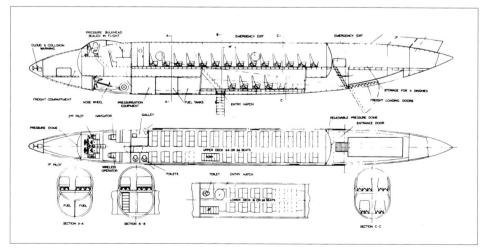

**The rather sleek-looking Avro Type 718 military transport project of August 1951.** Avro Heritage

**Rearward-facing seating arrangement for the 80-90-seat version of the Type 718.** Avro Heritage

## Avro Type 722 Atlantic

This final unbuilt development of the Vulcan, the Type 722 Atlantic, is almost certainly the most well known because the project received quite a lot of publicity in the aeronautical press at the time it was proposed. Preliminary data was first published in June 1953, when Avro's Sir Roy Dobson stated that 'airlines all over the world have been asking for details of the inevitable sequel to the Vulcan…'. A brochure prepared by Avro in September noted 'the performance requirements for a civil aircraft are in many respects similar to those for a long-range bomber, in that both must carry a large payload over a long range in the most efficient manner possible'. The high cruising speed essential to the bomber for military reasons was of value also to the civil type to give minimum journey times and high utilisation. Subsequent to its first flight the Vulcan had demonstrated outstanding capabilities and it was natural, therefore, to consider the possibility of basing a civil aircraft on the same configuration. This led to the Atlantic long-range, delta wing jet airliner.

The 722's operating Mach number and cruising altitude were not the same as those of the bomber and, of course, the fuselage capacity needed to be much greater. These differences affected the wing size and wing loadings, which were also therefore different from the bomber. Nevertheless, the basic aerodynamic configuration was retained to maintain the excellent handling qualities of the Vulcan at both ends of the Mach number range. Flight testing had shown that the Vulcan's low-speed properties were 'truly outstanding', and the delta could also easily achieve Mach 0.90 at height.

The Atlantic had four engines, Olympus, Rolls-Royce Conway or any other engine of equivalent thrust, placed some way out along the wing (when the initial data was released in June 1953 these sat alongside the fuselage). All of the fuel was in the wings, the delta allowing a large volume to be carried near the aircraft's CofG without having to resort to tanks in the fuselage. The fuselage itself was circular with an outside diameter of 12ft 6in (3.81m) and was fully pressurised to give sea level conditions in all stages of flight. The flight crew comprised two pilots seated side-by-side, a navigator and, if required, an engineer. The main passenger accommodation was divided into two cabins by a centrally positioned galley, and space below

the floor was utilised mainly for baggage. Two entrance doors were sited on the port side, one serving the forward cabin with the other at the rear of the aft cabin. The wing's control surfaces were very like the Vulcan's with elevators and ailerons, each split into two halves, occupying most of the trailing edge. Powerful airbrakes were provided on the wing forward of the engines near the front spar and a descent from 40,000ft (12,192m) could be accomplished in less than three minutes. A brake parachute was fitted in the tail cone for emergency landings.

Span was 118ft 9in (36.2m), overall length 143ft 0in (43.6m) and gross wing area 4,262ft² (396.4m²). With one hundred passengers on board, and 87,410 lb (39,649kg) of fuel (= 10,920gal/49,652 litres), the Atlantic's all-up weight was 204,900 lb (92,943kg). A maximum of 120 passengers could be carried but the fuel would have to be reduced to 60,112 lb (27,267kg) to compensate, thereby cutting the range. Taking one hundred passengers from London to New York at a cruising speed of 600mph (965km/h), against an 83mph (134km/h) headwind and with full BOAC safety and flight allowances, the still-air range on the westbound crossing was estimated to be 5,950 miles (9,574km). The cruising altitude was in excess of 40,000ft (12,192m). Despite the publicity, no orders were placed for the Atlantic.

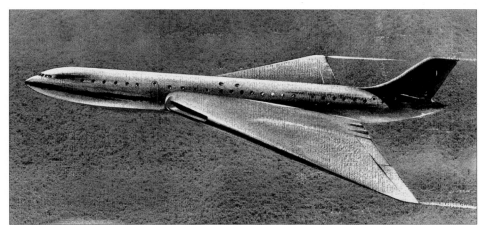

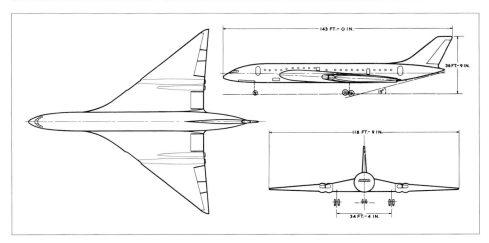

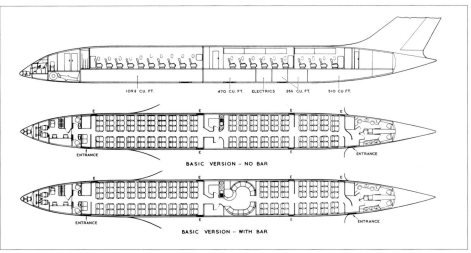

**This impression of the Type 722 Atlantic was first released to the public in June 1953 and shows the engines next to the fuselage as per the Vulcan.**

**By the time a new Atlantic brochure was completed in September 1953, in time for the Farnborough Show, the engines had been moved further away from the fuselage. This allowed the leading edge wing roots to be blended into the fuselage.** Avro Heritage

**The seating arrangements for the September 1953 Atlantic, with and without a bar. Note again rearward-facing seats.** Avro Heritage

# Chapter Four

# Service History

**Background to Service**

The V-Bomber Force was intended to deliver the British nuclear deterrent and began its existence in January 1955 with the entry into service of the Vickers Valiant. The Avro Vulcan B.1 followed in June 1957 and the two types were joined by the Handley Page Victor B.1 in 1958. The intended use of these three aircraft types was as high-altitude deliverers of nuclear weapons, with conventional bombing as a secondary role. The intention was to reach their assigned targets at an altitude of at least 50,000ft (15,240m) prior to dropping their weapon. As more powerful versions of the Olympus engine became available these were fitted to the Vulcan, enabling the originally specified height-over-target to be comfortably exceeded in later years. The delta-wing planform provided a useful margin of manoeuvrability at high altitudes, enabling the Vulcan in theory to avoid many types of NATO fighter that it met during exercises. When the Vulcan first went into service, it was fitted with a T4 (Blue Devil) optical bombsight in the under-fuselage

bomb-aimer's blister, but the T4 was removed quite early in the aircraft's career, with reliance being placed instead on the Navigation and Bombing System (NBS). The NBS consisted of an H2S Mk.9A radar, coupled to a Navigation and Bombing Computer (NBC). This system is described elsewhere in the book.

Part of the credibility of a 'deterrent' force is dependent on one's enemy believing that it exists and means business. Therefore, an early priority for the V-Bomber squadrons was to travel the world showing themselves off to all and sundry, as evidence that the Force was in being, and that it could readily deploy to remote locations should that need ever arise. While this activity could be regarded as mere 'flag-waving', it did play its part in making both friend and potential foe believe that the force's potential was real.

Although Bomber Command never operated in the manner of the USAF Strategic Air Command, which in times of high alert maintained nuclear-armed aircraft in the air 24 hours per day, many other airfields had Operational

**This official publicity photo shows two Vulcan B.1s in formation with Vickers Valiant BK.1s of Bomber Command during 1958, not long after the Vulcan had entered front-line service.** MoD PRB.13805 via Phil Butler

Readiness Platforms constructed, to enable groups of four V-Bombers to be dispersed from their main bases in an emergency, each group able to take off within the four-minute time limit from receipt of a missile attack warning or 'Quick Reaction Alert' (QRA). Amongst others considered, these airfields included Ballykelly, Bedford (Thurleigh), Boscombe Down, Brawdy, Bruntingthorpe, Burtonwood, Coltishall, Cranwell, Elvington, Filton, Kinloss, Leconfield, Leeming, Leuchars, Llanbedr, Lossiemouth, Lyneham, Macrihanish, Manston, Middleton St George, Pershore, Prestwick, St Mawgan, Stansted, Valley, Wattisham and Yeovilton – in other words, virtually all airfields in the UK with runways of sufficient length for V-Bomber operation. The main Vulcan bases generally had runways of 9,000ft (2,743m) length, but some

This photograph shows Vulcan B.1 XA906 of No 83 Squadron at the Gaydon Battle of Britain display on 14th September 1957. The aircraft is in the original all-over white colour scheme with the standard roundels and fin flashes. No unit markings are worn. via Phil Butler

This image of XA913, taken at Gaydon on 19th September 1959, shows an aircraft of No 101 Squadron, the second front-line unit to form. The aircraft wears a Squadron badge on its fin and remains in the white colour scheme with the 'full colour' national markings. via Phil Butler

XH477, shown here, is an aircraft of No 44 Squadron at the Gaydon display on 20th September 1958. It wears the Waddington Wing marking on its fin and wears a Squadron badge behind the fuselage roundel. via Phil Butler

A detail shot showing the nose of a Vulcan B.1 in the first 'all-white' scheme. The Squadron badge aft of the roundel is of No 83 Squadron. This location was a favoured position for application of the unit badge, although it might alternatively appear on the crew door, or (occasionally) on the aircraft's fin. via Tony Buttler

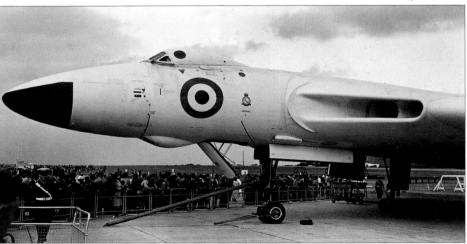

of the V-Bomber dispersal bases had shorter runways – Aldergrove, Hurn and Shawbury, which also figured in the 'dispersal' lists for a period, each only had 6,000ft (1,829m) runways. Each airfield had a group of two or four dispersals built immediately adjacent to the take-off point of a suitable runway, and from time to time most received a clutch of V-Bombers during Bomber Command exercises. Note that the airfields included civilian airports, and a few (such as Burtonwood) were airfields that had otherwise fallen out of everyday use. A typical Exercise during which 'Dispersal' was practised was 'Mayflight V' in May 1962, when Scampton Vulcans were dispersed to Middleton St George and Burtonwood, while Waddington aircraft flew to Coningsby, Leconfield and Leeming and crews from Waddington were moved to Finningley to man Vulcans from No 230 OCU. A similar 'Mickey Finn' exercise in September of the same year sent Waddington Vulcans to Leeming and Leconfield and Scampton ones to Lossiemouth, Middleton St George and Yeovilton, while OCU ones went to Coningsby.

The main types of regular exercises may be summarised as:

- **Mayflight** – a scheduled Bomber Command event which involved generation of the entire force, dispersal, a period on stand-by (with practice changes in readiness state) and then a scramble – selectively airfield by airfield.
- **Mick** – was a Bomber Command no-notice generation exercise, which stopped short of dispersal.
- **Mickey Finn** – superseded 'Mayflight' and was a Bomber Command no-notice generation, dispersal, QRA and scramble practice. On one memorable occasion the Bomber Controller scrambled the whole force simultaneously so that something like ninety aircraft from nine Vulcan and two Victor squadrons were launched at once, according to one participant's recollection.

This formation shot shows XA909, XH475 and XH476, all of No 101 Squadron, in the first 'all-white' scheme. The furthest aircraft, XA909, has the small Orange Putter tail-warning receiver radome at the rearmost tip of its fuselage. None are carrying unit markings. Avro 467-8-A via Tony Buttler

Another photo taken at Gaydon, this time during the Battle of Britain Day display on 17th September 1960, showing Vulcan B.1 XH499 of No 617 Squadron. It remains in the original white colour scheme, with the unit badge aft of the fuselage roundel. via Phil Butler

This photo of Vulcan B.1A XH478 was taken at Finningley during the 1962 Battle of Britain display and shows an aircraft of No 101 Squadron. This example is now in the 'anti-flash' white scheme with toned-down pastel roundels, fin flash and Waddington Wing badge. Evident is the enlarged tail section of the B.1A, housing the Red Steer radar-warning receiver, while the aircraft also has an air-to-air refuelling probe on its nose. via Phil Butler

Opposite page:

Avro Vulcan B.2 XJ781 in the 'anti-flash' scheme. This shot was taken while the aircraft was in service with No 83 Squadron. The only unit marking is the Squadron badge aft of the fuselage roundel. via Tony Buttler

This is an early shot of XH558 in the 'anti-flash' scheme in which it was delivered, possibly taken on a test flight before delivery, as there are no unit markings. A V Roe A-2-16 via Tony Buttler

- **Kinsman** – was a station-sponsored event involving just one of its squadrons doing what amounted to a mini-'Mayflight'.
- **Edom** – was the exercise nickname used to order changes in readiness state for all aircraft on stand-by. The normal condition, which applied to the permanent peacetime QRA force of one aircraft per squadron or the entire force following its generation, required a take-off within fifteen minutes (Readiness State 15 – RS15) which permitted crews to be in ready-rooms or their bunks. RS05 was cockpit readiness, which could be (and sometimes was) sustained for hours, and RS02, which involved starting engines and (for free-fallers but not Blue Steel-armed aircraft) taxying to the end of the runway

When the Victors and Vulcans were assigned to SACEUR in 1963, NATO events and terminology began to intrude and by the later years of that decade individual squadrons were practising their dispersal options via an Exercise 'Index', instead of a 'Kinsman'; MINEVALs were larger scale station-level equivalents with 'Mick' and 'Mickey Finn' being replaced by Part 1 and Part 2 TACEVALs, plus 'Active Edge' as an additional SACEUR-instigated generation exercise.

The V-Force was never dispersed in anger, although it was generated and armed, with crews held at cockpit readiness for a time, in response to the Cuban missile crisis of 1962. During this alert, Coningsby had seven Vulcan B.2s available, Finningley seven B.2s, a B.1A and five B.1s, Scampton twenty-three B.2s and Waddington five B.1s and twenty-two B.1As, a total of seventy. 'Available' aircraft included four receiving minor repairs at their bases and five available for recall from modification at Bitteswell.

Between 1962 and 1969, the QRA commitment was as described above. While a more relaxed posture was adopted after the RN had

assumed responsibility for maintaining the deterrent, the V-Force was still required to be able to resume its alert status at short notice and to cover the targets it had been allocated within SACEUR's overall war plan – a capability that it was required to demonstrate via TACE-VALs. This involved a certain amount of juggling of crews to ensure that, while some were away on detachments or leave, there were others who had studied their targets on a back-up basis. Similarly, the condition of aircraft undergoing maintenance had to be closely monitored to ensure that sufficient numbers could be recovered and generated, within the specified time, to cover the assigned targets.

The original 'nuclear deterrent', which entered service with the Vickers Valiant squadrons, was the Blue Danube atomic bomb, and this was also the armament of the Vulcan B.1 when it first entered service. The Blue Danube was supplemented in 1958 in the Vulcan squadrons at Finningley and Scampton by an 'interim' half-megaton fission bomb code-named Violet Club, pending the delivery of 'Yellow Sun Mk.1' in 1960. Meanwhile, under 'Project E', the Waddington squadrons had received American Mk.5 bombs, although their operational value was severely limited by US custodial considerations which precluded armed aircraft being dispersed. In 1962, the

A rare photograph of a Vulcan B.2 (XM612, taken in 1964) wearing the 'Castle' badge briefly worn by the Coningsby Wing before the units transferred to Cottesmore. The badge was modelled on Tattershall Castle near RAF Coningsby. Phil Spencer

XJ783 is seen here in the static display at the US Armed Forces' Day event at Sculthorpe on 19th May 1962. It is another B.2 aircraft of No 83 Squadron, with the badge aft of the roundel as the only unit marking. Although the national markings have been 'toned down' those seen in later years were even paler shades, especially for the blue of the roundel. via Phil Butler

XM575, seen in the static display at the Paris Salon on 15th June 1963, wears the three lightning-bolt fin marking of No 617 Squadron in (toned-down) red on its fin. The other markings are also paler than those seen in earlier pictures. Phil Butler

XH563, seen here at the Lossiemouth 'Navy Day' in 1962, is another 83 Squadron aircraft, again showing the very pale version of the 'toned-down' markings. via Phil Butler

American weapons provided for Victors and Vulcans were replaced by 'Yellow Sun Mk.2' with its Red Snow fusion warhead, although US weapons continued to be employed by SACEUR-assigned Valiants until these aircraft were withdrawn from service in 1965.

The need to accelerate the 'scramble' time of the V-force led to a number of developments all with the aim of getting the maximum number of bombers airborne within the time allowed by the 'four-minute warning' that was deemed to be the maximum time that the defence radar system (primarily the Ballistic Missile Early Warning System that relied on radars in Alaska and Greenland and at Fylingdales in Yorkshire) would be able to give. Some of these developments were improvements in infrastructure such as the provision of Operational Readiness Platforms (ORP) adjacent to the runways at both the main bases and selected dispersal airfields. Use of these eliminated taxying time allowing immediate take-off in response to an order from the Bomber Controller at High Wycombe, who was connected directly to crews in their cockpits via a dedicated network of telephone lines terminating in telescramble cables plugged into individual aircraft. This system provided a considerable degree of redundancy and could be backed up by radio changes in alert state also being relayed, for instance by air traffic control on a local frequency. Another innovation was the introduction of the ability to start all four engines at once. The original system relied on large numbers of batteries on a trolley and was demonstrated publicly at the SBAC Show in 1960 when four V-bombers were simultaneously started and scrambled. The types were changed each day, first up being the Vulcans of No 617 Sqn which were all airborne within 1 minute 45 seconds of the word 'Go'. This was later replaced by an integral 'rapid air' system which gave a similar capability without the

complication of the external trolley. The trial installation having been made on B.1 XA899, Avro's began to install the system in B.2s beginning with XJ782 in November 1962, the modification being completed in early 1963.

Because of the increasing capability of Warsaw Pact defensive systems, work had been going on to develop Blue Steel, which was a rocket-powered missile, to be carried by the Mk.2 versions of the Vulcan and Victor as a 'stand-off' weapon that could be launched beyond the range of enemy anti-aircraft defences and, because of its high-altitude, high-speed flight profile increase the chances of a successful strike. The Vulcans of the Scampton Wing were armed with Blue Steel from 1962 until 1970. An interesting sidelight on Blue Steel was that it was guided by an Inertial Navigation System (INS), which was inherently more accurate than the Navigational Bombing System of the Vulcan itself. Thus, Blue Steel-equipped aircraft used inputs from the missile's INS to feed the aircraft's Bombing and Navigation System (BNS) which meant that it was, in effect, a major source of navigational data during the carriage phase. Blue Steel became available for use in 'a national emergency' in September 1962, although it was not declared to be fully operational until February 1963, when the system was unveiled to the Press at Scampton.

Blue Steel's 'Achilles Heel' was the time it took to prepare it for operations. This was partly due to the safety precautions dictated by the missile's extremely unstable, and thus very dangerous, fuel (High Test Peroxide) and frequent technical difficulties encountered while trying to persuade the systems in the missile and the aircraft to communicate with each other. In the early days it could take twelve hours or more to prepare a missile/aircraft combination but this had been significantly reduced by October 1963 when Blue Steel armed aircraft began to be committed to QRA and during Exercise Nursemaid in 1964 eight Blue Steels were deployed in a simulated dispersal basis (that is, they were flown in an operational state, as if they were to be delivered to dispersal airfields), and actual dispersals followed in later exercises.

In a war situation it would be considered an option to drop an unfuelled Blue Steel as a free-fall bomb in the event that there was insufficient time to complete the rather hazardous fuelling process, or to do the same in other circumstances when system malfunctions prevented its planned launch.

A longer-range 'Blue Steel Mk.2' had been cancelled, but it was intended to replace it by arming the Waddington Wing with the Douglas WS-138A Skybolt missiles (later re-designated AGM-87A). However, technical failures during trials in the USA led to the US government cancelling the Skybolt programme in November 1962, leaving the V-Force in the lurch, and ultimately causing transfer of the nuclear deterrent role to the Royal Navy with the procurement of the Polaris missile from the USA and the construction of the nuclear-powered submarines required to launch them. Nevertheless, the V-Force retained its nuclear role with its Blue Steels and Yellow Suns being progressively replaced by the WE177B during the later 1960s.

Following the Soviet success in shooting down Gary Powers' U-2 overflight with a guided missile on 1st May 1960, a new assessment of the probable anti-aircraft missile threat led to a change of role for the V-Force: this time to attack at very low level 'under the radar', only emerging near the target to 'toss' their weapons. Thus, this required the V-Force to fly at low level (nominally 250ft [76m]), so as to

avoid detection by enemy radar, with a climb to 12,000ft (3,658m) near the target to release their Yellow Sun, until the parachute-retarded WE.177B became available for low-level delivery. Blue Steel remained in service, and was subsequently modified to permit low-level launch in place of the high-level delivery for which it had originally been designed. In the absence of a long-range stand-off weapon to carry the warhead, the WE.177 was to be dropped as a free-fall weapon. Low-level flying training of the Vulcan B.1A units began on 1st April 1963, with their low-level role declared operational on 1st June 1963. The Vulcan B.2 units followed, with training beginning on 1st January 1964 and their operational role declared on 1st May of the same year. The change in role resulted in the former white colour scheme being changed to a tactical camouflage on the upper surfaces of the aircraft to make them less visible to higher-flying opposition. The first B.2 to receive the camouflage was XM645, but no doubt some B.1As received theirs earlier.

Further weapon development flying cleared the actual release of the various nuclear and conventional weapons (including the Blue Steel missile) at low level. In the case of the conventional bombs, these were also provided with retarding parachutes to ensure that the aircraft was well clear of possible shrapnel damage from their explosion. The V-Bomber Force continued to act as the United Kingdom's nuclear deterrent until 1969. Following the transfer of this responsibility to the Royal Navy's Polaris-armed submarine fleet in June of that year, the V-Bombers continued to operate in support of the NATO and CENTO treaty organisations, with both nuclear and conventional weapons.

The new role had severe implications for the airframe lives of all the aircraft involved. The aircraft had all been designed to climb to 50,000ft (15,240m), deliver their weapons, and return to base at high level. The punishing effect of high speed low-level flight in possibly turbulent air had not been considered as a design case, and led to extensive investigation of each type of aircraft by their respective design authorities. In the case of the Vulcan the resulting fatigue-life assessment was extremely thorough, even involving the removal of Vulcan B.2 XM596 from the production line to become a grounded fatigue test airframe. The aim was to identify modifications that would increase the life to 12,000 flying hours in the low-level role.

Because of the need for continuous training in this role, much of the remaining lives of the Vulcans were spent flying along the UK low level route or in Canada, where aircraft flew from Goose Bay in Labrador. Goose Rangers were normally done on an individual crew basis. Low-level training was also carried out over Libya (via El Adem, Malta and/or Cyprus Rangers) and the Akrotiri Wing subsequently flew over Iran, the Gulf, Italy, as well as circuits of Cyprus itself.

**This official photograph, taken not long after the transition to the low-level role, shows two Vulcan B.2s at low level, one (a Finningley aircraft) in white and the other (XM645) in the newly-applied disruptive grey/green camouflage.** MoD PRB 27210

**XJ783 is shown here at Luqa, Malta, during its service with the Near East Air Force Bomber Wing at Akrotiri. NEAFBW Vulcans of Nos 9 and 35 Squadrons were frequent visits to Malta during this period.** via Phil Butler

The operating profile for 'toss bombing' a nuclear bomb (before low-level release of the WE.177B was cleared for use) involved the following:

- Approach target at up to the $V_{NE}$ of 415 knots (768km/h) at tree-top level
- Make a 2G pull-up to climb at 25° to the horizon
- Open bomb doors
- Release bomb at 12,000ft (3,658m)
- Within four seconds, close bomb doors and initiate a 2G turn to be tail-on to the explosion
- Dive to gain maximum speed, then climb away at full power.

This very precise operating requirement was behind the 'low-level training profile' that was imposed on V-Bomber crews once the low-level role became the norm. The profile was slightly less rigorous than that required in a real 'hot war' situation, primarily to preserve the fatigue life of the airframes. The profile also varied slightly depending on the Mark of aircraft and the weapon load. The low-level practice was normally flown at 500ft (152m), rather than the 'tree-top' height that would have been aimed for in a real emergency, and the normal speed was 240 knots (445km/h) rather than the 400+ knots (743+km/h) required by the war profile. Fuel management was required to maintain the wing tanks full for as long as possible (so the bomb-bay tank normally fitted in addition to any bomb-load would be used first).

One of the roles of the V-Force was the provision of strategic reconnaissance, using both conventional cameras and radar. Thus the Valiant entered service in a photo-reconnaissance role with the formation of the second squadron on the type and Victor similarly took on 'radar reconnaissance' duties very early in its career. Although A V Roe produced schemes for a photo-reconnaissance version of the Vulcan, these did not proceed to production (Chapter Three). However, the Vulcan did, in turn, eventually take over radar reconnaissance duties from the Victor when the remaining Victor SR.2 aircraft were needed for conversion to flight-refuelling tankers, and then later even supplemented the Victor in its flight-refuelling role. The B.2[MRR] maritime reconnaissance Vulcans carried an F.95 camera mounted in the bomb-aiming blister in place of the original optical bombsight, and indeed it was a normal fit on the standard bombers as a means of scoring simulated bombing runs.

Each of the V-Bomber types, after the necessary preliminary trials at their manufacturers and at experimental establishments (primarily RAE Farnborough and A&AEE Boscombe Down), entered service at an Operational Conversion Unit (OCU). As training courses graduated from the OCUs, their members formed the personnel strength of successive operational Squadrons. The V-Bombers, being larger, heavier, and needing longer runways than their predecessors were deployed at extensively re-developed Bomber Command airfields. In the case of the Vulcan these were initially at Waddington (OCU May 1956), Finningley (October 1957) and Scampton (May 1958). With the introduction of the B.2 version, a new Vulcan base was established at Coningsby, although this Wing moved to Cottesmore (a former Victor base) later. Full details of the various flying units are given in Appendix Two, starting with the experimental establishments and trials units. The contemporary Royal Air Force structure of Group, Wing, Squadron and Flight organisation then follow, with the Operational Conversion Unit inserted ahead of the list of Squadrons.

The first Vulcan squadron, No 83, formed from the first OCU training course in May 1957, remained at the OCU's base of Waddington near Lincoln, with a nominal establishment of eight Vulcan B.1s that was built up to full strength during the year. The unit quickly gained much publicity for the V-Bomber Force,

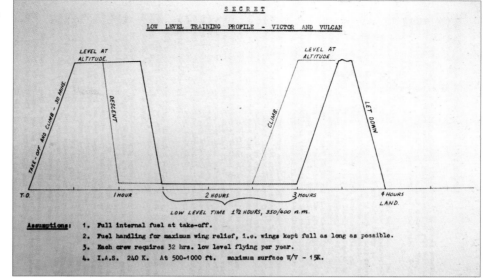

**Details of the training flight profile, taken from TNA document AIR 20/11306.**

and the Vulcan in particular, by making high-profile flights to the four corners of the world. The Vulcan had received adverse publicity with the earlier loss of a No 230 OCU Vulcan, following the crash of XA897 at London Airport at the end of a return flight from New Zealand and Australia on 1st October 1956, but the success of many overseas 'flag-waving' sorties initiated by No 83 Squadron soon displaced any memories of the unfortunate crash at Heathrow. Within eighteen months of the unit's formation, Vulcans of the Squadron had made 'official' visits to Kenya, Southern Rhodesia, Argentina, Brazil, Canada, Pakistan, Malaya, the Philippines and Ceylon, as well as sending an aircraft to the Paris Air Show in June 1958 and providing the Vulcan for a daily 'V-Bomber' formation at the SBAC Show at Farnborough in September. Although it may now seem odd to have considered a visit to Argentina as a priority for the V-Force, the actual event was the inauguration of a new President of Argentina, at which there were senior political dignitaries from

**XL446 of No 35 Squadron shows off its camouflage during an air display.**
C G Harden via Phil Butler

Left: **XM656 is seen here dropping 1,000 lb (454kg) parachute-retarded bombs on a flight from Cottesmore during the qualification trials for clearance of this weapon for the low-level role.** via Tony Buttler

Opposite page:

**A nice view of Waddington Wing B.2 XM597 during a low-level pass with undercarriage lowered at an air display. The black aerial at the top of the fin is for the ARI 18228/1 Radar Warning Receiver, for which this was the 'Trial Installation' aircraft in 1971. This equipment was later fitted to many Vulcans.** via Phil Butler

**This photograph taken at Waddington showing XM600 and another aircraft well illustrated the nose refuelling probe fitted to the Vulcan and the small nose radome for the General Dynamics Terrain-Following Radar which all Vulcans received for the low-level role.** via Phil Butler

more than sixty countries present, with the Vulcans taking part in a large flypast comprising much of the strength of the Argentine Air Force, so it was by no means a low-key event.

In addition to taking part in Bomber Command exercises and training, 'Lone Ranger' deployments of one or two aircraft had been sent to Bahrein and to Butterworth in Malaya, the latter as a trial 'reinforcement' to the Far East Air Force, and such V-Bomber deployments to British bases around the world became a very frequent occurrence. With so many distractions from routine, it was perhaps no surprise that the Vulcans in the 1958 Bomber Command Bombing and Navigation competitions did not do well, with the Valiant squadrons taking the first seven places in the ratings, followed by No 83 and then the Vulcans of the more recently formed No 101 Squadron. This meant that no Vulcan crews qualified to represent Bomber Command in the USAF Strategic Air Command competitions in the following year (although two aircraft had participated in the 1957 SAC Competition on a 'trial' basis). Both the RAF and USAF Competitions involved Navigation and Electronic Warfare exercises as well as the dropping of practice bombs against range targets, with marks awarded for accuracy. The Vulcans fared better in later years, although in several Bomber Command competitions the Victor squadrons took top marks, until development improved the Vulcan's radar system to its full potential. Deployment Exercises of one or more aircraft were frequent, at first called 'Lone Ranger' exercises as already mentioned. These expanded to include 'Western Rangers' (to the USA), 'Goose Rangers' (to Goose Bay for low-level exercises), and even 'Blue Rangers'. The latter were Vulcan ferry flights of Blue Steel missiles to Edinburgh Field in Australia where the missiles would be subject to trial firings by No 4 Joint Services Trials Unit. Ferrying by Scampton Wing Vulcans was preferable to using the

USAF C-124s which had carried several of the early missiles to Australia, and also enabled the Vulcan crews to see what the JSTU was doing with the missiles – as well as combining a 'Lone Ranger' element of exercising other aspects of deployment.

No 83 Squadron flew the Vulcan B.1 until August 1960, when it handed over all its aircraft to the reforming No 44 Squadron. The 'number-plate' was then handed over to a newly formed No 83 Squadron, equipped with the Vulcan B.2 at Scampton, which received its first new aircraft in December 1960. No 83 became one of the three units of the Scampton Wing, which in due course became equipped with the Blue Steel stand-off bomb. The squadron remained at Scampton until it was disbanded in July 1969, immediately after the main nuclear deterrent role was taken over by Royal Navy's Polaris-armed nuclear submarines.

The second Vulcan front-line unit was No 101 Squadron, formed at Finningley in October 1957 with B Mk.1s. It moved to Waddington in June 1961 in an exchange with the Vulcan OCU that moved in the reverse direction. It retained B Mk.1s (by then modified to B.1As) until January 1968, when they were the last of that version to be retired from front-line service and were replaced by B.2s. The Squadron disbanded in August 1982.

No 617, the Dam Busters, was the third Squadron to be formed with the Vulcan B.1, on 1st May 1958 at Scampton, inaugurating that base's association with the Vulcan which lasted until March 1982, with the disbandment of No 27 Squadron. Vulcan B.2s arrived in September 1961 and the unit received the Blue Steel-equipped B.2A during 1962, which the squadron flew until the weapon was finally withdrawn in 1971 (although flying with the missile ceased rather earlier). No 617 remained at Scampton until it disbanded in December 1981.

The fourth Vulcan squadron was No 44, formed at Waddington, as stated above, by the

handover of No 83 Squadron's B.1s in August 1960 (effectively the 'old' No 83 was renumbered to 44, and a 'new' No 83 was formed). The B.1s were duly modified to B.1A standard until replaced by B.2s in November 1967. The Squadron remained at Waddington until it was disbanded on 31st December 1982.

The fifth Vulcan squadron to form was No 27 which came into being at Scampton on 1st April 1961. With the other units of the Scampton Wing (Nos 83 and 617) it became equipped with the Blue Steel stand-off missile when this first entered service in September 1962. The unit disbanded on 29th March 1972, but was reformed on 1st November 1973 with the Vulcan B.2[MRR] at Waddington to take over part of the Strategic Reconnaissance role previously carried out by the Victor SR.2s of No 543 Squadron at Wyton when the latter aircraft were required for conversion to flight refuelling tankers. The B.2[MRR] remained with the squadron until it was disbanded on 31st March 1982.

The sixth Vulcan squadron was No 50, which formed at Waddington on 1st August 1961, initially with Vulcan B.1 and B.1A, their first batch of aircraft being transferred from No 617 when that unit received its B.2s. No 50 began to receive the B.2 version in December 1965, with the final B.1A leaving in November 1966. During 1982, the remaining six B.2 aircraft were converted to K.2 configuration and the unit transferred to flight refuelling duties until final disbandment on 31st March 1984. It was the last operational Vulcan squadron.

The seventh squadron to form was No 9 which received its first B.2 at Coningsby in April 1962, having been officially formed as a unit on 1st March. The unit moved to Cottesmore, a former Handley Page Victor base, on 10th November 1964 and remained there until moving to Akrotiri in Cyprus on 26th February 1969 where it became part of the Near East Air Force Bomber Wing. The Squadron returned to the UK to be part of the Waddington Wing in

January 1975 and stayed there until disbandment on 9th April 1982.

The eighth squadron to receive the Vulcan was No 12, which also formed with the Vulcan B.2, on 1st July 1962 at Coningsby. It moved to Cottesmore with the rest of its Wing in November 1964. It was the shortest-lived of the Vulcan squadrons, being disbanded on 31st December 1967.

The ninth and last Vulcan squadron in chronological order was No 35, which received its Vulcan B.2s from January 1963, (being officially formed on 1st December 1962). It formed the third Squadron of the Coningsby Wing, and moved to Cottesmore with its fellows in November 1964. No 35 moved to Akrotiri on 15th January 1969, a few days ahead of No 9 Squadron,

and remained there until returning to the UK on 16th January 1975 to join the Scampton Wing. No 35 was disbanded on 28th February 1982.

During a typical year (1962), Vulcans of the operational Squadrons accumulated 15,355:45 flying hours.

During a typical year (1962), Vulcans of the OCU and the eight operational squadrons then flying, accumulated 15,355:45 flying hours. This equates to approximately seventy aircraft in use by the end of the year, with their crews flying about 250 hours per year. This number of annual hours was typical, although it might vary a little from year to year.

Throughout its early service the operations of the Vulcan were closely allied to those of the USAF's Strategic Air Command (SAC), since

the plans of the two air forces were closely coordinated. Later the Vulcan was assigned to SACEUR and SHAPE called the shots – it was SHAPE that did the de-confliction with SAC's SIOP. If the Cold War had become 'Hot', the V-Force would have attacked targets in the Baltic States and other areas of western Russia to pave the way for SAC Boeing B-52s following them from bases further away.

As well as their participation in the annual SAC 'Giant Voice' Bombing Competitions, many Vulcan flights were made to the USA for exercises and visits to events such as air displays. From 1977, frequent visits were being made by Vulcans and their crews to the ranges surrounding Nellis Air Force Base in Nevada for 'Red Flag' exercises, where USAF aircraft and those from other NATO Air Forces flew against simulated Warsaw Pact targets with realistic threats from equipment designed to replicate Soviet air defences.

Although, apart from the years when two Squadrons were part of the Near East Air Force in Cyprus, the Vulcan Squadrons were part of Bomber Command, there were many deployments to RAF bases in Commands outside the UK, not just the 'Lone Rangers' but also groups of (typically) four aircraft deployed to Malta, Cyprus, Bahrein, and even Singapore and Malaya. The most significant of the latter was probably 'Operation Chamfrom', reinforcing the Far East Air Force during the Indonesian 'confrontation' (1964-66) when an undeclared war was effectively being fought in North Borneo. The Vulcans never took an active part in the confrontation, but Indonesian knowledge of their deployment no doubt gave their President reason for restraint in his actions.

The real demonstration of the Vulcan's worth perhaps only came in the twilight of its career, during the Falklands War in 1982, when the last Vulcan squadrons were reprieved from disbandment at the time of the Argentine junta's invasion of the Falkland Islands. The story of the 'Black Buck' operations to bomb the runway on Port Stanley Airfield and later to attack Argentine radars with Shrike homing missiles, will probably be more familiar to readers than many other aspects of the Vulcan's history, but for completeness we will summarise it here. The space available in this series of books does not allow a full account of all the activities of the Vulcan Squadrons, but that of 'Black Buck' does bear repetition.

This photograph of XM650 at its Waddington dispersal shows the 'Panther' badge of No 1 Group aft of the roundel, indicating that this aircraft had participated in a SAC Bombing Competition in the USA. This may indicate why the Waddington Wing marking has been deleted from its fin. via Tony Buttler

A rather menacing head-on view of a camouflaged Waddington Vulcan B.2 at its dispersal. Note that there is a flat-plate aerial mounting for 'Red Shrimp' (one of the Vulcan's several radar 'jammers') below the engine jet pipes on the starboard side of the aircraft. via Tony Buttler

A shot of a Scampton Wing Vulcan B.2A, XL320 airborne with a Blue Steel missile. The aircraft is camouflaged, following the transfer of missile-equipped aircraft to the low-level role.
Ministry of Defence via Terry Panopalis

This view shows Vulcan K.2 XJ825 of No 50 Squadron at an air display, probably in 1983. It wears the Waddington Wing marking and the 'running dingos' of No 50 Squadron on the fin.
via Phil Butler

This photograph shows Vulcan B.2[MRR] XH534 of No 27 Squadron over the North Sea, one of the unit's favoured patrol areas being the oil rigs in that area. Ministry of Defence via Terry Panopalis

When the invasion took place on 2nd April 1982, only three Squadrons of Vulcans remained in being, all based at Waddington and all three being due for disbandment by the end of June. On 9th April Waddington was placed on stand-by for possible involvement in the recovery of the islands. Five crews who had flown in the most recent 'Red Flag' exercise (in February 1982) were chosen, with six Vulcans selected for possible deployment (that is, one per crew plus a spare). In the event only five of the six aircraft were used. The chosen aircraft were those which had the 'Skybolt' attachment points and internal 'plumbing' fitted, because these items greatly facilitated the work needed to suit them for the task in hand. The adaptation work involved reactivating their air-to-air refu-elling equipment (still fitted, but not used for some years) and fitting an improved Inertial Navigation System. They were also fitted with additional radar jamming pods (Westinghouse AN/ALQ-101) with wiring runs along the Sky-bolt internal ducting. The crews began practis-ing air-to-air refuelling and the aircraft had their light grey undersides overpainted with a coat of Dark Sea Grey. Aircraft XM598 and XM607 deployed to Wideawake, the airfield on Ascen-sion Island, on 29th April. The first 'Black Buck' mission was launched at about midnight on the following day (30th April/1st May), both aircraft taking off amidst a flock of eleven Victor K.2 refuellers needed to support the sortie. XM598 had been intended as the primary aircraft, but because of a technical problem had to return to base, with the reserve aircraft, XM607, taking over. The task was to drop a stick of twenty-one 1,000 lb (454kg) bombs diagonally across the Port Stanley runway to ensure that at least one bomb would hit the runway. This intention was achieved, although a repeat sortie made by XM607 launched on 3rd May failed to hit the runway. The two Vulcans then returned from Wideawake to Waddington. The next task was aimed at destroying the Argentine radars on the Falklands, which were causing problems for the Royal Navy Sea Harriers. Trials took place over the Cardigan Bay bombing range using Martel missiles fired from XM597, but it was decided to use AGM-45 Shrike radar-hom-ing missiles (obtained from the USAF in Europe) in their place, carrying missiles mounted on two pylons attached to the Skybolt

**XM647 of the Akrotiri Wing is shown flying over Cyprus in 1973 during the time that Nos 9 and 35 Squadrons formed the Near East Air Force Bomber Wing.** Ministry of Defence via Terry Panopalis

**XM612 of No 101 Squadron at Nellis AFB in Nevada during a 'Red Flag' Exercise.** Ministry of Defence via Terry Panopalis

**XM612, one of the 'Black Buck' aircraft, on the Wideawake hardstanding, Ascension Island during May 1982. This example did not actually fly in a Black Buck operation itself.** Ministry of Defence via Terry Panopalis

under-wing hard-points. XM597 and XM598 were flown to Wideawake on 26th and 27th May to carry out this next operation. After an in-flight refuelling problem on 28th May, XM597 flew to the Falklands again on 30th May, carrying out an attack that caused slight damage to the main surveillance radar aerial. A further attack was then launched on 2nd June, again by XM597, this time carrying four Shrikes. This time two missiles were launched, destroying one of the radars controlling one of the anti-aircraft batteries near Port Stanley. On the way back to Wideawake the Vulcan's refuelling probe broke off, meaning it had to divert to Rio de Janeiro, short of fuel. It was still carrying two Shrikes, only one of which could be jettisoned, which caused something of a problem for the diplomats once the Vulcan had landed safely at Rio. A final 'Black Buck' bombing sortie was made on 11th June, by XM607. Meanwhile, six of the other operational Vulcans at Waddington were being progressively modified to become K.2 refuelling tanker versions, to equip No 50 Squadron and thereby extend the Vulcan's operational life until 31st March 1984.

# Chapter Five

# Trials Aircraft

## Engine Test-Beds

Successive versions of the *Bristol Olympus* turbojet powered all production versions of the Vulcan, although the first prototype had flown with the other main British turbojet engines of the time (the Rolls-Royce Avon and Armstrong Siddeley Sapphire). Several Vulcan B.1 and B.2 aircraft participated in the development flying of successive versions of the Bristol Olympus engine, which made its first Vulcan flight in the second prototype, VX777, on 3rd September 1953. Production Vulcans flown in the course of further Olympus development included:

| | | |
|---|---|---|
| XA889 | Mk.104 (B.Ol.1/2) | Jan 1958 - Oct 1958 |
| XA891 | Mk.200 (B.Ol.6) | Aug 1958 - Jul 1959 |
| XH538 | Mk.201 | Jun 1963 - Mar 1965 |
| XH557 | Mk.300 (B.Ol.21) | Apr 1961 - Jun 1964 |
| XJ784 | Mk.301 | Mar 1961 - Jul 1962 |

XA889, XA891 and XH557 spent much of their time with Bristol Siddeley Engines at Filton, the remaining two aircraft being mainly flown by A V Roe/HSAL at Woodford.

The Olympus Mk.200 and 300 engines were effectively prototypes for versions that went into service as the Marks 201 and 301 in production Vulcan B.2 aircraft. The Mk.301 engines were generally used in the later production aircraft (XM serial numbers), conferring a higher engine thrust at the expense of increased fuel consumption.

One weakness of the first generation of jet engines was smoke, or rather the smoke trail laid down by the aircraft. With a four-engine type like the Vulcan this brought problems because, if viewed against a bright sky or sunlit cloud, it permitted the bomber to be spotted very early (as highlighted in Chapter Seven). In fact, the smoke could be seen by others before the aircraft itself became visible, and the problem was made worse by humid conditions. The RAF rejected the solution adopted by the USAF, which was to introduce a chemical fuel additive that was very effective in cutting visible smoke but also very toxic. Vulcan B.2s XH558 and XL392, fitted with Olympus 201s, were used for the trials in 1971 and 1972, which

**Vulcan B.2 XH557 seen landing at Bristol Siddeley's Filton airfield in 1961 while testing the Olympus Mk.300 engine that (as the Mk.301) later saw service mainly in the Blue Steel-equipped Vulcan B.2As at Scampton. It wears the 'toned-down' fuselage roundels and no roundels or serial numbers below the wing.**
Bristol Siddeley E48596 via Phil Butler

involved checking the smoke produced and the changes in engine performance (particularly tendency for flame-outs and difficulty in relighting) after the fitting of various modified fuel injectors. (One of the authors remembers welding some of these experimental ones while working for Lucas Aerospace at the time!) The trials resulted in all Olympus 200-series engines in Vulcans being modified to receive the final version of the burners. Similar burner trials on Olympus 300-series engines in XM648 took place in 1975, but the modifications were not introduced to the fleet having the later engine series, possibly after cost-benefit analysis relating to the Vulcan's planned withdrawal date.

The *Bristol Olympus 22R* (otherwise the Mk.320) was the version intended for the British Aircraft Corporation TSR.2 strike aircraft. This engine was installed in Vulcan B.1 XA894 in a nacelle below the fuselage having bifurcated air intakes. The intake configuration was reportedly intended to allow evaluation of the engine performance at slow airspeeds, when the Vulcan might have its undercarriage down with the nose undercarriage interfering with intake airflow, but it seems more likely that the configuration was required to replicate the airflow of the final TSR.2 installation. XA894 arrived at Filton for conversion on 18th July 1960 and made its first flight with the Olympus 22R engine in February 1962. Test flights continued until the aircraft was destroyed on 8th December 1962 when it caught fire after an uncontained turbine failure during engine ground running. By this time nearly eighty hours of flight time had been accumulated on this version of the engine.

The *Bristol Olympus 593* was the engine for the BAC/Aérospatiale Concorde airliner, being a further development of the Olympus 22R. The Vulcan allotted to test this version was XA903, which arrived at Filton on 3rd January 1964 for conversion. The test engine was mounted below the fuselage in a similar manner to the 22R installation on XA894, but with a single 'straight-through' intake, essentially identical to a Concorde engine pod. The first flight with the Olympus 593 was made on 9th September 1966. At a later stage of the trials, a water spray rig was fitted below the nose of the Vulcan to enable water and ice ingestion tests to be carried out. The tests continued for a number of years, building up over 400 hours of Olympus 593 flight time before their completion in 1971. XA903 was then re-allotted for trials of the Rolls-Royce (Turbo-Union) RB.199 intended for the Panavia Tornado.

The *Bristol Siddeley BS.100* was a large turbofan lift/thrust engine with Plenum Chamber Burning (PCB) intended to power the Hawker Siddeley P.1154 vertical-take-off fighter aircraft, which was an enlarged, supersonic development of the P.1127 Kestrel. The engine was based on the core of the Olympus 200 series. The Vulcan B.1 XA896 was allotted to carry out flight trials of this engine and was delivered to Rolls-Royce at Hucknall on 25th May 1964 for conversion on behalf of Bristol Siddeley Engines. The BS.100 would have been carried in a pod below the fuselage in a similar manner to the Olympus test-beds. Work on the conversion ceased with the cancellation of the P.1154

Another photo showing the Olympus 593 test-bed XA903 on an early test flight.
Rolls-Royce via Terry Panopalis

This view shows the Conway and Spey Vulcan, XA902, at Hucknall in October 1962, not long after its first flight with two Rolls-Royce Speys in the inboard engine positions.
Rolls-Royce HP7311 via Tony Buttler

XA903 in its final form as the RB.199 test-bed, seen here taking off at Filton. Rolls-Royce via Terry Panopalis

in February 1965 and XA896 was scrapped. The *Rolls-Royce Conway* was a low-by-pass turbofan, rather than a pure turbojet. It made its first Vulcan flight in the re-engined first prototype, VX770. The aircraft was converted to R.Co.7 Conways at A V Roe's Langar works in 1956 and was delivered to Rolls-Royce at Hucknall on 24th August 1957. This aircraft was destroyed in a tragic accident during the Battle of Britain flying display at RAF Syerston on 20th September 1958, killing the crew. Following the crash, which had resulted from a structural overstress during the display, a second Vulcan (XA902) was also re-engined with the Conway to continue and complete the planned trials. Although the Conway had been seriously considered as the powerplant for further developments of the Vulcan (Chapter Two), its main military application was to power the Vulcan's rival, the Handley Page Victor B.2.

Vulcan B Mk.1 XA902 replaced the Vulcan prototype VX770 as a test bed aircraft for the Rolls-Royce Conway engine, its conversion beginning at Woodford in December 1958. XA902 arrived at Hucknall following this conversion on 17th July 1959. It was fitted with Conway R.Co.11 engines, this rating becoming the Mks 102 and 103 for service in the Handley Page Victor. The maximum thrust of these engines was between 16,500 lb (73.3kN) and 16,900 lb (75.1kN) at 9,990rpm.

The tests, which were programmed in six-hour flights, involved cruising at 40,000ft (12,192m). However, the cruise rpm of the Conway at this height meant that the aircraft's maximum speed would be exceeded, which would take this Mk.1 through its airframe limits. Because of these limitations it was decided to operate the engines at Boeing 707 airliner ratings, which were slightly less than the R.Co.11; so only two of the engines were operated at high rpm (9,370rpm), the other two at a lower figure; the climb was made at 9,570rpm. It was this structure/power limit problem that made VX770 break up in the air in 1958 during a display – the prototype's structure was by no means as strong as that of a production Vulcan and so its Mach limit was correspondingly less.

The maximum all-up weight of XA902 with four Conways was the same as a standard Vulcan Mk.1, around 160,000 lb (72,576kg), and according to *Flight* magazine in January 1960 this aircraft was frequently flying eighteen hours in a day. In all, it flew a total of 1,021 hours with Conways in place, with some of the flying being carried out from Malta as well as from Hucknall. When XA902 was originally allotted for Conway trials, it had also been intended to test the later RB.163 Spey engine.

With the Conway tests essentially complete, the aircraft was then converted to take *Rolls-Royce Spey* engines in the inboard positions, while retaining the outer Conways. It made its first flight in this form on 12th October 1961. The Spey engine was used in the DH.121 Trident and BAC 1-11 airliners, and in military form in the Blackburn Buccaneer Mk.2 and the HS.801 Nimrod. XA902 was retired in October 1962.

After retirement XA902 was taken by road to RAF Dishforth in March 1963. This final task was a feasibility study to see if it was practical to transport Vulcans in this manner, should there be a need.

The *Rolls-Royce (Turbo-Union) RB.199* was the engine intended for the Panavia Tornado and the former Olympus 593 test-bed, XA903, was chosen to carry out flight trials, with the RB.199 in a pod below the fuselage, superficially similar to that used for the Olympus. However, the pod was closely modelled on the starboard side of a Tornado fuselage, and at a later stage of the trials included the Tornado gun pod containing a Mauser 27mm cannon. XA903 was ferried from Filton to Cambridge on 4th August 1971 for conversion work to be carried out by Marshalls of Cambridge. The aircraft was delivered to Rolls-Royce on 9th February 1972 and made its first flight with the RB.199 on 19th April 1973. An interesting and unique feature of the trials took place in January 1976, when XA903 was flown to A&AEE Boscombe Down for firing trials of the Mauser cannon. These trials were carried out in firing butts, although the object was to determine whether ingestion of the products of shell propellants affected engine performance. (In earlier years, British fighter aircraft such as the Swift and Hunter had suffered problems from 'gun-smoke', which required engine fuel system modifications.) A total of 285 flying hours were built up with the RB.199 engine before XA903 was retired in February 1979, when it was the last Vulcan Mk.1 to fly.

## Automatic Landing and Instrument Development

This broad heading actually covers all development of the Autopilot Mk.10 and its associated Military Flight System, which then led to Automatic Landing *per se*. For some years, the development of automatic landing capability for the V-Bomber Force had been an Operational Requirement (OR.947), aimed at introduction during the service of the Vulcan and Victor Mark 2 versions. The requirement was finally abandoned, but only after a very large proportion of the necessary equipment had been developed and test-flying for system clearance had been carried out. The Autopilot Mk.10B and the associated version of the Military Flight System intended to achieve the capability were installed as standard in the Vulcan Mark 2, and further development (as the Mk.10C) enabled the Belfast C.1, Argosy C.1 and other transport aircraft to achieve the full capability (required for these transport types by OR.988). The work done over several years on the Vulcan B.1 development aircraft and on early B.2 versions proved that the system did indeed work, and it certainly smoothed the development path for the overall system to be cleared for use on the military transport types. This in turn enabled the system to be developed and cleared for use by civilian airliners, starting with the DH Trident, and subsequently (with airborne equipment nowadays available from several manufacturers) for almost all airliners in use today. The principles used by these civilian systems had been established by the earlier military development work, and the main difference incorporated in the civilian systems was the fail-safe 'redundancy' of triplicated (Triplex) system architecture that reduced the risk of system failure to the minimal level needed for certification while the aircraft equipped with the system carried fare-paying passengers to safe landings in minimal visibility. Although the capability is now available from a number of different autopilot suppliers, this pioneering work was done by Smiths Aircraft Instruments Ltd (latterly Smiths Industries Aerospace).

The Mk.10 Autopilot for the RAF was essentially similar to the Smiths SEP.2 type that had been developed for use in civilian transport aircraft such as the Bristol Britannia and Vickers Vanguard, although it also replaced the SEP.1 in some Comets and Viscounts. The initial Mk.10 work was carried out on the Vickers Varsity twin piston-engine crew-trainer (G-APAZ) used by Smiths Instruments to test the equipment. The work was done under two separate contracts [6/Instruments/4829/CB.16(A) for the Mk.10A Autopilot and 6/Instruments/21652/CB.16(B) for the 'Military Flight System']. This arose because the development was, initially at least, of two quite separate systems that gradually became closely integrated into a single entity, with the incorporation of extra features such as 'Autothrottle' as the development work proceeded. The definitive development, as fitted to the production Vulcan B.2 (and the Handley Page Victor B.2), was the Mk.10B autopilot. The later Mk.10C met the requirement for automatic landing by the Short Belfast and AW Argosy military transports. However, earlier work on the integration of the Vulcan's original Mk.10 autopilot in conjunction with the Navigation and Bombing System (NBS) had begun with the Vulcan B.1 XA894, prior to any specific work on the 'autoland' requirement.

Following development flying in the Varsity during the period from October to December 1958, the equipment was then fitted to Avro Vulcan B Mk.1 XA899 for further flying at Boscombe Down and Bedford (Thurleigh) under the supervision of the Blind Landing Experimental Unit (BLEU). The aircraft itself was initially on the strength of the Aircraft & Armament Experimental Establishment, whose pilots shared the flying with BLEU personnel during the first stage of trials. The trials continued at the BLEU from February 1959. At the start, the autopilot was the Mk.10A with various modifications being added progressively. The Mk.10B, the intended standard autopilot for the Vulcan B.2, was not installed in XA899 until September 1960, although the first fully automatic landing had been accomplished at Thurleigh on 22nd December 1959 with a modified Mk.10A unit.

The Automatic Landing System ('Autoland') comprised equipment on the aircraft enabling its automatic pilot to be coupled to signals from suitable Instrument Landing System (ILS) ground stations. These signals gave the autopilot directional (azimuth) information from the ILS Localiser and height data from the ILS Glidepath transmitter to enable the aircraft to land without input from the pilot. Such a system had been demonstrated at the TRE at Defford in 1945 using the Boeing 247 DZ203, but much had happened in the meantime, with input from the RAE's Blind Landing Experimental Unit, Smiths Aircraft Instruments and several other contributors to enable a proper 'operational' system to be put into service. The 1945 Defford trials had led to the formation of the BLEU. The final stages of this work (applying to the Vulcan B.2 and Victor B.2) were then carried out to meet OR.947. The military Autoland system required the use of 'leader cables' installed on either side of the runway and extending 5,000ft (1,542m) back from the downwind end of the runway to enhance the azimuth signals from the ground equipment, but later civilian systems were able to dispense with this complication as ongoing refinement of the ILS installations eliminated the need for the leader cables. The overall system allowed the aircraft to approach the runway from any direction at between 1,000 and 2,000ft (305 and 610m) to pick up the ILS localiser signals. From this point the autopilot could direct the aircraft through a number of stages until power was cut by the 'auto-throttles' 20ft (6m) above the runway threshold. The 'auto-throttle' feature enabled the aircraft to be flown at a set airspeed and rate of descent in a way that was more stable and repeatable than could be readily achieved by a pilot.

The official clearance trials of the Mk.10B Autopilot (and associated Military Flight System Mk.1B), flown on XH533, did not begin until May 1963. The first series of trials, which lasted until August of that year, involved fifty-three automatic landings at Boscombe Down and Bedford. The trials had been somewhat delayed by the need to install Murphy 'magnetic leader cables' on the ILS ground installations at both sites during the early phases of the work. XH533 had Olympus Mk.201 engines installed for these trials, although system clearance would have later required the system to be cleared also for the Mk.301 Olympus (to ensure that the 'auto-throttle' features were not altered by the change in airframe and engine characteristics – the Mk.103 aircraft having altered air intakes as well as the more powerful engines). The trials typically involved a take-off from Boscombe Down, followed by ten automatic landings at Thurleigh and then a return to Boscombe Down. The trials were carried out at different landing weights/Centre of Gravity positions to give a proper spread of results for the statisticians, and were predominantly at Thurleigh because of the Blind Landing Experimental Unit's kine-recording facilities at the latter airfield, which enabled accurate filmed records to be made of any variation in aircraft performance during the landing. The trials continued until the 'autoland' requirement for the Vulcan and Victor was cancelled in 1967, with the last foray of XH533 to Bedford being on 27th June 1967. During the previous eighteen months this aircraft had made at least ninety-seven automatic landings at Thurleigh. By that time the A&AEE pilots had started on autoland 'clearances for service' of each individual Vulcan B.2 from the Scampton Wing, but only that of XL319 (making eight landings carrying a

This photograph of all-white B.2 XH538 shows one of the two main 'Skybolt' trials aircraft. It lacks the normal enlarged fuselage tail-end of the B.2, although that was fitted to this aircraft at a later date. A V Roe A-2-75 via Tony Buttler

Blue Steel) was completed before the programme was cancelled. As mentioned earlier, the military 'autoland' scheme required the installation of magnetic leader cables at airfields such as Scampton, where it was to be employed, a feature which became redundant with the later civilian systems as ILS system performance was improved. The 'Autoland' capability requirement was finally cancelled by the time that the transfer of the nuclear deterrent role to Royal Navy submarines was in sight, but the work which had been carried out by the Vulcan (and Victor) bombers had, by then, laid the groundwork for the civilian Autoland systems pioneered by the DH.121 Trident, which in turn was the forerunner of systems in daily use by almost all types of modern civilian airliners today. A related development programme was the 'Take-Off Director' (TOD) trial, referred to in Chapter Seven, which used similar technology to 'Autoland' to enable take-offs to be made in zero visibility. This was purely a research programme that never reached an operational stage.

The Military Flight System (MFS), which was ultimately fitted to all Vulcans, was essentially the military version of the civilian Smiths Flight System (SFS), originally developed for application to civilian transport aircraft. It was also further developed for military use on board Smiths' Varsity research aircraft, G-APAZ, before being flown aboard a Vulcan. As eventually developed this became part of an integrated whole with the Mk.10B autopilot.

However, it started life as a completely separate project to integrate the information from several separate cockpit instruments in order to simplify the displays seen by the pilot, particularly during 'blind flying'. The two instruments that resulted from the development work were the Beam Compass and the Director Horizon. Together, these two items replaced the artificial horizon, gyro magnetic compass, flight director indicator, flight director heading selector, autopilot heading selector and the ILS deviation indicator. The military system also incorporated the steering pointer of the Bomb Direction Indicator. Each part of the system was duplicated, so that the pilot and co-pilot had separate instruments operating independently, powered by separate power supplies. Any discrepancy between the indications given by the pilot's and the co-pilot's instruments was flagged up, since that might indicate a system fault. The system also provided heading information to the aircraft navigator via a Track Control Unit, which also received information from the Navigational Bombing System and the Doppler Radar.

The main flight trials of the fully integrated Autopilot Mk.10B and the Military Flight System were carried out with Vulcan B.2 XH533. In the main, the flying was directed at analysing the performance and accuracy of the system in varying weather conditions, in order to establish statistical reliability figures to qualify the auto-landing system, but much of the work was

A 'formation' shot of Vulcan B.1 XH478 refuelling from Vickers Valiant BK.1 tanker WZ376 during a flight from A&AEE Boscombe Down in 1959 during the C(A) Release trials to clear the Vulcan to undertake in-flight refuelling in service. The view shows the Vulcan with an 'Orange Putter' tail-warning radar, an uncommon fit on the aircraft. via Phil Butler

also directed at developing the interface between the MFS, Autopilot and the Vulcan's existing 'Navigational Bombing System'.

Other enhancements of inputs to the MFS (such as the Sperry Heading Reference System, HRS Mk.2, that replaced the Mk.7B compass) were carried out on XH538, which was one of the two aircraft involved in testing aspects of Skybolt missile systems. The HRS Mk.1 was originally related solely to Skybolt, but was found to be an improvement on the existing instrumentation, so that development was continued after the cancellation of the Skybolt missile. The HRS enabled significantly more accurate bombing results to be obtained from the H2S/NBS equipment.

### In-Flight Refuelling
When the Vulcan first entered service it was not equipped for in-flight refuelling, but this capability was added as one of the features of a 'retro-fit' carried out quite early in its career. The whole Vulcan fleet was equipped with nose-mounted refuelling probe, after trials had been carried out at A&AEE Boscombe Down, with Vulcan B.1 XH478 used as the receiver from the Valiant BK.1 tanker WZ376. These trials were conducted between June 1959 and April 1961. Similar clearance trials were later conducted on the Vulcan B.2 with XH538 during January-March 1961. The primary purpose for providing a flight-refuelled capability was to enable ferrying to and from overseas bases – although the only real use 'in anger' was to allow the 'Black Buck' missions during the Falklands War in 1982.

The use of the Vulcan as a tanker itself did not follow until 1982, many years later, when the Handley Page Victor tanker fleet was near the end of its life and the expanding Lockheed Tristar and BAC VC-10 tanker fleets were still in the throes of conversion from other roles. The

clearance trials at Boscombe Down for the tanker role were conducted by XH558 in the latter part of 1982, refuelling other Vulcans and all other service types such as the Jaguar, Tornado and Harrier.

### Rocket-Assisted Take-Off Gear (RATOG)
One of the very first modifications envisaged for the Vulcan B.1 (but also to be applied to the Vickers Valiant and Handley Page Victor B.1) was the application of Rocket-Assisted Take-Off, to enable full-weight take-offs to be made from shorter runways or in tropical conditions, where take-off performance might be degraded by high ambient temperature. The requirement was to be met by fitting two de Havilland D.Spe.4A Spectre Mk.10211 rocket jettison units, each providing 8,000 lb (36.6kN) of static thrust, below the wings of the Vulcan. The B.1 XA889 was allotted for trials with this system in May 1959. The trials were intended to start with dumping trials of the High-Test Peroxide (HTP) fuel at Woodford, to assess possible airframe contamination, to be followed by fitting of dummy RATOG nacelles for jettisoning trials. The trials were to be concluded by ground firing of the units at Boscombe Down. However, following twenty-five test firings on a large Vulcan structural test specimen at the Hatfield base of the de Havilland Engine company, the programme, and orders for sixty-five Vulcan modification kits, were cancelled in August 1959.

### Blue Steel
The Blue Steel 'stand-off bomb' was a rocket-powered missile designed by A V Roe. It was to be carried in service by the Vulcan B.2A and the Handley Page Victor B.2A, although dummies, and development missiles, were also carried by the Vickers Valiant and earlier Vulcans and

Victors. The development trials were conducted in the UK and also at the Long Range Weapons Establishment in Australia. The missile had a nominal range of 150 miles (241km) and was powered by a Bristol Siddeley Stentor rocket motor, fuelled by HTP (High-Test Hydrogen Peroxide) and kerosene. The various versions of the missile design were identified by 'W' (Weapon) type numbers, commencing at W.100, with the operational missile being the W.105. These numbers were those used by A V Roe Weapons Division at Woodford, which was responsible for the development and production of the missile.

The trials in Australia began in August 1957 with two-fifths scale unpowered models being dropped by a Valiant, followed in February 1958 by a powered scale model. In the meantime, Vulcan B.1 XA903 had been allotted in May 1957 as one of the carrier aircraft for Blue Steel development and was extensively modified to carry the missile. XA903 arrived at Edinburgh Field in Australia on 16th November 1960 to participate in trials with No 4 Joint Services Trials Unit that involved dropping unpowered and launching powered missiles before returning to the A V Roe site at Woodford in February 1961. XA903 also carried out launches in the UK, both before and after its excursion to Australia. Earlier, XA893 had been involved in various items of 'mock-up' work in connection with Blue Steel, but it did not fly with the missile. No 4 JSTU was based at Edinburgh Field, near Adelaide in South Australia, from

**This photograph shows a Blue Steel missile in front of the Vulcan B.1 trials aircraft, XA902, at A V Roe's Woodford airfield.**
Avro Heritage Centre P01313

| Codename | Installation No | Equipment Purpose |
|---|---|---|
| Green Satin Mk.1 | ARI 5851 | Ground Position Indicator feeding the Navigational Bombing System |
| Green Satin Mk.2 | | Improved GPI system |
| Orange Putter | ARI 5800 | Radar Warning Receiver, fitted to some Vulcan B.1 |
| Green Palm | ARI 18074 | VHF Jammer aimed at Warsaw Pact fighter control system |
| Blue Diver | ARI 18075 | UHF Jammer, replacing Green Palm |
| Red Shrimp | ARI 18076 | Jammer for Warsaw Pact long-range radars |
| Blue Saga | ARI 18105 | Radar Warning Receiver |
| Red Light | ARI 18146 | X-Band Jammer to counter Warsaw Pact fighter radars |
| Red Steer Mk.1 | ARI 5919 | Radar Warning Receiver |
| Red Steer Mk.2 | ARI 5952 | Radar Warning Receiver, replaced Mk.1 |
| (No name) | ARI 5959 | General Dynamics Terrain-Following Radar |
| (No name) | ARI 18228/1 | Radar Warning Receiver |

which flights were made with all three types of V-Bomber over the Woomera ranges. The main Vulcan B.2 involved was XH539, which was based in Australia from December 1961 to January 1964. The last Australian launch was in October 1964.

Boscombe Down cleared the carriage and release of Blue Steel after a successful series of trials had been made between November 1961 and January 1962. A W.100A Blue Steel fitted with an instrumented pod was used for the majority of the carriage trials, the weapon's High Test Peroxide (HTP) and Kerosene fuel tanks being filled with either sand or a water/glycol mixture to the missile's correct weight and CofG. A Type 102A weighted dummy missile was used for the remaining carriage trials and for the release trial. The limits for carriage were the same maximum height, speed and manoeuvre as for the aircraft, with release at 0.84 IMN in straight and level flight (+/-5°) at 50,000ft (15,240m) +/-5,000ft (1,524m). The operational clearance of Blue

Steel was passed during 1962 in stages, for example carriage with HTP and operation of most of the missile's systems in August and carriage with an operational warhead and launch in emergency conditions in October. Further trials of Blue Steel were conducted by Squadron B Mk.2 aircraft in conjunction with No 18 Joint Services Trials Unit at RAF Scampton, including the launching of two 'qualification' missiles by Vulcans and two by Victors.

**Electronic Equipment**

During most the years of the Vulcan's development and service, almost all weapon systems and ancillary equipment were identified by codenames for security reasons, the so-called 'Rainbow Codes', arising from the first word of the codename always being a colour of the rainbow. The main items of electronic equipment are listed in the table above. Many Vulcans were involved in trials of electronic equipment, references to which will be found in many individual aircraft histories in Appendix 1

# Chapter Six

# In Detail

The Avro Vulcan's construction followed the accepted manufacturing practice of the time, using an all-metal structure that was reasonably conventional. The aircraft itself had a mid-position cantilever delta wing, a single swept fin and there was no horizontal tailplane. The earlier chapters have explained how the bomber started life with a true delta wing with the leading edge swept back at an angle of almost 50° and with only a relatively small tip chord. However, the Vulcan B Mk.1 wing was modified by the introduction of compound sweepback, obtained by increasing the chord at a point about three-quarters of the span out from the centre-line. On the inboard portion this was faired by a straight line to a point about semi-span, the sweep angle being reduced to 42°, and outboard at 53.5° through to an increased tip chord. The 'breaks' that resulted from this alteration were positioned at points that would ensure that the structural alterations forward of the front spar were kept to a minimum. The original pure delta wing had an aspect ratio of 2.84 and the modified B.1 wing an aspect ratio of 2.78.

The Mk.2's wing took this development even further by adding yet more pronounced compound sweep to the leading edge, as shown in the drawing. This also added an extra 12ft (3.66m) to the span. The leading edge was brought even further forward and the resulting aerofoil section showed a markedly drooped nose. These changes brought with them a general thinning of the outer wing and, of course, a larger wing area which was used to counteract the increases in this version's operational weight and ceiling. The extra thrust made available from more powerful marks of the Olympus powerplant offered increased operating altitudes but an inevitable increase in compressibility effects, so a local reduction in thickness/chord ratio from the additional span paid a useful dividend. B Mk.2's wing aspect ratio was 3.1 and the thickness/chord ratio for both B.1 and B.2 wings was 10% at the root (that is, the centre section/outer wing joint), but at the tip it was 8% on the Mk.1 and 5% for the later version.

Vulcan's wing was built in three main components – a centre section constructed integrally with the fuselage together with two outer sections (port and starboard). A straightforward two-spar structure was applied using the boom and web method of manufacture. The underside of the centre portion had cutouts for the bomb and engine bays and the wheel wells.

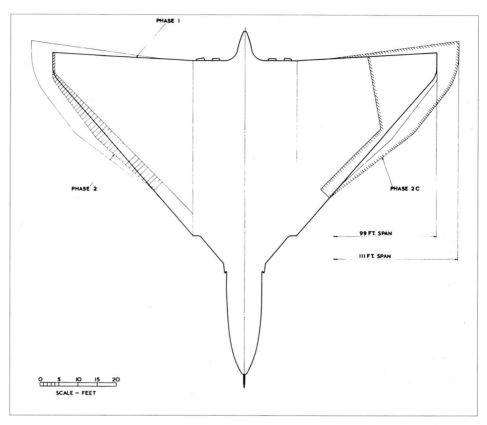

Planview drawing showing the three different wings flown on the Vulcan – the original pure delta, the small additional leading edge extension on the Phase 2 wing as used by the B Mk.1, and the more extensive Phase 2C wing of the B Mk.2. Avro Heritage

Most of the loads across the underside of the fuselage had to be carried by the lower spar booms, but over the top portion of the bay the loads were transferred by a series of relatively close spaced arch beams. At the transport joint between the centre section and outer wings all of the bending loads were taken by the bottom spar joints, but on the top surface these loads were partially absorbed by the surface skin and stringers. The front and rear spar centres formed the fore and aft boundaries of the bomb bay and the section above them was built-up with those arch beams, formed mainly using T-section top and bottom booms together with plate webs. The inter-spar part of the outer wings used a system of closely spaced ribs with angle booms and pressed plate webs stiffened by vertical members. The innermost rib formed the outer boundary of the main undercarriage wheel-well and, as such, was an especially sturdy structure in order to take the undercarriage loads into the wing box. The whole of the wing was covered in light alloy skin.

The manufacture of the large swept dorsal fin and rudder, swept at an angle of 49° 30' on its leading edge, was achieved in a similar way to that of the outer wings. It used two built-up spars, closely spaced interspars and light alloy sheet plating and, to improve the directional stability, the fin fairing was extended along the fuselage. For landing, electrically-operated, three-position, rotating-slat-type airbrakes were mounted in the mainplane above and below the engine air intakes. These would extend above and below the wing and in addition, for braking after touchdown, there was a large Irvin-designed ribbon brake parachute housed in the upper fuselage tail.

The aircraft's structure was composed primarily of aluminium light alloy but magnesium alloy was also used to a substantial degree in the movable trailing edge control surfaces; the intention here was to keep the weight of the control surfaces to a minimum and reduce the problem of mass-balancing. On the Mk.1, in the

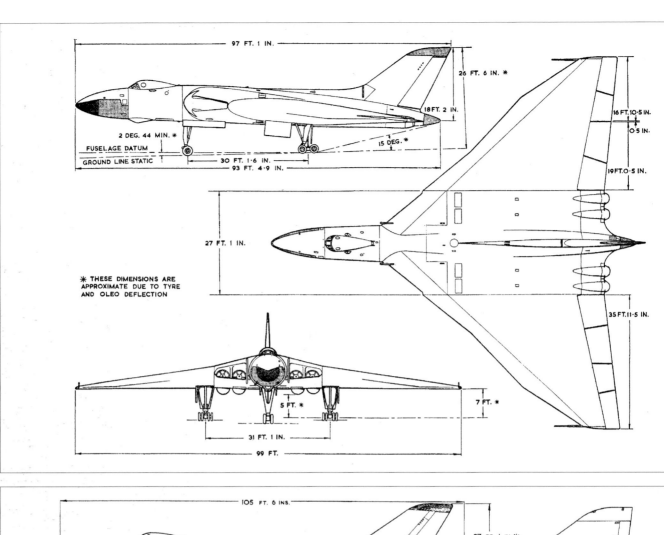

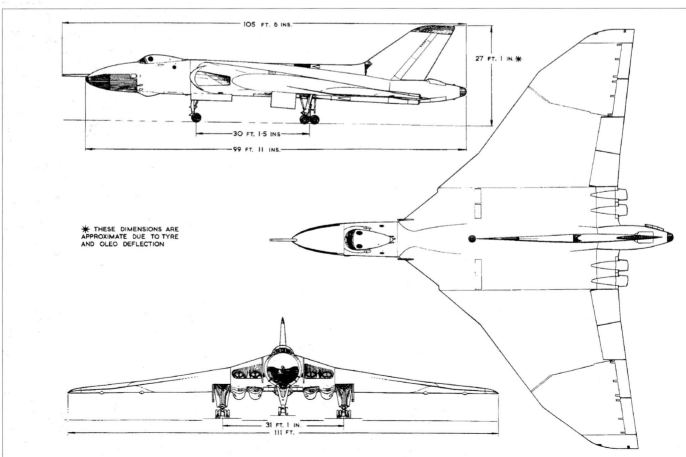

absence of a conventional tail unit, the elevators were mounted in the outer wings and extended from the centre-section wing transport joint to a main hinge rib slightly more than halfway along the wing trailing edge; the ailerons extended outboard from this rib to the wingtips. All of these surfaces – ailerons and elevators and also the rudder – were separate and built around a single spar that carried the necessary hinge fittings. There was a fully powered duplicated control system for the elevators and ailerons and these surfaces were split into separate portions (two ailerons and two elevators per wing), each powered by its own unit. Both ailerons and elevators were aerodynamically balanced.

The wing trailing edge control surfaces were altered for the Vulcan Mk.2 with its larger span. Basically these now comprised four elevons on each outer wing. The outboard elevons were balanced by means of mass balances carried on outrigger arms situated near each hinge, while the inboard elevons (and the rudder) embodied Westland-Irvine type forward sealed balances. Each elevon was operated independently by its own electro-hydraulic power unit. As a result the control configuration was quite different between the two marks of Vulcan, as can be seen on their three-view drawings.

Vulcan's circular-section fuselage employed an all-metal, semi-monocoque, stressed-skin structure that incorporated transverse frames braced by longitudinal stringers together with two fabricated ribs that formed the support for the arch-shaped formers of the bomb bay. The nose radome, housing the complex and extensive electronic apparatus that had to be installed in the modern V-Bomber, was formed as a single moulding of fibreglass-Hycar sandwich. At the time of its appearance this radome was thought to be the biggest one-piece unit of its kind yet made in Britain, and possibly in the world. The upper portion of the nose used orthodox metal construction.

The fuselage itself was built in four pieces – the nose fairing plus front, centre and rear sections. The front constituted the crew's pressurised compartment and the centre section was, of course, the wing centre section described above, which extended from the rear bulkhead of the crew compartment to a point aft of the rear spar. The forward part of the cen-

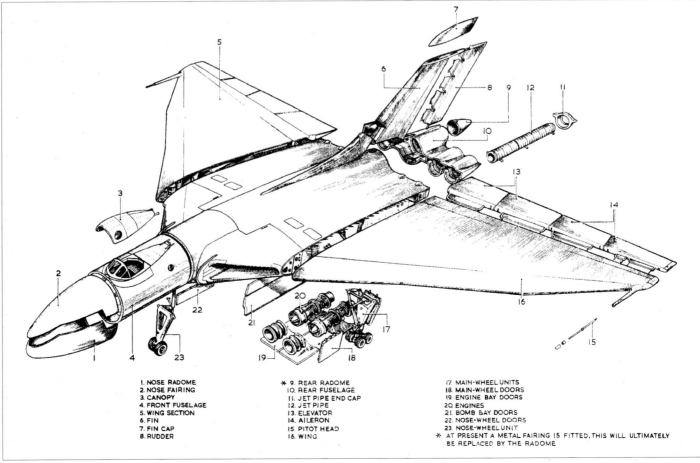

| | | |
|---|---|---|
| 1. NOSE RADOME | ✳ 9. REAR RADOME | 17. MAIN-WHEEL UNITS |
| 2. NOSE FAIRING | 10. REAR FUSELAGE | 18. MAIN-WHEEL DOORS |
| 3. CANOPY | 11. JET PIPE END CAP | 19. ENGINE BAY DOORS |
| 4. FRONT FUSELAGE | 12. JET PIPE | 20. ENGINES |
| 5. WING SECTION | 13. ELEVATOR | 21. BOMB BAY DOORS |
| 6. FIN | 14. AILERON | 22. NOSE-WHEEL DOORS |
| 7. FIN CAP | 15. PITOT HEAD | 23. NOSE-WHEEL UNIT |
| 8. RUDDER | 16. WING | ✳ AT PRESENT A METAL FAIRING IS FITTED, THIS WILL ULTIMATELY BE REPLACED BY THE RADOME |

re section above the nosewheel contained fuel, but the rest formed an extensive bomb compartment. Two strong ribs formed the side walls of the bomb bay, separating it from the inboard engine bays, and these took the weight of the bomb load into the main spars. Between this structure and the crew cabin came the nosewheel bay. Beneath the bomb bay was a pair of bomb doors which, to minimise drag when they opened, folded upwards inside the bomb compartment. The outsides of the centre section contained the engines, jet pipes and airbrakes. The fuselage rear section embodied the rear supports and outlets for the jet pipes and a cone-shaped fairing at the end covering the tail-warning radar scanner.

The Vulcan Mk.2 had an extended and bulged tail cone that housed a large volume of electronic equipment and its power sources, including a Red Steer radar head in the extreme end. This standard large cone was first installed on the second production aircraft (XH534). In due course the rush conversion of several B.2 Vulcans into K Mk.2 tankers saw the ECM cone emptied of its electronics so that the upper portion of the hose drum unit (HDU) could take their place. The lower half of the HDU was fitted beneath and covered by a box-shaped cover, with three lights on each side for guidance purposes. An additional fuel tank was fitted in the bomb bay but the Vulcan K.2 only ever operated as a single-point tanker.

Vulcan's own fuel was carried in fourteen pressurised bag-type tanks contained in magnesium alloy compartments, four in the fuselage in the forward end of the centre section and another five flexible tanks in each wing. The tanks were arranged in groups so that each engine was normally fed by a particular group. However, cross-feed was provided so that, in an emergency, any engine might receive fuel from any tank or group of tanks. An in-flight refuelling capability was made available to the Vulcan as a receiver aircraft from the sixteenth production aeroplane onwards, the probe being installed in the nose.

Turning to the aircraft's weaponry, Britain's first atomic weapon was called Blue Danube. As noted in Chapter One its warhead and systems were housed in a shell derived from the 12,000 lb (5,443kg) 'Tallboy' conventional 'iron' bomb used during the final years of World War Two. This could be carried inside the Vulcan bomb bay. However, relatively few examples of Blue Danube were manufactured before the weapon was taken out of service in 1962 and replaced by Blue Steel.

Chapter Three has noted how the Vulcan B.1 was unsuited to carry the Blue Steel stand-off bomb. For a Mk.2 to carry Blue Steel its existing bomb bay doors had to be removed and replacing by a special set of new doors with a contoured recess that formed a housing for the missile when it was loaded. The services to the missile passed through these doors and there were also separate upwards-opening doors in the bomb bay rear end to accommodate the missile's upper fin. Once the missile had been released these rear doors would be shut. Inside the bomb bay two crutch frame assemblies and a carrier beam had to be installed to take Blue Steel, there being no bomb carrier as such.

The four Olympus jet engines were housed in pairs in two bays inside the centre section and between the front and rear spars. They were bounded by the bomb bay rib and the centre section/wing transport rib, each pair being fed by a common near-rectangular intake. In addition, each of these engines was

housed in its own separate compartment and surrounded by firewalls. On the prototypes the huge air intakes had to absorb over twenty-two tons of air per minute, and the intakes were even larger on the B Mk.2 to satisfy its much more powerful engines. The jet pipes were underslung and emerged from the centre section to extend slightly beyond the trailing edge. Vulcan's thick delta wing offered great flexibility for fitting alternative engine installations and more advanced engines. Indeed new marks of Olympus or other types of power unit were substituted with relatively little difficulty.

The Vulcan had five crew members housed in a cockpit designed to a standard pattern laid down for all V-Bomber aircrew. Admittance to this compact flightdeck, by means of a folding ladder, was made through a hatch cut beneath the nose of the fuselage just forward of the nose leg. This took the crew to an intermediate level where three rearward-facing seats were available for the air electronics officer (right-hand seat when facing aft), navigator (centre) and radar operator (left). The two pilots then had to climb up a second ladder to a higher level to get to their stations, which were the only positions to have ejection seats. The three aircrew to the rear never had the luxury of such a facility, all they had available to them were parachutes, and so they always knew that getting out in a emergency would probably be difficult to say the least. In 1959 A&AEE Boscombe Down declared that ejection seats would be the only sure

This page:

**The first version of the Olympus engine, shown here at around the time it was chosen to power the Vulcan, offered a thrust of 9,750 lb (43.3kN) for a weight of 3,520 lb (1,597kg). The Olympus 101 used by the B Mk.1 weighed 3,650 lb (1,656kg).**

**A dummy Avro Blue Steel guided weapon photographed on 11th September 1960 on display at that year's Farnborough Show.** Eric Morgan

Opposite page:

**With the fuselage and wing relatively complete, it is time to fit the engines. Some of the electronics and radome are still to be installed.** Avro Heritage

**Section drawing showing the principal components that made up the Vulcan B Mk.1.**

method of escape for the rear crew because of probable fluctuating g-loads and the aircraft's attitude, making movement from the rear position difficult. The Establishment strongly recommended that such seats should be fitted very quickly, but they never were, and ever since that decision has been the source of enormous controversy. Each pilot had parallel-motion-type rudder pedals and a fighter-type single-grip control column or stick, rather than the old spectacle style of control column used in the past in wartime piston bombers. A prone bombing station was provided in a blister below the cabin.

The Vulcan was fitted with a tricycle undercarriage, each main unit having a liquid-spring shock absorber and a four-wheel eight-tyre bogie. These were retracted hydraulically both forwards and upwards into their mainplane housings outboard of the power units. The steerable nose-wheel unit was fitted with twin wheels and was retracted with a single jack, upward and backward, into the fuselage nose. Structurally, the main undercarriage for the B Mk.2 was different to the Mk.1. The undercarriage was designed by Dowty and to date was one of the most impressive to have come out of the famous company.

Such was the power of the nuclear bombs that much thought went into ensuring that the bombers themselves were protected from the effects of the nuclear thermal flash generated by their own weapons. Studies related to the protection of V-Bombers from thermal flash had shown the inherent dangers of applying national, registration and other markings to these aircraft in colours of low reflectivity value. It was even suggested that an aircraft experiencing a high degree of thermal flux might well return to base with such inscriptions as 'Don't Step Here' cut neatly through the outer skin. It was discovered that black was the worst colour for conducting heat, followed closely by red and also it was clearly not sufficient to paint over such markings just before an operation. White paint over black or red still retained much of its conductivity and in fact, to get the full benefit, the white finish needed to age for two or three months before it was exposed to heavy thermal flux. Vickers Valiant aircraft used for Operation Grapple (the drop testing of British thermonuclear devices [hydrogen bombs] over the South Pacific in 1957) had in general used green for national markings in place of black and pastel shades.

In fact the two Vulcan prototypes were painted white with normal dark markings and early production Vulcan B Mk.1s were for a period painted in an overall silver finish. However, soon after entering service these Mk.1 aircraft were switched to white overall but, for some time while the discussions continued, they still retained roundels and fin flashes in the standard shades of red and blue. Eventually all three V-Bomber types had white colour schemes with their roundels and markings 'toned down' to paler shades for nuclear duties. Following the reassignment of the V-Bombers to a low-level (non-nuclear) strike role in the 1960s, the Vulcans were repainted in disruptive green/grey tactical camouflage.

The radio and electronic equipment on the B Mk.2 included a high frequency (HF) transmitter-receiver wireless, two radio altimeters (high-range and low-range) giving automatic indications to the pilots, instrument landing system (ILS) landing aids, automatic direction finding (ADF or radio compass), and an ultra high frequency (UHF) and twin very high frequency (VHF) installation which was remotely controlled by the pilots for airfield control purposes. The radar installations comprised Gee, H2S, IFF (identification, friend or foe), NBC (the Navigation and Bombing Computer) and ECM (electronic countermeasures). Except for the omni-type IFF aerial and the VHF aerials, no external aerials were fitted. The HF transmitter-receiver was fed with signals from a resonant slot in the aircraft fin, the ADF utilised parabolic and probe type aerials in the fuselage, metal strips and a box aerial in the mainplane supplied the ILS landing aids, and the H2S used a rotating scanner in the nose.

A set of four Vulcan B Mk.2 main undercarriage forgings, produced on the 12,000-ton press at High Duty Alloys in Redditch. These components were made as a solid die forging in high strength aluminium alloy. In the soft 'as-forged' condition they were then sent to Dowty for rough machining – primarily the drilling of various large holes. In this form, as seen here, they were then returned to HDA for a heat treatment operation to give them their optimum strength properties. After that, back to Dowty to become part of a Vulcan leg. High Duty Alloys

Close-up of a B Mk.2's nose leg – in this case XL360 preserved at the Midland Air Museum.

The defensive ECM electronics on the Vulcan comprised powerful jammers, a radar warning receiver, tail warning radar, infra-red flares and chaff stored in the wing in large quantities. These included the Green Palm VHF communications jammer (at the time of its introduction the Soviet's defence network was based on VHF equipment) and Blue Diver and Red Shrimp barrage jammers. During the 1960s the passive radar warning receiver was Blue Saga, but in the early 1970s this was replaced by the much better state-of-the-art ARI.18228 receiver. The electronic warfare (EW) suite was completed by the Mk.1 Red Steer tail warning radar mounted in the tail cone. This was later replaced by the far superior Red Steer Mk.2.

It wasn't just the Vulcan's shape and aerodynamics that were such a step forward, the manufacturing process for such a large aeroplane had to cover some new ground as well. In general the construction techniques used in the Vulcan were pretty straightforward, but a great deal of ingenuity from Avro designers and engineers went into the production planning and some of the detail processes. Primarily the problems generated in building the bomber were associated with its size because the sheer bulk of this aircraft, and the unusual shape of

some of its components, had in many cases made them difficult to make. For most of the larger sub-assemblies that were built at Chadderton, some extremely sturdy jigs had to be provided. In fact these were rather larger than might normally have been expected because of the soft nature of the undersoil at the Chadderton factory, which was not particularly stable as a working surface. Consequently, the larger jigs had to be built on very substantial steel rafts to give them a solid base, but this gave an added benefit because it meant that all of the main jigs were then transportable.

The biggest and most complex of the sub-assemblies was, of course, the centre section which, as a complete unit without its leading and trailing edge portions, measured about 30ft (9.15m) long by 26ft (7.92m) wide. The initial batch of these massive items were transported as single pieces to the final assembly line at Woodford some 16 miles (25.7km) away. They were moved in the early hours, complete

with Police escort, and all of the lamp-posts along the A6 from Manchester to the Stockport area had to be hinged so that the lorry and its load could pass freely. It was Avro who paid for these modified lamp-posts. However, the difficulties in moving such a large chunk of metal brought a redesign and in due course the inter-spar assembly was modified. Its structure was now arranged so that, after manufacture at Chadderton, it could be split down the centre line into two more easily handled portions for despatch to Woodford. When the whole centre section had been reassembled at Woodford, the entire unit was lifted out of its jig by overhead crane and positioned onto a mobile trolley. This was then moved further down the line to receive its crew cabin, outer wings and fin. With the airframe virtually complete and much of its equipment in place, the aircraft then received its undercarriage which allowed it to be moved along on its own. The powerplants were one of the last items to be installed.

## Technical Data

| | 707 | 707A | 707B | 707C | B Mk.1 | B Mk.2 |
|---|---|---|---|---|---|---|
| **Powerplant** | | | | | | |
| lbst (kN) | 1 x 3,500 (15.6) Rolls-Royce Derwent 5 | 1 x 3,600 (16.0) Rolls-Royce Derwent 8 | 1 x 3,500 (15.6kN) Rolls-Royce Derwent 5 | 1 x 3,600 (16.0) Rolls-Royce Derwent 8 | 4 x Bristol Olympus 11,000 (48.9) Mk.101 or 12,000 (53.3) Mk.102 or 13,500 (60.0) Mk.104 | 4 x Bristol Olympus 16,000 (71.1) Mk.200 or 17,000 (75.6) Mk.201 or 20,000 (88.9) Mk.301 |
| **Dimensions*** | | | | | | |
| Span, ft (m) | 33' 0" (10.1) | 34' 2" (10.4) | 33' 0" (10.1) | 34' 2" (10.4) | 99' 0" (30.2) | 111' 0" (33.8) |
| Length, ft (m) | 40' 2" (12.2) | 42' 4" (12.9) | 41' 3½" (12.6) | 42' 4" (12.9) | 97' 1" (29.6) | 105' 6" (32.2) |
| Height on ground, ft (m) | 11' 3" (3.4) | 11' 7" (3.5) | 11' 7" (3.5) | 11' 7" (3.5) | 26' 6" (8.1) | 27' 1" (8.3) |
| Gross wing area, ft² (m²) | 366.5 (34.1) | 408 (37.9) | 366.5 (34.1) | 408 (37.9) | 3,554 (330.5) | 3,964 (368.7) |
| **Weights** | | | | | | |
| Gross weight, lb (kg) | 8,600 (3,901) | 9,800 (4,445) | 9,500 (4,309) | 10,000 (4,536) | 167,000 (75,751) | 74,080 (33,603) |
| Fuel load, lb (kg) | | | | | 75,056 (34,045) | 204,000 (92,534) |
| Military load, lb (kg) | | | | | 1 x 10,000 (4,536) or 21 x 1,000 (454) bombs, 1 x Blue Danube | 1 x 10,000 (4,536) or 21 x 1,000 (454) bombs, 1 x Blue Steel, 1 x 7,250 (3,289) Yellow Sun Mk.2 |
| **Performance** | | | | | | |
| Max level speed, mph (km/h) | | 403 (648) | | 403 (648) | 620 (998) at height | 640 (1,030) at height |
| Operational ceiling ft (m) | | | | | 55,000 (16,764) | 60,000 (18,288) |
| Range, miles (km) | | | | | 3,000 (4,827) | 4,600 (7,401) |

* Dimensions given for the Vulcan B Mk.1 also apply to the Avro 698 Prototype.

# Memories

**Vulcan B Mk.2 XM597's nose and intake detail in close-up.** Barry Jones

**Avro 707B VX790 lands after another Farnborough display.** Barry Jones via Terry Panopalis

The authors have spoken to several former aircrew who flew either the Avro 707 scale-model test aircraft or various examples of the Vulcan itself. Their observations and memories have been collected together here to give something of an idea of just what it was like to fly, and indeed live with, Britain's Famous Delta Bomber.

To start us off, **Group Captain Ted Mellor** was an RAE pilot who flew the Avro 707. He was a Flight Lieutenant with Aerodynamics Flight RAE (Farnborough and Bedford) between 1955 and 1958, and retired as a Group Captain in 1984. He remembers: 'Given that they provided no particularly hairy moments I would say that the 707A and 707B were comfortable to fly; "pleasurable" might be stretching it a bit. As might be expected the A was altogether "tauter" in flight than the B and had a dinky early auto throttle mode. It was some surprise to me how slowly, and at what an angle, the B could be flown, albeit with a lot of stick movement for not a lot of effect. My logbook tells me that most of my 707B flying was side-slip tests under asymmetric drag and weight conditions (wingtip parachutes, weights in the wing). Now what was all that about?

In fact I rarely flew the 707A. The serviceability of some of these prima donnas was measured in flights per year (single figures). I digress, but I remember the Shell Film Unit hanging around for weeks to get some air-to-air of the Fairey Delta 2 supersonic research aircraft, and finally deciding that they would "come back next summer". The 707B did have one unavoidable vice – it didn't want to land. As it entered the "ground effect" (where the ground was close enough to affect the pressure pattern and hence the aerodynamics) it experienced a significant nose-up pitching moment. Thus whereas in most aircraft, having initiated the round-out one would continue to pull the stick back as the speed decreased, the B required the stick to be frozen or checked forwards to "push" the aircraft on to the ground. Using a normal technique would result in you leaping smartly back to 100ft (30m) or so, where a late correction would trigger a classic dynamically unstable (over control) pitch oscillation. Sadly I believe that is exactly what caused its demise after it had been retired to the Empire Test Pilots School for the students to mess about with.'

**An unidentified Avro Vulcan B Mk.2.** Barry Jones

Moving on to the Vulcan itself, **Squadron Leader Joe L'Estrange** flew fighters for most of the early part of his RAF career, but later on was transferred to the V-Force to fly Mk.2 Vulcans. He remembers the switch to bombers as quite a shock, but in due course he served with Nos 35, 44 and 50 Squadrons, and spent time with No 230 OCU as well.

'You get a "feeling" for most of the aircraft that you fly, but some more than others and this was certainly the case with the Vulcan. It proved quite a change from the fighters I was used to and I was not too enamoured when I was told that I was joining the V-Force. My feelings changed when I found that the Vulcan had a much better performance than some of the fighters I had flown. I thoroughly enjoyed flying it.

Admittedly, sitting in the cockpit was like being in an upstairs bedroom looking out through a letterbox – this was because I was used to an all-round view from a fighter cockpit. But you got used to this and learnt to handle it. The cockpit layout was pretty reasonable and gave no problems. However, it had been designed in part by Roly Falk who was a tall chap, and so smaller folk like me had to stretch a bit to reach some items. In fact the cockpit was quite a tight fit for all of the instruments, which of course were the old-fashioned dials, gauges and switches – none of the modern computerised equipment was available as yet.

Overall this was not as good as a fighter-type arrangement and if one had had to go to war, I would have preferred a Boeing B-47 Stratojet style of cockpit. Nevertheless, the Vulcan had one of the better cockpit layouts and having a control stick was great – much better than the old wheel-type of control. One point I never liked, however, was the crew in the back not having ejection seats.

The Vulcan was a lovely aircraft to handle. It had lots of power and the control was good both at low and high speeds. At low all-up-weights and with a bit of luck it was possible to initially outmanoeuvre Hawker Hunter and Gloster Javelin fighters; but not for long. However, in a war situation a Vulcan pilot would try and get away from any situation involving fighters rather than waiting around – he knew that he would not have much chance of coping.

Vulcan's rate-of-climb for its size and weight was excellent – nine minutes to 40,000ft (12,192m) at operational figures. The best height that I achieved in the bomber was 54,000ft (16,460m), and I remember crossing America at 50,000ft (15,240m) to keep out of the way of civil air traffic. Normally we cruised in the range 40,000ft (12,192m) to 45,000ft (13,716m).

As the Soviet Union's defences were improved, the stage was reached where Vulcan had little defence capability of its own, other than the ECM kit. The rear pod might throw off

a surface-to-air missile but, if we had to go to war flying at height and staying there, we would have been very lucky to get through and survive. Low level was better, but the chances of survival were still only 50/50 – very much a lottery. In a war the solution would be to get down on the deck as low as possible, but AA guns were still very dangerous. Later people started using hand-held missiles, which were even more dangerous – and this was at night too. Fitting Skybolt would have been a good move, had it worked, because with a stand-off missile like that we could have launched an attack from almost anywhere.

If the pilot could see clearly (that is, in daylight only) he could fly a Vulcan as low as 100ft (30m). A flying height of 500ft (150m) was still too high because the Vulcan could be seen by the enemy from some way away. Until the engine's combustion cans were changed, the Vulcan used to leave a trail of smoke. For example, in Cyprus (Akrotiri), if we made a dummy attack over the sea, people on the ground could see our smoke trials from a very long way off. This of course, gave them ample warning of our approach and the situation was not improved until new combustion cans were introduced that cured the smoke problem.

Vulcan, obviously, was a big aircraft and low down, at high all-up-weights and high speed, it

**Vulcan B Mk.2 XL317 flying over Lincolnshire countryside.** Dave Thomas via Barry Jones

**Mk.2s XJ824 and XM574 seen on the flight line.** Barry Jones

**XM597 photographed in the USA.** Barry Jones

did suffer a little in manoeuvrability because of 'G' limitations. However, if one kept the speed down one could get great manoeuvrability because the aircraft had powerful elevons along the rear of the wing and these gave excellent control. The Vulcan would not stall properly like a tailed aircraft and so the pilot could get a huge angle of attack – up to 40°. You could also get a high rate of descent, up to 4,000ft/min (1,220m/min) or more, which was a good way of getting down quickly in an emergency, but this did give a lot of buffet which affected the airframe's fatigue life. This was possibly how Ian McDougal got into Rio de Janeiro after his 'Black Buck' mission. He was flying at height, was very low on fuel, and this was a way to get down fast in the short distance to the airfield – in fact at the end he did not have enough fuel left for a circuit.

The advantages of the delta wing were many. With the requirements of height and range it helped a great deal. Compressibility effects were not so bad on a delta as they were on a tailed aircraft, and getting rid of the tail saved weight as well. The delta was an ideal answer to the specification because it could lift 200,000 lb (90,720kg) to altitude without trouble. Vulcan was also an extremely strong aircraft – a swept wing type would have needed additional strengthening to allow it to deal with aeroelastic effects. Also, Vulcan had good range and all of the kit could be fitted inside the wings.

The Olympus power unit was a first class engine that gave great reliability, despite the pounding that it took with the Vulcan. I had six thousand hours and twenty-one years using it and there was very little trouble, which gave great confidence in the powerplant as a whole. On the Mk.2 all four engines could be used at

maximum power, within the engine and airframe limitations, without worrying about overstressing the airframe. The airframe limits for the Mk.2 were Mach 0.93 for the 200 Series Olympus and Mach 0.92 for the 301. This difference came from alterations to the intakes for the more powerful engines. The Mk.2 at full power would of course continue to increase speed, but at Mach 0.94 the auto Mach trim actuator would become ineffective and the elevators would need to be at full upwards deflection to compensate. If you tried to go faster than that, there would be an increasing nose down change of trim and so you would have to throttle back to wait for the speed to drop.

I remember in 1952 when taking an Instructor's course, that a group of us visited Bristol Engines at Filton when the original Olympus was undergoing testing on the bench. The early jet engines in our fighters did not respond very quickly to opening the throttle, but this early Olympus could have its throttle pushed to fully open and the engine picked up its thrust beautifully. Little did I realise then that I would be using the Vulcan's uprated Olympus on my first flight in the bomber, which took place on 8th February 1963. However, when flying the Vulcan we still treated the throttle reasonably gently (unless we needed to get away from a situation very swiftly) because this helped to reduce the stresses on the engine.

Dropping bombs from a Vulcan at high level was very different from the days of piston bombers because the aiming was now mostly done by radar, rather than bomb-aiming equipment. I did do some practice drops from a Vulcan flying at 200ft (60m), but that sort of low-level work was much more fun in a de Havilland Hornet or Vampire fighter. In fact, in a Vulcan one really needed to be at least 2,000ft

(610m) above the ground, or to have parachute-retarded bombs, to ensure that the aircraft was not hit by shrapnel from the exploding iron bombs.

The most enjoyable and satisfying flying was experienced when flying for air displays. Ideally, this was done at low fuel states and speeds about 130 to 165 knots (241 to 306km/h), which permitted maximum manoeuvrability without exceeding 'G' limits. A series of wing-overs and steep turns resulted in a tight display in front of the crowd. I flew many of these displays over twenty-one years, both at home and abroad. Wherever the Vulcan went it was a great crowd pleaser because of its good looks and for its ability to perform directly in front of the audience.

All in all the Vulcan was a first-class jet. It had the equivalent of a thin wing (based on width of chord), which satisfied the need for high speed, but it also had a large wing section which gave high lift. Thus the bomber had all the qualities required for range, height and speed (within the limits), and with its delta wing it could carry more fuel. Vulcan was a lovely aircraft to fly from the moment I first got into it. I felt comfortable with her all of the time – it was great to have an aircraft in which one had absolute confidence.

Finally, it was converted into a flight refuelling tanker and, yet again, performed the task to great effect and without any problems. From the pilot's point of view I found that I got a lot of satisfaction from providing for thirsty aircraft of different types. I am now looking forward to seeing '558 getting airborne in the very capable hands of Dave Thomas. I'd give an arm and a leg to be on that first flight but I don't think that they would want an octogenarian getting in the way.'

**Vulcan air display at Akrotiri.** Joe L'Estrange

**Near East Air Force view of Vulcan B.2s taken in 1973 – XL391 (left), XJ854 and XJ783 (right).** Barry Jones

**Air Vice-Marshal Nigel Baldwin** flew the Vulcan in Cyprus. The item that follows was originally delivered at the RAF Historical Society's Spring 2006 seminar, called *The RAF in the Mediterranean Theatre Post-WW II*. It describes his time as a Flight Commander flying Vulcans out of Akrotiri in the early 1970s with No 35 Squadron. The authors are grateful to Air Vice-Marshal Baldwin and the RAF Historical Society for allowing us to reproduce the text of this lecture here.

'For the RAF, in the early 1970s, there were some major changes afoot. Most important was the fundamental change in NATO doctrine from that of massive retaliation to flexible response. That meant the end of QRA – Quick Reaction Alert – for me and my Vulcan and Victor colleagues at Waddington, Scampton, Cottesmore, Marham and Wittering. (QRA, of

course, had meant one crew from each squadron, with a nuclear-armed aircraft, on fifteen minutes alert, twenty-four hours a day, seven days a week.) The change in doctrine also led to the run-on of the Vulcan force including two squadrons dedicated to CENTO.

Now the Vulcan force would retain its laydown nuclear strike ability but with greater flexibility. It would also retain its twenty-one 1,000 lb (454kg) bomb conventional role. The Canberras of Nos 6, 32, 73 and 249 Squadrons were stood down at RAF Akrotiri in January 1969. They were immediately replaced by eight Vulcan B Mk.2s of 35 Squadron from Cottesmore; on 19th March, eight more followed from IX Squadron, also from Cottesmore. It was declared from London that the force was to be a strike (code for 'nuclear') force for CENTO – that was to be their primary role. This did not

stop a BBC report to the contrary (an assertion was broadcast that the Vulcans would be a NATO asset).

Nos 9 and 35 Squadrons were set up at Akrotiri at the southeast end of the airfield, both squadrons being commanded by Wing Commanders. An overarching HQ Bomber Wing, also under a GD Wing Commander, and with supporting navigation, radar bombing, and airborne air electronic staff officers, was established nearby. That Wing Commander also commanded the first- and second-line engineering support – so very similar to the centralised servicing at the UK's V-Bomber bases that we had all grown up with. A slight digression here but many had argued for years for the greater efficiencies that would ensue if at least first- and some second-line tradesmen could 'belong' to the flying squadrons rather than to the Station's centralised engineering establishment. People like to belong – and most ground crew would have preferred belonging to a famous squadron like IX or 35 than to an amorphous mass. By the time ten years later I was OC 50 Squadron at Waddington, I had three engineering officers (including the first female V-Force Junior Eng Officer) and a hundred airmen tradesmen and, most importantly, an Aircraft Servicing Chief (ASC) for each of 'my' aircraft. Becoming known as semi-autonomous servicing, this became the standard.

But back to Akrotiri: here the aircraft were 'owned' by HQ Bomber Wing who "employed" all of the ground tradesmen and allocated an aircraft to the Squadron crews. Many of the training exercises were planned by HQ Bomber Wing too – that sometimes led to disagreements not least between the Wing Comman-

ders, and sometimes even the Squadron Leader Flight Commanders got involved! Being a Near East Air Force (NEAF) asset, we were commanded and controlled by the CinC NEAF at Episkopi and not by the AOCinC Strike Command at High Wycombe. On the other hand, because the two NEAF Vulcan squadrons were obviously only a small part of the whole of the RAF's V-Force, and so far away from the centre of the UK-based logistic chain, there was much dialogue and sometimes inevitable tensions between the respective HQ staffs.

When I arrived on 35 Squadron in November 1970, as a soon-to-become Squadron Leader Flight Commander, the squadron had been at Akrotiri for nearly two years and was well established with full ground and flying training programmes in place – all monitored from the HQ at Bomber Wing and at Episkopi.

The V-Force, by this stage, was well into flight simulation. Since the earliest days of the Vulcan, all pilots had been trained on, for the time, sophisticated simulators at the Operational Conversion Unit (OCU). Once operational on the squadrons, all pilot teams of captain and co-pilot had to do a three-hour exercise every month to retain their operational category. So it was recognised in MOD that if squadrons were going to be deployed permanently to Cyprus, the cost of dismantling, transporting, and re-siting a simulator would just have to be accepted. And so it was. (The alternative of flying back to the UK every month was just not practicable.) During my time, much imaginative work was done to link up the navigators' ground trainers (that of the nav plotter and the nav radar) and that of the AEO (the fifth member of a V-Force crew: the Air Electronics Officer) with that of the pilots. Thus practice war missions could be flown and this much improved the training and testing of critical crew cooperation, especially during the tense moments when attacking a heavily defended target.

Flying training around Cyprus was, of necessity, very limited. At home, we had got used to flying the UK low-level route – essentially enter low level near the Isle of Wight at EP3, usually at 500ft (150m) above ground level (agl), across Dorset and Somerset, up through Wales and the Lake District to the western isles of Scotland, clockwise back down across the Lowlands and the Yorkshire hills to about abeam Doncaster and then turn port and exit to the south of the River Humber. In Cyprus, the geography was much more constraining. Having done an almost obligatory two-hour high-level navigation stage (usually to the west of Crete and back at about FL450 using limited nav aids), we then descended abeam Akrotiri under Gata radar to enter a 250 mile (400km) or so low-level route anticlockwise around the island, again usually at 500ft (150m) agl.

We began the low-level stage near Ayia Napa just south west of Famagusta – in the days when Ayia Napa was a quiet fishing village

with pristine sands and not a squaddie in sight – attacking, with an F95 camera, two or three targets, often a glistening white-painted village church. To keep aircraft airframe fatigue consumption as low as possible, we usually cruised along at 240 to 250 knots (445 to 463km/h), the aircraft's engines set at not much more than idling and certainly no more than 80%, then accelerated to 350 knots (649km/h) as we ran into the target. Once we approached the end of the route, we ran into Episkopi bombing range (in easy sight of the CinC and his staff at HQ NEAF) and dropped a 28 lb (12.7kg) practice bomb on to the sea target. Bombing accuracy was assessed in real time by a Range Safety Officer – often a squadron junior aircrew officer. We would then set up a low-level pattern and usually complete six attacks before recovering to Akrotiri for thirty to forty minutes CT – continuation training in the instrument and visual circuit, mainly for the pilots of course.

Nowadays when we travel by air to Cyprus, we land at the substantial airfields of either Larnaca or Paphos. Back in the 1970s, only Nicosia (a joint RAF and civil airfield with an 8,000ft [2,440m] runway) was available for us as a Plan 2 diversion, so we always had to keep sufficient fuel for the hop there – some 60 miles (96km) but with the Troodos Mountain range in the way. We also used the military airfields of Adana in southern Turkey and Souda Bay in Crete as much more distant Plan 1 diversion airfields. But they were very seldom used not least because the weather factor at Akrotiri, certainly by Lincolnshire standards, was usually wonderful. Nevertheless, we were always conscious that Akrotiri's one runway could be blocked – probably by an impecunious English Electric Lightning of No 56 Squadron who always seemed to be in need of a 'priority' landing. Or by a magisterial Shorts Belfast of Air Support Command who always expected landing priority. Had the one runway been blocked, most of us had calculated that we could get the Vulcan down safely on the 60ft (18.3m) wide parallel taxiway (which, considering the Vulcan had a wheel span of just over 32ft [9.75m], now I am older I realise might have been a bit difficult on a dark night in a cross wind…).

While the weather *was* wonderful, for at least half of the year if not more, that meant it was hot. Akrotiri had a reliable 30°C midday temperature; Nicosia was even hotter. Cockpit temperatures on the ground and while flying the low-level route soared. We coped by using lightweight flying suits, air-ventilated suits, and had large cold air trolleys which blasted freezing air into the aircraft while we did the start-up checks – which usually took an hour unless the aircraft had been primed for an alert. There was a rule that, once the door was closed, we had to be airborne within fifteen minutes. We then normally climbed to above FL 400 – in about fifteen minutes and, during the two-hour high-level navigation stage got as cold as we could bear before descending for a couple of hours

or so at low level. Frost used to form on the inside of the cockpit blister. Dehydration was a huge concern: we carried several two-gallon plastic bottles of orange juice and drank it constantly while airborne. None of it seemed to come out at the other end.

We planned most squadron flying with early morning take-offs – not too difficult in NEAF when the working day, even for staff officers, began at 0700. The low-level turbulence built up heavily by midday and aircraft fatigue management became a fine art. Each aircraft's consumption of FI, that is the fatigue index, was closely monitored from a white 'black box' in the bomb bay roof and recorded – by aircraft and by individual captain's name. Graphs were conspicuously displayed at HQ Bomber Wing so everybody soon knew who the rough and the smooth were.

One major difference between NEAF and No 1 Group was the approach to fighter affiliation exercises. In the United Kingdom, there were strict rules such as bank angle not to exceed 30° during manoeuvre. In NEAF there were no such restrictions. Moreover, to the south of Akrotiri lay a large restricted area which we could book to exercise with our Lightning friends of 56 Squadron (or the occasional visitors when 56 was away). It also meant that, unlike in the UK, we could de-brief together afterwards. At home, it was difficult to use communications jamming to confuse the fighter controllers; there were fewer restrictions in Cyprus. To give the Lightnings a hard test, we could exploit the Vulcan's extraordinary manoeuvrability at high altitude, using low IAS, high power, and maximum peacetime 'G' to fly steep climbing turns with remarkably small turning radii. If the Lightning *did* manage to creep astern, we could jam their AI radar to prevent missile release. We learned a lot about fighter evasion from these sorties: usually a well flown Vulcan could outmanoeuvre a *single* Lightning but a well flown *pair* of Lightnings would usually win out – if, that is, they had sufficient fuel.

In order to widen the training available, and being denied the Goose Bay, Labrador, and Ranger flights to USAF Strategic Air Command low-level routes out of Offutt AFB in Omaha, we used to send an aircraft back to the UK every Monday – alternating IX and 35 week by week – to land and stay at Waddington: a 1 Group Vulcan base. We would plan to fly three trips Tuesday to Thursday around the UK low-level route, have a long weekend catching up at home, and delivering oranges and Cypriot wine, and then return to Akrotiri on the Monday. Each squadron crew was scheduled a UK Trainer every six months.

Relations with our UK hosts were not always as smooth as they should have been. They reached a nadir during my time when, on one occasion, we taxied in to the usual NEAF Vulcan parking slot near the control tower at Waddington to read out of the cockpit window a large, newly painted notice, signed ostenta-

**Vulcan cockpit – pilot's instruments and controls.** Avro Heritage

tiously by the Waddington Station Commander, to the effect that, although visiting aircraft were welcome at his station, they should not expect to get any engineering assistance from his ground crew! Mind you, this charming thought might well have come about because, back at Akrotiri, the then OC Bomber Wing had decreed that any visiting Vulcans from Waddington were to be parked at the dispersal as far from where 'his' Vulcans were parked as was geographically possible! Happy days.

Other airfields welcomed us, whether it was the Shah of Persia's Tehran/Meherabad, Malta's RAF Luqa, Bahrain's RAF Muharraq; or indeed Mauritius' Plaisiance International – where for my crew a huge crowd was waiting for us. I was on national TV with two hours of landing (and being asked why I was bringing nuclear weapons to Mauritius). On departure day we were given the whole of Mauritian airspace to fly around the island at low level before setting off for RAF Gan in the Maldives on the way back home to Akrotiri.

There was an early expectation that the Vulcans would roam all over the Middle and Near East, and to the Far East. The aircraft had long legs and a high cruising speed (certainly for the time – two hours to Malta; three and a half hours to Bahrain on the Northern CENTO route over Turkey and Iran; then four hours to Gan in the

Maldives; then four more to Singapore/Tengah). In addition to Mauritius, I got as far as New Zealand with my crew. And, in an extraordinary venture out of the run of the mill, both IX and 35 Squadrons adopted Cheshire Children's Homes in Ethiopia and were able to take the aircraft, on alternate years, to that desperate country laden, not with bombs, but with medical supplies (especially to combat polio) and toys for the children. The now Air Vice-Marshal Ron Dick, who captained the first Vulcan visitor, tells me that it is the only time he has ever seen hardened Vulcan crew chiefs in tears.

From many of these airfields, we were able to mount low-level training exercises. Probably the most productive were those based on RAF Luqa in Malta, Tehran/Meherabad in Persia, and RAF Masirah in Oman, usually with detachments of four aircraft for a week or a fortnight. From Luqa we would fly low-level routes, sometimes using the Vulcan's simplex Terrain Following Radar (TFR), attacking targets with the F95 camera, around Sicily and up the west coast of Italy into the Plain of the Po. From Tehran we would go around the moon-like, uninhabited plateaus of Iran – from Masirah, all over the desolate and mountainous areas of Oman. Excellent training, and wonderful alternatives to the soon to become 'old hat' anti-clockwise around-Cyprus route.

And then there were Command and Station readiness exercises when, just as in Strike Command back in the UK, all aircraft and crews had to be generated in the nuclear strike role to a very tight timescale. Held at immediate readiness over several days, the exercise would invariably conclude with a mass fly-off – sixteen Vulcans scrambling would get everybody's attention. On one occasion I recall our imaginative station commander, the then Air Cdre John Stacey, ordered the Akrotiri air traffic controllers to feign 'death' and go off-air for our recovery. Sixteen Vulcans recovered to the visual circuit and landed sequentially at Akrotiri controlled only by an Aldis lamp from the tower. Very exciting and something that would never have happened at a UK V-Bomber base!

Like all Strike Command operational stations, RAF Akrotiri had an annual surprise visit from the STC TACEVAL (Tactical Evaluation) team reinforced, in our case, with staff officers from HQ NEAF. My colleague Kevan Dearman, who was a flight commander on IX Squadron, recalls our first TACEVAL experience: all Vulcan crews were generated in the normal way in the strike (nuclear) role, but he and about half a dozen others were sent off to RAF Luqa in

Malta to exercise that role. The remaining Akrotiri crews were re-generated in the conventional role with seven live 1,000 lb (454kg) free-fall bombs (this was before we had the retarded tails). After a Hi-Lo profile, the target was a specially prepared raft in the sea some distance from Akrotiri. The attack, known as a CJ, required the aircraft to run in fast at low level and pull up and level off at 2,500ft (762m) above sea level just before release. All the crews were tired, hot and weary after several days on alert and coping with intruder activity organised by one of the resident British army regiments from Episkopi or Dhekelia. However, to everyone's surprise, the lead Vulcan in the stream sank the target with its middle bomb. The resulting delay while a new target was laid, with the aircraft circling in the heat, was not welcomed but the Station Commander, John Stacey, was ecstatic – and Akrotiri scored a creditable TACEVAL result.

I referred earlier to the 'old hat' anti-clockwise low-level route around Cyprus that too many crews got blasé about. After we had all landed after one Command exercise, Air Cdre Stacey called a station exercise just as we were shutting down (and expecting to get back to the Ski Club on Ladies Mile), and we were told we were re-generating in the conventional role that is, twenty-one 1,000 lb (454kg) bombs. For the fly-off for that exercise a couple of days later, our exhausted armourers and crew chiefs de-loaded the real bombs, and replaced them with 28 lb (12.7kg) practice bombs. However, here's the really imaginative change – the Station Commander ordered the Wing Nav Officer, my namesake Simon Baldwin, to find us targets on the Cyprus low-level route but we were to fly that route clockwise that is, backwards. That really set the cat amongst the pigeons – and the bombing results were awful. It was from this fly-off that we returned to Akrotiri with a 'silent' air traffic control tower.

So, in summary, for those of us at Akrotiri in the early 1970s, times were good. It was especially so for those of us who had had only Lincolnshire and perhaps Rutland in our address book. I remember a very positive visit by the new Prime Minister, Edward Heath (his predecessor Harold Wilson had never visited the RAF anywhere). The CENTO Alliance, although a bit suspect politically, gave us a good excuse to range over the Middle East. Akrotiri, with its Air Commodore station commander, Vulcan Bomber Wing operating quite independently of Strike Command in the UK, its Lightnings of 56 Squadron, Hercules of 70 Squadron, Wessex helicopters, RAF Regiment Wing and Bloodhound surface-to-air missiles of 112 Squadron, was an exciting place, even if all the aircraft were left out in neat packages on the dispersals at night despite Colonel Gaddafi up the road with his Soviet *Badgers*. There was real synergy at Akrotiri, not least because, certainly for the first time in my experience, just about all the elements of air power were together on one station.'

**Wing Commander 'Jeff' Jefford** was directly associated with the Vulcan for over ten years, and for a period was Nigel Baldwin's navigator. He operated initially with Blue Steel and later in the free-fall bombing role, ultimately logging over two thousand hours on type.

'Starting with the Canberra, one of the fundamentals of post-war Air Ministry bomber procurement policy appears to have been that, whenever possible, navigators were to be buried in the bowels of an aeroplane and denied any external visual reference. This was in marked contrast to the opposition's practice, the navigator's station on a typical Soviet bomber of the 1950s, the Ilyushin IL-28 and Tupolev Tu-16 for example, having generously-glazed bay windows, providing a magnificent panoramic view of the passing countryside. See also what the Americans did with the Canberra once they got their hands on it. The ultimate expression of the British philosophy was manifested in the V-Bombers whose navigators were required, not only to work in the dark, but to do it facing backwards, leading to spatial disorientation and providing bags of scope for misunderstandings as to whether a left turn meant "my left, or yours?". The basic rules of the game were simple – navigators were supposed to estimate where the aeroplane *might* be and every now and then announce this to Biggles, who would look out of his window and award the guess marks out of ten. This policy prevailed for many years, even the designers of the BAC TSR.2 seemingly being persuaded to treat glass as a strategic commodity which was in short supply. This may be a fanciful interpretation but it is a fact that for several years this particular navigator was fortunate enough to fly over much of the world, courtesy of the RAF's Canberras and Vulcans, without actually having been able to see very much of it.

During the quarter of a century that the Vulcan flew with the RAF the art of practical air navigation was transformed into a science. When the bomber entered service in the 1950s, it required two men to monitor and manage the state-of-the-art navigation and bombing equipment and to handle any of the potential failures to which the kit was prone while guiding the aeroplane to its destination, sometimes by reference to the stars, and, if appropriate, dropping a bomb on it. The Vulcan's equipment had been updated somewhat by the 1980s, but it was still an analogue system based on 1950s (even 1940s) technology. By the 1980s any self-respecting combat aeroplane had a remarkably accurate digital nav/attack computer supported by an inertial platform and/or a solid state Doppler radar, the overall system having an insignificant failure rate. Pending the air force's finding the money for a fleet fit, the contemporary navigator (only one by this time, assuming that there was still a seat for him – the writing was already on the wall for this honourable trade) was probably saving up his pocket money to buy a personal Global Positioning System from a shop in the local High Street, and he had no use whatsoever for astro, because there was nowhere to stick his sextant – at least, nowhere very comfortable.

So what did the passage of those twenty-five years mean for the average Vulcan nav, or pair of navs? The Nav Radar is the easier of the two to deal with, as his kit did not change significantly. He was responsible for operating the H2S Mk.9A radar, the result of a dozen years of development work applied to the H2S Mk.1 of World War Two. It could provide fixes to a notional accuracy of the order of 200 yards (183m) and could deliver bombs within about 400 yards (366m), although a high degree of skill was required in order to achieve consistently good results. When attacking a 'no-show' target, it was possible to use another object, one that would give a positive radar return, by measuring the N/S and E/W distances (up to a maximum of 40,000 yards [36,575m] in each plane) between the target and the selected response and inserting these into the equipment; the Nav Rad then aimed at the 'offset' response, while the aeroplane actually tracked towards the real target.

The north-oriented radar picture was displayed on a 9in (22.9cm) diameter cathode ray tube and could be 'stabilised', that is, fed with groundspeed so that the ground appeared to stand still while the centre of scan, the 'aeroplane', moved across it. The rotation of the 6ft (1.8m) wide aerial could be restricted so that it scanned only a narrow sector, rather than the full 360°, thus minimising the radiation that could betray the aircraft's presence while increasing the frequency with which a particular response was illuminated; the aerial's depression angle could also be adjusted, 'tilted', to improve the definition of a particular response by optimising the amount of energy being directed at it. The display could be viewed at a variety of scales between 1:1M and 1:1/8M; from high level it could paint a map with a radius of about 180 miles (290km) and at the other extreme the set could be adjusted so that an airfield response (often the actual runway but, if not, at least the arc of the adjacent hangars) was about 2in (5.1cm) long – certainly good enough to make a reasonable stab at an approach.

Allied to the H2S was the Navigation and Bombing Computer (NBC), the combination of the two constituting the Navigation and Bombing System (NBS) – (not to be confused with the Bombing and Navigation System – the BNS – which embraced additional elements, including the sources of heading and velocity inputs). The NBC did exactly what its name suggests and, while the radar itself was relatively trouble-free, the computer elements, several dustbin-sized containers full of gears, cams, bicycle chains, pieces of 35mm film, electrical relays and so on could cause problems. There were a number of ways in which these 'calculators', as they were known, could fail and for each of these failures there was a specific limited procedure that required the Nav Rad to compensate for the malfunction. Since bomb-aiming with a 100% serviceable set of equipment was 'easy', the periodic routine training programme dictated that a large proportion of practice attacks had to be carried out using these fall-back options.

At low level, apart from providing fixes, the H2S could also assist in terrain-following at night or in poor visibility, since any ground ahead of, and higher than, the aircraft would obscure returns from more distant features – a, so-called, 'cut off' situation. When this occurred, the pilot was advised to climb until the aircraft was high enough to permit the radar to 'see' past the obstruction to the next feature, thus ensuring that it would fly over, rather than into, the first one.

While the Nav Rad's equipment may not have changed very much, the bombs did and he was the designated weapons expert within the crew. The Vulcan B Mk.1's Release to Service would have permitted it to have delivered a Blue Danube or Violet Club atomic bomb, or an American weapon supplied under Project 'E' (the US Mk.5, euphemistically referred to in British documentation as the 'bomb, HE HC 6,000 lb'). By the time that the B Mk.2 entered

service, these early arrangements had been superseded by the homegrown Yellow Sun Mks.1 and 2, followed, on three squadrons, by Blue Steel, all of these being replaced by the WE177 from the late-1960s onwards. Training flights, simulating all of the safety precautions and controlled release procedures associated with such weapons, were flown using dummy rounds. Bombing accuracy was initially assessed by ground-based radar units although, once the force had adopted wholesale 'below the radar' low level tactics, scores were based on vertical photographs taken by an F95 camera installed at the visual bomb-aiming station.

In the conventional role, the bomb bay could accommodate up to twenty-one 1,000 lb (454kg) 'iron' bombs which could be dropped singly or as a stick of variable length with the usual range of fuses and tail units to permit detonation above, on contact with or below the surface as required. Live bombing practice was carried out using 25 lb (11.3kg), and later 28 lb (12.7kg), practice bombs plus an occasional allocation of thousand pounders. Visual aiming was done (by the other navigator) using a T4 bombsight, although this procedure was only

practical at medium or high level and the adoption of (almost) exclusively low-level tactics meant that it had largely been abandoned in favour of radar-aiming by the mid-1960s. Conventional bombing was gradually allowed to fade away however, few, if any, 1,000 lb (454kg) bombs being provided in the late 1970s and the commitment was quietly dropped altogether in 1980 – two years before it was actually needed, at very short notice, in the Falklands.

Unlike that available to the Nav Rad, the equipment provided for the other navigator, the Plotter, did change over time. In the early days he was able to monitor the aircraft's progress via a Ground Position Indicator (GPI) Mk.4A furnished with heading from a magnetically monitored gyro-compass (an element of the Smiths Military Flight System – the MFS) and velocities from a Green Satin Doppler radar. Accuracy of the computed position decayed with time and the GPI was periodically reset against fixes obtained from the H2S or GEE Mk.3. More traditional navigational aids included astro and a Marconi AD7092D radio compass, which could furnish CONSOL counts and could sometimes be persuaded to provide bearings on ground

## The Nav Rad Operator's Station

While there was no 'trade demarcation' as such, it is generally true to say that the area outlined by the (superimposed) white lines on the left of the picture (starboard side of the aeroplane – we are facing backwards) was the Nav Rad's playground, while that on the right was the Plotter's affair with the bit at the top of mutual interest, since it was a read-out of information generated by kit largely under the control of the Nav Rad but also of considerable interest to the Plotter. The toys bleeding off on the extreme right were the province of the AEO. The Nav Rad's area is dominated by the Indicator Type 301, the H2S cathode ray tube and its associated controls for adjusting the picture; the box above it is an R88 camera which could take photographs of the screen. In front of the Ind 301 is the Control Unit (CU) 626 – a 'joystick' that was used to 'move the picture around' and, on a bombing run, was connected to the autopilot so that the Nav Rad could actually steer the aeroplane.

The Ind 301 is flanked by the CU595 to the left and the CU585 to the right. The CU595 permitted the 'tilt' of the aerial to be altered and controlled the direction and arc of sector scan. The CU585 was used to select the functions offered by the NBC ('fix', 'stab', 'home' or 'bomb') and provided a means of inserting 'internal' offsets of up to 20,000 yards (18,290m) N/S and E/W; a second set of 'external' offsets, of up to 40,000 yards (36,575m), was available via the CU12558, which was fitted in the desk (under the removable lid which is evident in the photograph). The circular unit mounted on the upper panel was the Radar Altimeter Mk.6A, most of the dials to its left being temperature read-outs from the bomb bay, most of them specifically provided in connection with Blue Steel. The dial at the top was a pressure read-out associated with the NBC and the rectangular hole beneath it is where the control panel for the True Airspeed Unit should be. The large 'shared' panel, the so-called 'Nav Panel', displayed the information being used/produced by the NBC, including track, groundspeed or true airspeed and the wind velocity, expressed in Cartesian co-ordinates, that is, its N/S and E/W components.

While most of the Nav Rad's kit stayed the same throughout the life of the Vulcan, the Plotter's displays changed over time. The picture shows a Blue Steel aeroplane still fitted with GEE, which means that it dates from about 1963 – only two of these black boxes would still be present in a similar photograph taken ten years later. Taking the Plotter's panel from the bottom and working up, the first two boxes are, on the left, Green Satin Mk.2 and the GPI Mk.6. Above them are: on the left, GEE Mk.3 (with the small circular screen and sundry knobs and tits below); in the centre the Inertial Navigation Control Unit and, on the right, the Store Control Panel, both of the latter being concerned with the missile. There was a third missile box (the Inertial Navigation Monitoring Unit) located, somewhat

inconveniently, under the lid of the Plotter's desk. On the canted, upper panel the individual dial displayed forward throw (for free fall bombing), flanked by the Track Control Unit (which combined magnetic heading with variation and drift to provide an output of true track, which was used, among other things, to orientate the H2S display). Above that are four dials displaying indicated airspeed, altitude, true track and outside air temperature. The top row comprises a relative bearing indicator (that is, the read-out from the radio compass – the control unit for which is *just* visible on the roof) and four fuel contents gauges. Missing from this picture is the Ground-speed Selector Unit, which ought to be occupying the small vacant oblong slot above the Inertial Navigation Control Unit. ('Jeff' Jefford)

These two views of XA890 were taken on 9th September 1955, during the SBAC display at Farnborough. Note the Avro logo on the fin.
Phil Butler

based transmitters (or the nearest cu-nim). By the mid-1960s GEE had been supplanted by TACAN, the Doppler had been upgraded to the Green Satin Mk.2 and the original GPI was being replaced by the Mk.6. Designed by Elliott Bros, the GPI Mk.6 probably represented the pinnacle of analogue computing technology; tailored to meet the specific demands of the Blue Steel system, it ultimately became the standard fit for all Vulcans, including free-fallers.

Blue Steel represented a significant technological advance in that it introduced the RAF's first inertial platform and, until the missile was actually released, the platform's output was available to the navigator in the carrier aircraft and he could integrate this with information derived from other sources to feed his equipment with the ideal combination of data. Because the missile's free flight time would have been measured only in minutes, long-term accuracy was not a requirement and the velocities produced by the inertial system tended to decay relatively rapidly with time. So long as the missile was on board, therefore, the platform was effectively slaved to the output of the aircraft's Doppler but it could become the primary source whenever the Doppler 'unlocked'. Conversely, the heading output of the platform was far better than that provided by the, essentially magnetic, compass fitted in the aircraft.

The need to upgrade the heading source had long been recognised and by the late 1960s, just as Blue Steel was being withdrawn, the gyro-magnetic compass was being progressively complemented by the Heading Reference System Mk.2, which was purely gyro-based and very accurate. This eventually became the standard fleet fit, thus providing all Vulcans with the precise heading information that had previously been confined to the missile carriers. At much the same time the means of measuring drift and groundspeed had been further improved by the introduction of Decca Doppler 72. The new Doppler was a solid-state device with no moving parts, which went some way towards eliminating some of the less desirable characteristics of the occasionally temperamental Green Satin which it replaced.

So much for the equipment; what of the procedures? So long as all of the kit performed to specification, an operational sortie should have been no problem at all. With the GPI being fed by the Doppler, and with its read-out periodically refined by H2S fixes, a Vulcan crew could have found its way to any target within range and hit it with a more than adequate degree of precision, bearing in mind that it was delivering a nuclear weapon.

The snag was that the kit was prone to failure, which meant that it would often be necessary to revert to limited procedures. As a result,

in the course of routine training, both navs tended to spend much of their time working with one or other hand tied behind their backs. Reference has already been made to the Nav Rad's having to cope with equipment failures, some of which could degrade navigational information, and the Plotter's life could be further complicated by the loss of Doppler, problems with the Blue Steel's inertial system and so on. There were specific procedures laid down to paper over virtually any combination of cracks and most training sorties involved at least one element of dealing with a failure of some kind, often real, sometimes simulated.

While the TACAN would be routinely selected to a convenient station as a safety precaution, apart from international transits or airways flying, it was little used in practice because it was hardly likely to be available on a war sortie. Furthermore, once a Vulcan was more than 200 miles (322km) offshore it was out of range of TACAN and there was nothing to see on the radar screen so the primary fixing aid became astro, and astro had definite limitations, especially by day when, as often as not, the only available body was the Sun – which could furnish only a single position line. By night, calculating, shooting and plotting a classic two-star, seven-shot fix required *at least* twenty minutes from start to finish and was a laborious process, involving correcting for acceleration errors, a problem which was not significant in aircraft of lesser performance. All of this involved numerous arithmetical processes, any numerical errors tending to negate the whole exercise. Much has been

claimed with regard to the accuracy of astro but much of it has also been exaggerated. That is not to say that remarkable results were never achieved; they were, but the overall performance was far less spectacular, although this tended not to be publicised. For instance, while the final error of the winning crew in the annual Bomber Command Navigation Competition was usually measured in mere yards, the average accuracy was more conveniently measured in miles – and sometimes, in the case of the tail-enders, quite a lot of them. That said, so long as astro was available you were never 'lost'; but that is not the same as saying that you knew *precisely* where you were.

All of this astro business was somewhat academic, of course, because it would have not have been employed on an overland war sortie into the USSR. In fact, training aside, it was only necessary actually to resort to astro when making long trans-oceanic flights. While the traditional 'bomber establishment' clung to the mythical accuracy of celestial navigation, reality finally intruded in 1973 when No 27 Squadron re-formed in the maritime surveillance role, which meant that its crews needed to *know* where they were when operating for prolonged periods over the sea in high latitudes. It took some time for the equipment to arrive but the requirement was eventually satisfied by installing LORAN in the squadron's aeroplanes. Similarly, when the Vulcan was required to participate in Operation CORPORATE (the Falklands), the inadequacy of astro was again tacitly acknowledged when it became necessary to cobble together an OMEGA fit.'

**Flight Lieutenant John Farley** will forever be remembered for his work as the test pilot who tested and cleared the Hawker Siddeley Sea Harrier for service. However, during a period with the Royal Aircraft Establishment, he also experienced the Vulcan first hand, as part of the overall research undertaken in readiness for the Concorde supersonic transport.

'Concorde fans who have visited the Fleet Air Arm Museum will be aware of the part played in the development of Concorde by two single-seat research aircraft, the Handley Page HP.115 (XP841) and the BAC 221 (WG774), as both are on display alongside a Concorde prototype at Yeovilton. Perhaps less well appreciated is the role of Vulcan XA890.

Operated by the Aerodynamics Research Flight (Aero Flight) both the single seaters and the Vulcan flew from the Royal Aircraft Establishment airfield at Thurleigh, near Bedford, and in the mid-1960s played an important part in convincing the RAE scientists that their ideas for a supersonic transport using a slender delta wing were practical. Thanks to the lift produced by vortices over their top surfaces, slender deltas flying at low speeds can enjoy a remarkable margin from the stall. Indeed the stalling angles of attack (AoAs) can be more than double the angles we are used to with ordinary wings, and even then the "stall" may take the form of a departure in roll and yaw rather than a breakdown of lift. The bad news is that such AoAs lead to huge amounts of drag so that, long before the "stall", you need full throttle just to maintain speed in level flight. This speed is rather naturally called the Zero Rate of Climb speed or Vzrc. At Vzrc you cannot accelerate, climb or turn. The only way out is to reduce the

drag by lowering the nose, accepting a loss of lift and height in order to accelerate. From a pilot's perspective the manoeuvre is similar to a normal stall recovery.

This leads to the consideration of take-off speeds needing a margin above Vzrc rather than above Vs (the stalling speed). The snag is that on a multi-engined slender delta Vzrc literally leaps up if you lose an engine and require a very different pitch attitude from the one you had before the failure. To address such concerns, the Aero Flight boffins came up with a Take Off Director (TOD) proposal for Concorde that used the cross pointer director bars provided for the Instrument Landing System or ILS. On take-off this meant using the vertical needle to track the runway centre line and following the horizontal one to rotate at the correct speed and then capture the attitude that gave the desired margin above Vzrc during initial climb out. When an engine failed the system would at once start moving the horizontal bar down the display, directing the pilot to a new lower nose position, automatically taking into account the thrust and drag variations due to the particular all-up-weight and ambient conditions of the day.

While the HP.115 and the BAC 221 had similar aerodynamics to Concorde, they had totally different inertias. In the dynamic situation of a take-off the high-inertia Concorde was going to respond quite differently to the low-inertia single seaters, not because of its shape, but because of its very different weight. Hence the use of a Vulcan to develop the TOD.

The box that drove the TOD contained a suitable mix of accelerometers and rate gyros and was provided with inputs from the normal Vulcan pitot static system. The trial needed to

develop the laws, or mathematical equations that would determine just how the box moves the director bars as well as what to do about rotate cue. It was clear that different pilots were likely to respond to the instrument display in different ways, so we tried to adjust things so that the system could handle the full range of piloting techniques from smooth gentle corrections to large aggressive inputs. The normal right hand-seat Vulcan flight instruments were replaced by a panel that closely resembled that of the Hawker Siddeley Trident, then in service with British European Airways (BEA), including the actual Trident attitude and horizontal situation instruments. After some one hundred hours of development flying the Aero Flight pilots felt the laws were about right, so it was time to see what airline pilots thought of them.

I had strong views about this final and most important test phase, failed dismally to keep them to myself, and so got lumbered with the job. The flying supervision chain then swung into action regarding the need to indoctrinate the right hand seat visitor on purely Vulcan issues. They could foresee nothing but trouble with these flights and as Captain looked to me to cover all eventualities so that they might be fireproof, come what may.

Selling our work to airline pilots not used to the development scene, let alone the Vulcan required some thought. Used to the spacious and comfortable shirt sleeve environment of a Trident, or similar, such evaluators were not going to feel instantly at home trussed up in the right hand Vulcan bang-seat, looking through a porthole to the side and a letter box to the front. In fact if I was not careful, I suspected some might even change their minds before we got to taxi out. At best their minds were hardly going to be fully focused on the niceties of the TOD. Finally, there were a few Vulcan bits and pieces on the right which I could not see, let alone reach, and which I would have to rely on them operating correctly when appropriate. So I pondered all this and concluded that the sortie brief should only mention the Vulcan in passing and that all emphasis would be on the TOD. This approach left me with the need to operate this two-pilot cockpit without much help, so I decided it was time to call in a few favours in the hangar.

The idea was that my friends would make three Perspex sheets that fitted over the right hand side consoles. These sheets would have holes for the switches to stick up through and allow the gauges to be read. One panel was painted white and had the switches and gauges numbered 1 to 10, the second was blue 20 to 22 and the third yellow 30 to 37. This simplified the check list calls to the likes of 'Yellow panel 32 to ON' (or whatever). Thus the Vulcan brief boiled down to just mentioning that there

**Spectacular view of XA890 with wheels down and airbrakes deployed. It shows the original wing, which the aircraft kept throughout its life.**
Eric Morgan

The standard right-hand seat for the Vulcan
pilot. John Farley

were these three panels that I would ask them
to set from time to time.

As for the ejection seat, I explained they did
not need to know anything about it. I would
check it thoroughly and strap them in. I pointed
out we were only flying in the circuit and this
was Bedford, not a long-haul flight, and so we
had the luxury of the airfield and Air Traffic Control to ourselves. This meant we would land at
once in response to any conceivable emergency (desirable also for the poorly placed
team in the back looking at the nosewheel leg
through the escape hatch at 1,000ft [305m]). In
short they were about to fly in a delightfully
overpowered four-engine airliner that could
climb on one, at our very own private airstrip.
So let us talk about the TOD, which you are
here to try…

In the air they all loved it. As is the way of the
world the older captains looked very serious
the while and tried to come up with a significant
comment (as befitted their station in life), while
the young first officers said "want one" and a
week later sent a well-written report. My logbook contains the names of sixteen chaps who
enjoyed the TOD. They include such legendary
aviators as Dave Davis of the Air Registration
Board (ARB) and Brian Trubshaw. There was

one I especially enjoyed flying with, First Officer
John Millett from BEA, who had earlier been a
flying instructor of mine at Flying Training
School. I then felt a little of what Janis Joplin
described when she went back to a high school
reunion as a pop star and met again the teach-
ers who had virtually drummed her out of
school. Actually, if John reads this, we thought
he was one of the better ones. Good military
instructors need to be hard at times because
hard school works and military squadrons are
not exactly flying clubs.

It was a real pleasure to see how this diverse
bunch took to the kit. A typical sortie started
with them doing a normal take-off to see the
rotate demand and generally get used to the
display, then I would quickly pop it back on the
ground so that they could do five or six more
take-offs. On the second one I would chop a
throttle on initial climb out, the bar would dip
and off they went at the correct new attitude.
Then came a run with the first throttle chopped
at rotate and the second after unstick. Given
the right weather and evaluating pilot, I later
enjoyed chopping one before rotate, the second during rotate and a third as we left the
ground. Sitting alongside them and watching
as they climbed out over the valley at the end of
Runway 27 (RW27), with a rate of climb of
around 200ft/min (60m/min), on one engine, in
a strange type that they had not been briefed

on, said everything about the potential value of
a TOD.

So that was the part played by XA890. A
great ship and one of the few Vulcans that kept
the original straight leading edge. As aeroplanes go it is probably the only one I have
flown where I always felt I had plenty of wing,
whatever the manoeuvre. That wing and its low-
speed lift was in a class of its own, especially
when landing. Come to think of it, there was
one TOD visiting pilot who experienced the
truly awesome potential of all that wing area
and the occasion might be worth mentioning.

The chap, who shall be nameless, was a
senior examiner with the Civil Aviation Flying
Unit (CAFU), the unit charged with setting the
standards in civil aviation. Such worthies are
not known for treating trips as a jolly, but I
expected him to relax his examiner attitude a bit
on his day out in our Vulcan. Sadly I was to be
disappointed and by the end of the trip, I was a
tad peeved with being treated as a lower form
of aeronautical life. Sure I was only a flight lieutenant with two thin blue ones against his four
wide gold ones but it was my aeroplane! So I
decided to use some of the aforementioned
wing and show him in the process that there
were other people in the world who knew about
aeroplanes beside himself.

Downwind for the last landing, I quietly
remarked that the Vulcan had a lot of lift avail-

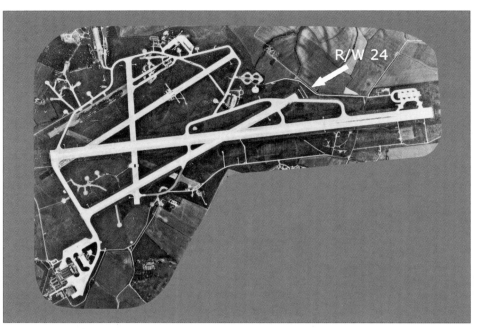

**Runway layout at RAE Bedford. The 'ORP' for dispersed Bomber Command Vulcans is shown at the North side of the right-hand end of the wider runway.** John Farley

**Beautiful image of three Vulcan B.2s in formation: XM597 nearest, XM852 and XM655.** Barry Jones

able and so did not need much runway for landing. I then took control and turned finals on RW24, which was half the width of the main one we had been using and much shorter. Vulcan buffs will know that the minimum threshold speed in RAF service was 125 knots (232km/h), a speed determined NOT by lift requirements but by the need for good lateral control in turbulence. The day was lovely, with not a turb anywhere, so by half a mile out I was nicely settled on finals for RW24 at 125 knots gear down and airbrakes out. At 100ft (30.5m), as the security fence slipped beneath our nose, I popped the chute, opened the bomb doors, stop-cocked the two inner engines and kept steadily raising the nose. The lovely monster reared right up and seemed to just hang in the sky before greasing on at a very low speed.

Lowering the nose and stopping, I pointed out that if he looked out his side he would see that we were still a little short of the centreline of RW27. Getting no response, I looked across to find him rigid in his seat and just staring out of the front. I suspect he was in shock as we had only used the stub of 24 or about 2,000ft (610m). Perhaps he thought he had died and was waiting to see some gates appear.'

Flight Lieutenant Tim Mason flew the Vulcan both in the RAF and at one of the UK's test establishments, this time A&AEE at Boscombe Down. He was actually the project pilot for the Vulcan 'Autoland' trials in 1966 and 1967, until the requirement was cancelled. Here the autopilot was linked to the Airfield's Instrument Landing System (ILS) to enable a 'hands-off' landing to be made from the start of the approach right through to touchdown.

'I arrived at A&AEE on 1st January 1966, by which time autoland trials on Vulcan XH533 were, I think, already under way. The Trial Instruction was No 1 of 1965, so the trial itself was due to start shortly thereafter, but I do not know the actual date. An autoland Vickers Varsity had spent some time at A&AEE in 1965 for familiarisation flying by the pilots concerned, and XH533 was the only Vulcan involved from A&AEE. There were two threads to the programme during 1966 – statistical data gathering using XH533 and the clearance of every early example of the B Mk.2 Vulcan for autolanding. Clearance for service use of the kit in Vulcan 2s was to be made on individual aircraft. My own involvement in the flying is given below, all flights from Boscombe Down:

| | |
|---|---|
| 7.3.66 | 9 autolandings at Bedford |
| 8.3.66 | 9 autolandings at Bedford |
| 9.3.66 | 11 autolandings at Bedford |
| | (all smooth, I record) |
| 14.3.66 | 12 autolandings at Bedford |
| 29.4.66 | 9 autolandings at Bedford |
| 24.5.66 | 10 autolandings at Bedford |
| 27.5.66 | 10 autolandings at Bedford |
| 12.1.67 | 9 autolandings at Bedford |
| 1.3.67 | 10 autolandings at Bedford |
| 27.6.67 | 8 autolandings at Bedford |
| | (The last of the trial autolandings). |
| 22.8.67 | tests of a rate-of-descent recorder |
| 25(?).8.67 | tests of a rate-of-descent recorder |

On 2nd October 1967 I flew XH533 to St Athan, never, I believe, to fly again.

Bedford was used because it had a flat runway and approach plus the benefit of extra facilities for tracking the aircraft. The system used leader cables and only the UK Military (I think) tried it – basic ILS performance and integrity improved considerably after the decision to install leader cables was made. 28th April 1966 was the date of the only autoland clearance flight of a Service Vulcan B Mk.2 – XL319 at Scampton. I note that it was the first with a Blue Steel (most probably a dummy) and that eight autolandings were made, all safe but with a tendency to land slightly left of the centreline. Shortly after the XL319 flight the requirement for clearance of autolanding in the Vulcan was cancelled.

Looking at some other points concerning the Vulcan, the T.4 bombsight was a visual bombsight in the blister under the nose; the nav/plotter had to lift a cover and lie prone with his full kit on (in theory) to use it. I only flew on one sortie when it was used, taking six hours to fly from Coningsby to Filfla (off Malta) and back to drop one 100 lb (45kg) practice bomb. This was on 31st July 1962 in XL386 of 9 Squadron as part of a Groupex, which means that other aircraft would have been involved. As far as I remember the T.4 was a development of the earlier Mk.14 sight, widely used. It would have used inputs from the nav equipment, for instance, heading, drift angle, true airspeed, accurate height and ground speed.

ODM stood for Operating Data Manual and included performance information on take-off, climb, cruise (level and cruise/climb), descent and landing on four engines. I seem to remember that limited data was included for three engines. When I was on 9 and then 35 Squadrons the data was calculated for Olympus 200 series engines (17,000 lb

XM594 touches down at Waddington, in the process giving a fine view of the Vulcan's wing-mounted airbrakes. Barry Jones

[75.6kN] static thrust). In autumn 1963 we started getting aircraft with 300 series engines (20,000 lb [88.9kN] static thrust), but I'm sure that we had no data for the more powerful motors on the basis that there was plenty of poke for take off and climb, while in the cruise the same speed (M=0.86) was used and the bigger engines throttled accordingly, and thus we could rely (?) on the existing figures. In practice, again to the best of my recollection, 300 series aircraft were more thirsty than the 200, and it was not usual to fly higher to gain any advantage. One reason was the unacceptable discomfort of having to wear the full high-level kit above 45,000ft (13,716m) for training. Incidentally, by the time I left 35 Squadron in January 1965 we were not permitted to use the full power of the 300 series, achieved by taking off and flying in "cruise" control (a switch on the throttle quadrant). I feel sure that the ODM trials on XL391 at A&AEE in 1965 were cruise performance measurements with the 300 series. On 2nd, 3rd and 7th February 1966 (at A&AEE) I flew XL391 on a trial which included three-engine cruise climb performance measurements.

The HRS (Heading Reference System) was a fancy name for a compass; it came into use after my time in Bomber Command and I don't recall any trials on it at Boscombe, although it is just possible that I was not involved. HRS replaced the compass system previously in use due to the unsatisfactory results of our brave boys in American competitions; later we did better and, I think, achieved very creditable results with HRS against B-52s.'

# Contracts and Airframe Histories

The prototype Avro 698 bombers and two batches of scaled models were ordered at the same time (serial numbers allotted on 22nd June 1948). These comprised: Two Avro 698s to Spec. B.35/46 (VX770 and VX777) on Contract 6/Aircraft/1942/CB.6(a); Two Avro 707s to Spec. E.15/48 (VX784 and VX790) on Contract 6/Aircraft/2205/CB.6(a); Two Avro 710s (VX799 & VX808) on Contract 6/Aircraft/2626/CB.6(a)

The larger half-scale Avro 710s were intended to represent the full-scale prototypes as closely as possible, but it was later decided to order a 'high-speed' Avro 707 in their place, resulting in an order for the Avro 707A (WD280 to Spec. E.10/49) to Contract 6/Aircraft/3395 on 6th May 1949, while the proposed Avro 710s were cancelled on 10th February 1949.

On 13th November 1951 three more Avro 707s were ordered, to Contract 6/Aircraft/7470/CB.6(a). These included two more 707A (WZ736 and WZ739) and an Avro 707C version (WZ744) with two side-by-side seats, intended as a conversion trainer. Ultimately, WZ739 was cancelled, while the other two aircraft spent their lives at the RAE.

## Aircraft Individual Histories

The individual histories have been compiled from the 'Movement Cards' (Air Ministry Form 78) held by the MoD Air Historical Branch, and available on microfilm from the Royal Air Force Museum at Hendon. Another set of these cards covers aircraft operated by the Ministry of Defence (Procurement Executive) and its predecessors such as the Ministry of Supply. The dates given should be regarded as 'indicative' rather than exact, since they may vary by a few days from the actual movement of an aircraft. Some information of a repetitive nature has been deleted – for example, movement to a 'Disposal Account' for repair or maintenance where the aircraft remained at its base and subsequently returned to the same flying unit. Also omitted are short-term exchanges between units where the aircraft later returned to the original unit. (Some exchanges of this nature only lasted for a single day).

'Categories' (Cat.) mentioned refer to damage assessments after an incident. Categories 1 to 3 indicate relatively minor damage and these have been omitted. Cat.4R indicates

**This photo shows XM649 of the Waddington Wing, flying a low-level over Lincolnshire.** A V Roe A2/1/201 via Tony Buttler

'Repair by Contractor' (or in some instances by an RAF Maintenance Unit), Cat.5 indicates a complete write-off, with a suffix letter or letters showing whether as 'scrap', 'components' (for spares recovery), 'ground instruction', and the like.

As mentioned elsewhere, during much of the Vulcan's service life the type operated at stations operating 'centralised servicing' and the individual aircraft were allotted to all the Squadrons of the Wing (for example, '27/83/617' for the Scampton Wing). However, these aircraft usually flew with and wore the markings of one of the Squadrons, even if they may sometimes have been flown by crews from another unit. Where this system applied, we have tried to show the final unit markings applied to each aircraft. Space and research time limits prevent us from recording all the markings that may have been worn over the life of each aircraft.

## THE SCALE MODELS

### Avro 707 (VX784)

| | |
|---|---|
| 4.9.49 | First flight at Boscombe Down by Eric Esler. |
| 6.9.49 | Delivered from Boscombe Down to Farnborough |
| 30.9.49 | Crashed near Blackbushe – Chief Test Pilot Eric Esler killed. (Total: 2:43 F/H) |

### Avro 707B (VX790)

| | |
|---|---|
| 6.9.50 | First flight at Boscombe Down by R J (Roly) Falk. |
| 24.10.50 | Accepted off Contract |
| 21.9.51 | Damaged in landing accident at Boscombe Down. |
| 27.9.51 | Arrived at Woodford by road, for assessment and repair |
| 16.5.52 | Authority to return to A V Roe at Boscombe Down after repair |
| 5.6.52 | To Dunsfold. |
| 10.9.52 | Transferred to RAE Farnborough – delta-wing research |
| 26.1.56 | Transferred to ETPS for test-pilot training, coded '19'. |
| 25.9.56 | Landing accident at Farnborough |
| 27.5.57 | By road to RAF Bicester for storage |
| 22.10.57 | By road to RAE Bedford |
| 3.11.57 | Struck off Charge at Bedford for use as spares source |

### Avro 707A (WD280)

| | |
|---|---|
| 14.6.51 | First flight at Boscombe Down |
| 9.9.51 | Loaned to firm for SBAC Show |
| 15.11.51 | Authority for short loan to RAE Farnborough |
| 20.11.51 | Returned to A V Roe at Boscombe Down |
| 18.5.52 | Boscombe Down to Woodford |
| 24.6.52 | Authority to take part in CFE Annual Convention at West Raynham, 30.6.52 to 4.7.52 |
| 29.8.52 | Loaned to firm for duration of SBAC Show |
| 2.7.53 | Loaned to firm for duration of Paris Salon |
| 17.8.53 | Delivered to RAE Farnborough. Position error measurement |
| 4.9.53 | Loaned to firm for SBAC Show |
| 14.10.53 | Delivered to Woodford. Delta-wing research at A V Roe |
| 27.10.55 | Delivered to A V Roe Bracebridge Heath – major servicing |
| 12.2.56 | Returned to Woodford |
| 6.3.56 | Delivered to Renfrew, en route to Australia by sea. |
| 3.5.56 | Loaned to Australian Aero Research Council |
| 10.2.67 | Struck off Charge for local disposal in Australia. Sold to Geoffrey Mallett, Melbourne |
| 15.5.99 | To RAAF Museum, Point Cook. Current in 2006. |

### Avro 707A (WZ736)

| | |
|---|---|
| 20.2.53 | First flight at Waddington (assembled at A V Roe, Bracebridge Heath) |
| 16.6.53 | Despatched to RAE Farnborough |
| 7.5.54 | Despatched to A V Roe for installation of powered controls |
| 12.9.55 | Arrived at NAE Bedford. 'Automatic approach' trials |
| 16.11.55 | Despatched to AIEU Martlesham Heath. Automatic landing trials |
| 9.4.56 | To RAE Bedford, control system assessment |
| 19.4.56 | Returned to AIEU Martlesham Heath |
| 30.11.56 | To RAE Bedford |
| 19.12.56 | Returned to AIEU |
| 26.7.57 | Continuation of automatic throttle trials at RAE (BLEU) Bedford |
| 24.5.62 | Delivered to RAE Farnborough as source of spares for WZ744. |
| 31.5.62 | Struck off Charge. |
| 7.12.64 | Allotted to RAF Colerne as 7868M for preservation Later to RAF Finningley and then RAF Cosford |
| 3.9.82 | To Manchester Museum of Science and Industry. Current in 2006. |

**A view of VX784 at Farnborough.**

**Spectacular view of VX770 being displayed for the camera.** Eric Morgan

### Avro 707C (WZ744)

| | |
|---|---|
| 1.7.53 | First flight, at Waddington (after assembly at A V Roe Bracebridge Heath works) |
| 27.8.53 | Loaned to firm for SBAC Show |
| 23.9.53 | Arrived at A&AEE Boscombe Down. Pilot familiarisation on deltas |
| 18.5.54 | To A V Roe, Woodford, installation of powered controls |
| 12.1.56 | Despatched to RAE Farnborough |
| 26.9.56 | To A V Roe, Woodford. Instrumentation for electrically-controlled signalling |
| 25.3.59 | To RAE Farnborough |
| 7.6.66 | Aircraft released |
| 2.2.67 | Allotted for preservation as 7932M |
| 17.4.67 | To RAF Colerne for preservation. Later at Finningley and then Topcliffe. |
| 13.4.73 | Transferred to RAF Cosford for the Aerospace Museum. Present in 2006. |

### PROTOTYPES

Two Avro 698 prototypes ordered on 22nd June 1948 to Contract 6/Aircraft/1942/CB.6(a):

### Avro 698 (VX770)

| | |
|---|---|
| 30.8.52 | First flight at Woodford by Roly Falk. (Rolls-Royce Avon engines) Loaned to firm for 1952, 1953, 1954 SBAC Shows. By April 1953 re-engined with Armstrong Siddeley Sapphires. |
| 18.1.55 | Accepted off Contract at A V Roe. |

| | |
|---|---|
| 8.6.56 | Allotted for fitment of Rolls-Royce Conway engines |
| 17.8.56 | To Langar for conversion |
| 24.8.57 | Delivered from A V Roe Langar to Rolls-Royce, Hucknall Conway engine development on Contract 6/Eng/9906/CB.13a |
| 31.8.57 | Loaned to Rolls-Royce for SBAC Show |
| 30.8.58 | Loaned to Rolls-Royce for SBAC Show |
| 20.9.58 | Crashed at RAF Syerston during Battle of Britain display, structural failure after being over-stressed. |
| 29.9.59 | Struck off Charge |

### Avro 698 Vulcan (VX777)

| | |
|---|---|
| 3.9.53 | First flight at Woodford. (Bristol Olympus engines) |
| 5.9.53 | Loaned to firm for SBAC Show. |
| 14.7.54 | RAE Farnborough – preparation for bomb-dropping trials |
| 27.7.54 | Cat.3 damage, overshooting runway. |
| 23.3.55 | Accepted off Contract. |
| 30.3.55 | To A&AEE. Preliminary flight trials |
| 26.5.55 | Returned to Woodford for trials with extended wing leading edge |
| 10.7.56 | Allotted for conversion to Mk.2 prototype (Contract 6/Aircraft/13262/CB.6(a) |
| 31.8.57 | First flight as Mk.2 aerodynamic prototype. Loaned to firm for SBAC Show in September. |
| 27.4.60 | Delivered from Woodford to Farnborough for ground vibration trials of armament and equipment. |
| 18.10.62 | Struck off Charge for disposal and scrapped at Farnborough. |

## PRODUCTION VULCANS

### 45 Vulcan B.1

XA889 to XA913 (25) to Contract 6/Aircraft/8442/CB.6(a), serial numbers allotted 22nd July 1952.

XH475 to XH483, XH497 to XH506 and XH532, (20) to Contract 6/Aircraft/11301/CB.6(a), serial numbers allotted 17th September 1954.

Almost all surviving Vulcan B.1s on operational Squadrons were converted to B.1A standard, with revised electronics including a tail-warning radar similar to that fitted to the B Mk.2. After 'Trial Installations' on XA895 at A V Roe, the remaining B.1A conversions were carried out at the Armstrong Whitworth Bitteswell site between 1959 and 1962.

### XA889

| | |
|---|---|
| 4.2.55 | First flight |
| 10.6.55 | Awaiting Collection. Handed over to MoS Air Fleet at Woodford |
| 18.6.55 | Made flypasts at the Paris Air Show, also on 19.6.55. |
| 3.9.55 | Loaned to firm for SBAC Show at Farnborough |
| 15.3.56 | Arrived at A&AEE Boscombe Down for official trials |
| 12.7.56 | Returned to A V Roe at Woodford – installation of Olympus 102 engines. |
| 19.7.57 | To Bristol Engine Co, Filton. Olympus 104 development work. |
| 31.8.57 | Loaned to A V Roe for SBAC Show at Farnborough |
| 28.11.57 | Bristol Engine Co. Trials of an Olympus 102 fitted with strain gauges |
| 3.1.58 | A V Roe – fitting of Olympus 104 engines |
| 4.2.58 | From Woodford to Boscombe Down. A&AEE clearance of Mk.104 engines. |
| 15.2.58 | Returned to Woodford. Completion of Olympus 104 trials. |
| 3.4.58 | From Woodford to Filton. Olympus 104 development work at Bristol Engine Co. |
| 28.10.58 | To Woodford for major servicing. |
| 22.5.59 | Allotted for RATO trials at A V Roe. |
| 25.11.59 | Re-allotted for engine development and structural strain gauge testing and tests of revised wing leading edge. |
| 30.11.60 | Re-allotted for full-scale fatigue testing at A V Roe |
| 19.11.62 | Despatched to A&AEE Boscombe Down for conventional armament trials. |
| 16.9.63 | A&AEE. Radio and navigation system trials |
| 22.7.65 | Escort for Buccaneer on transatlantic flight |
| 17.8.65 | ASV.21 radar trials |
| 25.8.67 | Struck off Charge as scrap at Boscombe Down |

### XA890

| | |
|---|---|
| 24.8.55 | First flight |
| 31.8.55 | Awaiting Collection and Handed over to MoS Air Fleet at Woodford |
| 1.9.55 | Loaned to firm for SBAC Display at Farnborough |
| 27.4.56 | Arrived at A&AEE Boscombe Down for radio and radar trials. |
| 5.6.56 | Returned to Woodford. Preparation for Phase 2 radio and radar trials |
| 19.7.56 | To A&AEE. Continuation of radio & radar trials. |
| 18.9.56 | To A V Roe. Modifications. |
| 7.3.57 | To A&AEE. Radio compass trials |
| 12.3.57 | Returned to A V Roe, Woodford. Preparation for armament trials |
| 7.2.58 | To RAE Farnborough. Trials with 2,000, 6,000 and 7,000 lb bombs. |
| 2.2.59 | To A V Roe, Woodford. Preparation of Red Beard Mk.2 trials. |
| 22.7.59 | Returned to RAE Farnborough. Continuation of armament trials. |
| 10.5.62 | Re-allotted for 'Rapid Blooming Window' and infra-red decoy trials. |
| 27.1.64 | To RAE Bedford. Trials of experimental take-off directors (TODs) |
| 26.10.68 | Arrived at A&AEE Boscombe Down. Electro-magnetic pulse trials. |

| | |
|---|---|
| 5.5.69 | Struck off Charge at Boscombe Down for non-flying trials. Fire-fighting training. |

### XA891

| | |
|---|---|
| 22.9.55 | First flight |
| 23.9.55 | Awaiting Collection and Handed over to MoS Air Fleet at Woodford. Performance investigation. |
| 31.5.57 | Despatched to A V Roe at Langar. Preparation for B.OI.6 Olympus 200-series trials. |
| 24.7.59 | Crashed near Beverley, Yorkshire. Cat.5(s) after major electrical failure. Five crew escaped. |
| 12.9.61 | Struck off Charge. |

### XA892

| | |
|---|---|
| 23.11.55 | First flight |
| 30.11.55 | Awaiting Collection and Handed over to MoS Air Fleet at Woodford. Armament trials. |
| 27.4.56 | To RAE Farnborough. Landing trials |
| 29.5.56 | Returned to A V Roe, Woodford. |
| 1.9.56 | Loaned to firm for SBAC Show at Farnborough |
| 29.11.56 | Arrived at A&AEE Boscombe Down from Woodford. Armament trials. |
| 24.6.58 | To A V Roe Woodford for servicing. |
| 4.11.58 | To A&AEE. Continuation of conventional armament trials. |
| 12.2.59 | To A V Roe for modifications. |
| 15.5.59 | To A&AEE. Continuation of trials. |
| 18.2.60 | To A V Roe. Modifications. |
| 20.9.60 | To RAE Farnborough. Nuclear weapon development. |
| 21.4.62 | Despatched to RAF Halton for Ground Instructional use. Allotted 7746M on 14.3.62. While at Halton, marked as '16' on its nose. Scrapped in July 1971. |

### XA893

| | |
|---|---|
| 16.1.56 | First flight |
| 24.1.56 | Handed over to MoS Air Fleet at Woodford. Electrical systems development. |
| 11.11.59 | Re-allotted for Blue Steel mock-up work and ECM aerial development. |
| 5.5.60 | Despatched to Gloster Aircraft, Moreton Valence. Blue Steel and X-Band aerial installation. |
| 17.10.62 | Released for disposal and later to RAF Abingdon. Nose used for ground instruction as 8591M (allotted 6.63), initially for the RAF Exhibition Flight, from April 1986 displayed at Cosford Aerospace Museum. Still present 2006. |

### XA894

| | |
|---|---|
| 9.1.57 | First flight |
| 18.1.57 | Handed over to MoS Air Fleet at Woodford. De-icing system and auto-pilot development. |
| 29.3.57 | To A&AEE Boscombe Down. Mk.10 Autopilot trials. |
| 2.5.57 | To A V Roe, Woodford. Autopilot development. |
| 5.9.57 | To A&AEE Boscombe Down. Intensive autopilot development trials. |
| 16.10.57 | To A V Roe for engine change. |
| 1.11.57 | Returned to A&AEE, continuation of trials. |
| 18.11.57 | To A V Roe. De-icing system clearance trials. |
| 14.10.58 | To A&AEE. Official trials of Autopilot and Navigational Bombing System. |
| 4.2.59 | To A V Roe for servicing. |
| 27.11.59 | To A&AEE. Continuation of trials. |
| 18.7.60 | Delivered from Boscombe Down to Filton. Bristol Siddeley Engines Ltd. Allotted for B.OI 22R Olympus development for BAC TSR.2. |
| 23.2.62 | First flight with B.OI 22R fitted. |
| 8.12.62 | Turbine disc failure during engine running started fire on the ground at Filton, aircraft destroyed. |
| 14.9.65 | Written off Charge. |

### XA895

| | |
|---|---|
| 12.8.56 | First flight |
| 16.8.56 | Delivered to 230 OCU. |
| 31.12.56 | Loaned to Handling Squadron, Boscombe Down. |
| 19.1.57 | Returned to 230 OCU |

| | |
|---|---|
| 5.3.58 | Arrived at Woodford from Waddington. Allotted for ECM TI and flight trials |
| 27.9.60 | Arrived at A&AEE for electronic compatibility trials |
| 21.10.60 | Despatched to Woodford |
| 8.6.61 | Despatched from Woodford to BCDU Finningley |
| 11.5.65 | Arrived at RRE Pershore for development and trials of Red Steer Mk.2. |
| 6.9.65 | Despatched to Hawker Siddeley Aviation, Woodford. Trials of ARI 5952. |
| 17.1.67 | Despatched to 19 MU St Athan. |
| 19.9.68 | Sold as scrap to Bradbury Ltd. |

### XA896

| | |
|---|---|
| 30.1.57 | First flight |
| 4.3.57 | Awaiting Collection |
| 7.3.57 | 230 OCU. |
| 27.6.60 | 44 Squadron. |
| 6.9.61 | 230 OCU |
| 25.5.64 | Arrived at Rolls-Royce, Hucknall for repair and conversion to BS.100 flying test-bed for use by Bristol Siddeley Engines Ltd. Conversion abandoned when BS.100 engine cancelled in February 1965. |
| 25.10.66 | Struck off Charge. Scrapped at Hucknall. |

### XA897

| | |
|---|---|
| 10.7.56 | First flight |
| 20.7.56 | 230 OCU (on nominal strength, but not delivered to unit) |
| 1.10.56 | Crashed at Heathrow Airport during GCA approach in bad visibility, on return from overseas flight to New Zealand and Australia. |
| 3.10.56 | Struck off Charge as Cat.5(s), remains removed to 71 MU Bicester. |

### XA898

| | |
|---|---|
| 26.11.56 | First flight |
| 31.12.56 | Awaiting Collection |
| 3.1.57 | 230 OCU |
| 19.11.59 | 101 Squadron |
| 25.11.59 | 230 OCU |
| 23.7.64 | Allotted 7856M for No 1 SoTT, Halton |
| 26.8.64 | Struck off Charge as Cat.5(GI). Coded '30' at Halton. Broken up in August 1971. |

### XA899

| | |
|---|---|
| 16.2.57 | First flight |
| 28.2.57 | Handed over to MoS Air Fleet at Woodford. Development of Mk.10A autopilot. |
| 15.5.58 | Arrived at A&AEE Boscombe Down. Trials of new Flight Instrument System for V-Bombers. |
| 4.2.59 | Allotted to Blind Landing Experimental Unit. Trials of automatic landing system. |
| 9.2.62 | Despatched from Bedford to Woodford. Development of rapid engine start-up and take-off Systems. |
| 26.6.63 | Struck off Charge as Cat.5(GI) |
| 7.11.63 | Despatched to Cosford as an instructional airframe. Allotted as 7812M on 22.5.63 (initially for 1 SoTT, Halton, but move to Halton cancelled). Sold as scrap by August 1973. |

### XA900

| | |
|---|---|
| 7.3.57 | First flight |
| 25.3.57 | 230 OCU |
| 22.6.60 | 101 Squadron |
| 6.2.62 | 230 OCU |
| 22.2.62 | RAF Coningsby for mods. |
| 24.8.62 | 230 OCU |
| 17.11.65 | Allotted 7896M for No 2 SoTT, Cosford. |
| 24.2.66 | Struck off Charge, Cat.5(GI). Later to Cosford Aerospace Museum. Scrapped in early 1986. |

### XA901

| | |
|---|---|
| 19.3.57 | First flight |
| 31.3.57 | Awaiting Collection |
| 4.4.57 | 230 OCU |
| 19.11.59 | 617 Squadron |
| 25.11.59 | 230 OCU |

**This shot shows XA894 after conversion to the Olympus 22R test-bed, showing the bifurcated air intakes.** via Tony Buttler

**A lovely shot of an early Vulcan in silver: this time XA895, which had a long career on trials work.**

**This photograph is a staged publicity shot of early production Vulcan B.1s at Woodford, published as deliveries to the RAF were about to begin. The line-up includes XA898, XA893, XA892, XA891, XA889 and XA894.**
A V Roe C474 via Tony Buttler

| 27.6.60 | 44 Squadron |
| 9.7.62 | RAF Coningsby for mods. by A V Roe working party |
| 17.12.62 | 230 OCU |
| 24.11.65 | To Cranwell. Allotted 7897M for RAF College 17.11.65. Sold as scrap September 1972. |

**XA902**

| 13.4.57 | First flight |
| 7.5.57 | Awaiting Collection |
| 10.5.57 | 230 OCU |
| 3.12.58 | Delivered from Waddington to A V Roe, Woodford. Conversion to R-R Conway Mk.108 engines. |
| 17.7.59 | Arrived at Rolls-Royce Ltd, Hucknall. R-R Conway flight development. |
| 5.1.60 | Arrived in Malta (R-R Engine Development Section at Luqa). |
| 17.3.60 | Returned to Hucknall |
| 16.5.61 | Loan to Rolls-Royce for RB.163 Spey and Conway Stage 3, 3C and 4 development |
| 17.10.62 | Struck off Charge and returned to RAF for disposal |
| 7.3.63 | Airframe taken by road to RAF Dishforth |

**XA903**

| 10.5.57 | First flight |
| 31.5.57 | Handed over to MoS Air Fleet at Woodford. Blue Steel development trials. |
| 16.11.60 | Arrived at Edinburgh Field |
| 6.2.61 | Departed from Edinburgh Field on return to Woodford |
| 1.8.62 | Re-allotted to A V Roe for auxiliary power unit development |
| 3.1.64 | Arrived at Bristol Siddeley Engines Ltd, Filton. Conversion to Olympus 593 flying test-bed. |
| 9.9.66 | First flight with Olympus 593. |
| 4.8.71 | Arrived at Marshalls of Cambridge. Conversion to RB.199 flying test-bed. |
| 9.2.72 | Arrived at Rolls-Royce. |
| 19.4.73 | First flight with RB.199. |
| 23.1.76 | Authority given for move to A&AEE Boscombe Down. At A&AEE, ground firing trials of a Mauser 27mm. cannon were made from the RB.199 pod. |
| 22.2.79 | Arrived at RAE Farnborough – allotted for ground training use. |
| 19.7.79 | Struck off Charge. The nose of this aircraft survives in 2006 as an exhibit at the Wellesbourne Wartime Museum at Wellesbourne Mountford airfield near Stratford on Avon. |

**XA904**

| 31.5.57 | First flight |
| 13.7.57 | Awaiting Collection |
| 16.7.57 | 83 Squadron |
| 19.10.59 | AWA Bitteswell for B.1A conversion |
| 20.1.61 | 44 Squadron |
| 1.3.61 | Cat.4R flying accident at Waddington, re-categorised Cat.5(c). Power control failure, followed by landing off runway and collapse of undercarriage. |
| 12.12.61 | Nose of this aircraft allotted 7738M for transfer from No 71 MU to RAF Finningley. Scrapped in January 1974 |

**XA905**

| 26.6.57 | First flight |
| 11.7.57 | 83 Squadron |
| 7.7.59 | Cat.3R flying accident – repaired on site by 60 MU. |
| 16.10.59 | 44 Squadron, after repair. |
| 23.8.61 | 230 OCU |
| 10.9.64 | Waddington Wing |
| 23.7.64 | Allotted 7857M for RAF Newton (No 9 SoTT) and handed over 14.9.64. Scrapped at Newton 29.1.74. |

**XA906**

| 19.7.57 | Awaiting Collection |
| 12.8.57 | 83 Squadron |
| 6.1.59 | Declared Cat.3R, requiring 'Repair on Site' by A V Roe. |
| 2.4.59 | 44 Squadron, after repair |
| 5.3.62 | AWA Bitteswell for B.1A conversion |
| 16.8.62 | 44 Squadron Waddington Wing |
| 3.3.67 | 19 MU St Athan |
| 8.11.68 | Sold as scrap, Bradbury & Co |

**XA907**

| 29.8.57 | Awaiting Collection |
| 30.8.57 | 83 Squadron |
| 21.7.59 | Declared Cat.3R, requiring 'Repair on Site' by A V Roe. |
| 17.12.59 | 44 Squadron, after repair |
| 29.10.61 | AWA Bitteswell for B.1A conversion |
| 4.5.62 | 44 Squadron Waddington Wing |
| 2.2.65 | BCDU, Finningley |
| 12.10.66 | 19 MU, St Athan |
| 20.5.68 | Sold as scrap. |

**XA908**

| 28.8.57 | First flight |
| 17.9.57 | 83 Squadron |
| 24.10.58 | Crashed at Detroit, MI, USA, after failure of power controls. |
| 27.10.58 | Struck off Charge |

**XA909**

| 30.9.57 | Awaiting Collection |
| 1.10.57 | 101 Squadron |
| 22.1.62 | Whitworth Gloster, Bitteswell for B.1A conversion |
| 25.6.62 | 50 Squadron Waddington Wing |
| 16.7.64 | Cat.5(s) flying accident. Abandoned near Valley, Anglesey after engine explosion. |
| 23.7.64 | Struck off Charge. |

**XA910**

| 31.10.57 | Awaiting Collection |
| 1.11.57 | 101 Squadron |
| 21.6.60 | 230 OCU |
| 22.1.62 | 101 Squadron |
| 2.2.62 | AWA Bitteswell, B.1A conversion |
| 17.7.62 | 50 Squadron |
| 27.8.63 | Waddington Wing |
| 9.2.67 | 19 MU |
| 10.11.67 | RAF Cottesmore. Allotted as 7995M on 6.12.67. |
| 22.4.69 | To Ministry of Technology charge at RAF Cottesmore. |
| 27.5.70 | Struck off Charge, sold as scrap. |

**XA911**

| 31.10.57 | Awaiting Collection |
| 1.11.57 | 83 Squadron |
| 27.6.60 | 230 OCU |
| 12.1.62 | BCDU |
| 17.7.62 | Whitworth Gloster, Bitteswell. B.1A conversion. |
| 19.2.63 | Waddington Wing |
| 9.2.67 | 19 MU |
| 8.11.68 | Sold as scrap, Bradbury & Co |

**XA912**

| 13.11.57 | First flight |
| 30.11.56 | Awaiting Collection |
| 2.12.57 | 101 Squadron |
| 3.10.60 | Armstrong Whitworth, Bitteswell. B.1A conversion. |
| 19.3.61 | 101 Squadron |
| 7.8.63 | Waddington Wing |
| 6.3.67 | 19 MU |
| 20.5.68 | Sold as scrap. |

**XA913**

| 18.12.57 | Awaiting Collection |
| 19.12.57 | 101 Squadron |
| 21.3.61 | Armstrong Whitworth, Bitteswell. B.1A conversion. |
| 29.11.61 | 101 Squadron |
| 27.2.63 | Waddington Wing |
| 21.12.66 | 19 MU |
| 20.5.68 | Sold as scrap. |

**XH475**

| 10.1.58 | Awaiting Collection |
| 22.1.58 | 230 OCU |
| 28.2.58 | 101 Squadron |
| 27.4.62 | AWA Bitteswell. B.1A conversion |
| 24.9.62 | 101 Squadron Waddington Wing |
| 6.11.67 | Cat.5(GI) at Waddington, allotted as 7996M. 7996M was SoC on 2.4.76 at Waddington. |

**This detail of XA907 shows the tail section of a B.1A after conversion, with the enlarged tail-cone for the Red Steer radar.** via Tony Buttler

**XH476**
| | |
|---|---|
| 3.2.58 | Awaiting Collection |
| 5.2.58 | 101 Squadron |
| 29.11.61 | AWA Bitteswell. B.1A conversion |
| 7.5.62 | 44 Squadron |
| | Waddington Wing |
| 2.5.67 | 19 MU |
| 21.1.69 | Sold as scrap, Bradbury & Co |

**XH477**
| | |
|---|---|
| 29.1.58 | First flight |
| 17.2.58 | Awaiting Collection |
| 18.2.58 | 44 Squadron |
| 3.11.60 | AWA Bitteswell. B.1A conversion |
| 14.7.61 | 44 Squadron |
| 12.6.63 | Crashed at St Colme, Aboyne, Aberdeenshire. Flew into hill during low-level exercise. Cat.5(s). |
| 18.6.63 | Struck off Charge. |

**XH478**
| | |
|---|---|
| 14.2.58 | First flight |
| 31.3.58 | Handed over to MoS Air Fleet at Woodford. Orange Putter 'Window' installation trials |
| 16.4.58 | Authority to go to RAE Farnborough for bomb bay vibration trials |
| 3.8.58 | Returned to Woodford. |
| 9.10.58 | Despatched to A&AEE Boscombe Down. Orange Putter trials |
| 3.11.58 | To Woodford. TI of 'special containers' and fitment of anti-flash screens. |
| 15.6.59 | To A&AEE Boscombe Down. Flight refuelling tests. |
| 10.7.59 | Returned to Woodford. |
| 20.11.59 | To A&AEE. Flight refuelling tests. |
| 23.12.59 | Returned to Woodford |
| 20.4.60 | To A&AEE. Rebecca Mk.10 and flight refuelling tests in conjunction with Valiant WZ376. |
| . .60 | Returned to Woodford |
| 20.1.61 | To A&AEE. Flight refuelling tests. |
| 7.4.61 | Returned to Woodford |
| 25.7.61 | To Bitteswell. Re-fit to B.1A standard. |
| 9.2.62 | 101 Squadron |
| 7.10.63 | Waddington Wing |
| 20.4.66 | Loan to Ministry of Technology. Arrived at A&AEE. Trials of 1,000 lb retarded bomb. Later re-allotted for flight refuelling training at A&AEE |
| 27.3.69 | Delivered to RAF Akrotiri, allotted as 8047M on 5.3.69. |
| 1.11.70 | Struck off Charge. To fire-fighting use from 4.2.75. |

**XH479**
| | |
|---|---|
| 27.3.58 | Awaiting Collection |
| 31.3.58 | 101 Squadron |
| 12.5.61 | AWA Bitteswell. B.1A conversion |
| 25.1.62 | 101 Squadron |
| 22.10.63 | Waddington Wing |
| 13.6.67 | Allotted to No 1 SoTT, Halton, Cat.5(GI), as 7974M. Coded '21'. Scrapped on site 23.7.73. |

**XH480**
| | |
|---|---|
| 21.3.58 | First flight |
| 18.4.58 | Awaiting Collection |
| 22.4.58 | 44 Squadron |
| 22.6.62 | Whitworth Gloster, Bitteswell. B.1A conversion |
| 23.11.62 | 44 Squadron |
| | Waddington Wing |
| 10.11.66 | 19 MU |
| 19.9.68 | Sold as scrap, Bradbury & Co |

**XH481**
| | |
|---|---|
| 25.4.58 | Awaiting Collection |
| 30.4.58 | 101 Squadron |
| 7.10.60 | AWA Bitteswell. B.1A conversion |
| 5.5.61 | 101 Squadron |
| 6.4.65 | Waddington Wing |
| 8.1.68 | Cat.5(GI) for fire-fighting at Waddington. |

**XH482**
| | |
|---|---|
| 16.4.58 | First flight |
| 30.4.58 | Awaiting Collection |
| 5.5.58 | 617 Squadron |
| 1.8.61 | 50 Squadron |
| 30.3.62 | AWA Bitteswell. B.1A conversion |
| 3.9.62 | 101 Squadron |
| 12.10.62 | 50 Squadron |
| | Waddington Wing |
| 14.10.66 | 19 MU |
| 19.9.68 | Sold as scrap, Bradbury & Co |

**XH483**
| | |
|---|---|
| 16.5.58 | Awaiting Collection |
| 29.5.58 | 617 Squadron |
| 20.1.61 | AWA Bitteswell. B.1A conversion |
| 29.8.61 | 50 Squadron |
| 1.11.62 | Waddington Wing |
| 5.8.67 | Struck off Charge as Cat.5(GI) for fire-fighting practice at Manston. |

**XH497**
| | |
|---|---|
| 16.4.58 | First flight |
| 28.5.58 | Awaiting Collection |
| 30.5.58 | 617 Squadron |
| 1.8.61 | 50 Squadron |
| 9.1.62 | AWA Bitteswell. B.1A conversion |
| 19.6.62 | 50 Squadron |
| | Waddington Wing |
| 6.4.66 | 19 MU |
| 3.7.68 | Landing accident at Scampton after nosewheel detached, not repaired. |
| 21.1.69 | Sold as scrap, Bradbury & Co |

**XH498**
| | |
|---|---|
| 6.6.58 | First flight |
| 27.6.58 | Awaiting Collection |
| 30.6.58 | 617 Squadron |
| 1.8.61 | 50 Squadron |
| 6.10.61 | AWA Bitteswell. B.1A conversion |
| 30.3.62 | 50 Squadron |
| | Waddington Wing |
| 19.10.67 | Struck off Charge, Cat.5(GI). Allotted as 7993M for RAF Finningley, for 'crew drill training'. Disposed of 9.2.70. |

**XH499**
| | |
|---|---|
| 16.7.58 | Awaiting Collection |
| 18.7.58 | 617 Squadron |
| 1.8.61 | 50 Squadron |
| 10.5.62 | AWA Bitteswell. B.1A conversion. |
| 12.10.62 | 50 Squadron |
| 3.7.63 | Waddington Wing |
| 4.9.63 | Delivered from Waddington to HSAL Woodford. Handling, systems engineering and performance tests for low-level role. |
| 18.9.63 | To A&AEE Boscombe Down, Weapon release clearance for low-level operation. |
| 31.1.64 | Arrived at Bitteswell. Stage 2 installation of low-level role equipment |
| 16.4.64 | Arrived at A&AEE. Evaluation of Stage 2 equipment. |
| 13.10.64 | Arrived at Bitteswell. De-instrumentation. |
| 11.11.65 | Handed over to MoD. |
| 1.12.65 | Struck off Charge as scrap at HSAL Bitteswell. |

**XH500**
| | |
|---|---|
| 14.8.58 | Awaiting Collection |
| 18.8.58 | 617 Squadron |
| 13.7.59 | AWA Bitteswell. B.1A prototype conversion (with XH505) |
| 30.9.60 | 617 Squadron |
| 1.8.61 | 50 Squadron |
| 16.8.63 | Waddington Wing |
| 1.1.68 | Struck off Charge as Cat.5(GI), allotted to RAF Scampton as 7994M 28.11.67 for crew drill training. To fire-fighting training 29.9.76. |

**XH501**
| | |
|---|---|
| 2.9.58 | Awaiting Collection |
| 3.9.58 | 617 Squadron |
| 7.3.61 | AWA Bitteswell. B.1A conversion |
| 2.11.61 | 44 Squadron |
| | Waddington Wing |
| 12.10.66 | 19 MU |
| 8.11.68 | Sold as scrap, Bradbury & Co |

**XH502**
| | |
|---|---|
| 31.10.58 | First flight |
| 31.10.58 | Awaiting Collection |
| 11.11.58 | 617 Squadron |
| 6.10.61 | 50 Squadron |
| 14.8.62 | Whitworth Gloster, Bitteswell. B.1A conversion |
| 25.2.63 | Waddington Wing |
| 10.1.68 | Struck off Charge as Cat.5(GI) for fire-fighting at Waddington. |

**XH503**
| | |
|---|---|
| 31.10.58 | First flight |
| 18.12.58 | Awaiting Collection |
| 31.12.58 | 44 Squadron |
| 30.8.62 | Whitworth Gloster, Bitteswell. B.1A conversion |
| 6.3.63 | Waddington Wing |
| 6.12.66 | 19 MU |
| 8.11.68 | Sold as scrap, Bradbury & Co |

**XH504**
| | |
|---|---|
| 19.12.58 | Awaiting Collection |
| 31.12.58 | 230 OCU |
| 19.11.59 | 83 Squadron |
| 25.11.59 | 230 OCU |
| 21.8.61 | AWA Bitteswell. B.1A conversion |
| 2.3.62 | 101 Squadron |
| 19.7.63 | Waddington Wing |
| 4.1.68 | Struck off Charge, Cat.5(GI) for fire-fighting at Cottesmore. |

**XH505**
| | |
|---|---|
| 31.12.57 | Awaiting Collection |
| 16.3.58 | 230 OCU |
| 16.7.59 | AWA Bitteswell. B.1A prototype conversion (with XH500) |
| 6.10.60 | 617 Squadron |
| 1.8.61 | 50 Squadron |
| 16.8.61 | 44/50/101 Squadrons. |
| 9.1.68 | Struck off Charge, Cat.5(GI) for fire-fighting at Finningley. |

**XH506**
| | |
|---|---|
| 20.1.59 | First flight |
| 27.1.59 | Awaiting Collection |
| 20.4.59 | 44 Squadron |
| 25.1.60 | AWA Bitteswell. B.1A conversion |
| 31.10.60 | 617 Squadron |
| 1.8.61 | 50 Squadron |
| 17.9.63 | Waddington Wing |
| 10.1.68 | 19 MU |
| 8.11.68 | Sold as scrap, Bradbury & Co |

**XH532**
| | |
|---|---|
| 31.3.59 | Handed over to MoS Air Fleet. Safety assessment and survey following 'Yellow Sun' installation. |
| 15.4.59 | Authority to go to RAE Farnborough for flights with 'Yellow Sun'. |
| 1.5.59 | 230 OCU |
| 19.11.59 | 101 Squadron |
| 25.11.59 | 230 OCU |
| 15.3.62 | 101 Squadron |
| 28.5.62 | Whitworth Gloster, Bitteswell. B.1A conversion. |
| 15.11.62 | 101 Squadron |
| 19.6.63 | Waddington Wing |
| 11.3.66 | 19 MU |
| 8.11.68 | Sold as scrap, Bradbury & Co |

**89 Vulcan B.2**

XH533 to XH539, XH554 to XH563 (17) to Contract 6/Aircraft/11301/CB.6(a), as above.

XJ780 to XJ784, XJ823 to XJ825 (8) to Contract 6/Aircraft/11830/CB.6(a), serial numbers allotted 3rd March 1955.

XL317 to XL321, XL359 to XL361, XL384 to XL392, XL425 to XL427, XL443 to XL446 (24) to Contract 6/Aircraft/12305/CB.6(a), serial numbers allotted 8th February 1956.

XM569 to XM576, XM594 to XM612, XM645 to XM657 (40), to Contract KD/B/01/CB.6(a), serial numbers allotted 20th December 1957. (Of these, XM596 was used for ground trials and was never flown.)

Aircraft equipped to carry the Blue Steel missile with the Scampton Wing (which entailed much internal 'plumbing', and revised bomb doors to fit around the missile) were designated B.2A.

The B.2[MRR] was a version assigned to No 27 Squadron for the Maritime Radar Reconnaissance role. The aircraft concerned were B.2s with LORAN C navigation equipment in addition to the normal fit, and with the Terrain-Following Radar (by then fitted to all operational Vulcans for the low-level strike role) removed. The initial conversions were from the batch that had wing hard-points (intended for Skybolt), since the role definition included the fitment of atmospheric-sampling pods, attached below their wings, as and when required. The later conversions (XH537, and the XJ examples) dispensed with the provision of pods.

B.2(MRR) conversions: (9) XH534, 537, 558, 560, 563, XJ780, 823, 825.

K.2 conversions: (6) XH558, 560, 561, XJ825, XL445, XM571.

The K.2 version was produced at the time of the Falklands War when the existing fleet of Handley Page Victor K.2s was running out of fatigue life, much of their remaining flying hours being absorbed by supporting 'Black Buck' Vulcans and other aircraft en route to the Falklands and back again.

**XH533**

| | |
|---|---|
| 30.8.58 | First flight |
| 26.3.59 | Accepted off Contract and handed over to MoS Air Fleet at Woodford. Contractor's trials. |
| 20.5.59 | To A&AEE, Boscombe Down. Heavy load take-off measurements. |
| 5.6.59 | Returned to A V Roe, Woodford |
| 30.8.61 | Allotted for 'air-ventilated suit' trials at A V Roe |
| 10.5.62 | Despatched to A&AEE Boscombe Down. Automatic landing system, de-icing system and air-ventilated suit trials. (Return to Woodford not recorded) |
| 19.4.63 | Despatched from Woodford to A&AEE, further trials |
| 29.8.63 | To Hawker Siddeley Aviation Ltd. Fatigue life mods. and Automatic Landing System trials. |
| 30.5.65 | Arrived at A&AEE. Autoland trials. |
| 2.10.67 | To No 19 MU, St Athan for storage, following cancellation of the autoland trials. |
| 6.5.69 | Transferred to MoD for ground instructional use at No 4 SoTT (7 Engineering Squadron) as 8048M. |
| 15.10.70 | Sold as scrap, Bradbury & Co. Nose sold separately. |

**XH534**

| | |
|---|---|
| 18.6.59 | First flight |
| 17.7.59 | Awaiting Collection. Allotted to MoS Air Fleet. |
| 16.12.59 | A V Roe, handling and performance trials |
| 4.3.60 | Accepted off Contract. To A&AEE Boscombe Down for CA Release trials |
| 26.4.60 | Returned to Woodford |
| 5.8.60 | Allotted for Blue Steel and crew escape trials |
| 3.9.60 | Loaned to firm for SBAC Show at Farnborough |
| 12.10.60 | Despatched from Woodford to A&AEE. Temporary loan for Autopilot Mk.10A clearance. |
| 11.12.61 | To A&AEE for Blue Steel performance trials. |
| 3.4.62 | Returned to A V Roe. |

| | |
|---|---|
| 9.4.62 | To A&AEE. Continuation of trials. |
| 8.5.62 | To Woodford. High-Test Peroxide spray testing (that is, spray from Blue Steel fuel component) |
| 14.6.62 | To A&AEE. Trials re HTP spray. |
| 7.8.62 | Damaged at Boscombe Down when Fairey Gannet AEW.3 collided with it on the ground. |
| 26.8.63 | To Woodford for TI of bomb bay fuel tank installation. |
| 10.7.64 | To A&AEE. |
| 4.1.65 | To HSAL Woodford for return to standard. |
| 6.12.66 | 230 OCU |
| 29.3.72 | Station Flight, Scampton |
| 30.3.72 | 230 OCU |
| 7.4.72 | Hawker Siddeley Aviation, Bitteswell. |
| -.8.73 | Modification for MRR role [B.2(MRR)] |
| 22.8.74 | 27 Squadron |
| 7.8.81 | RAF St Athan |
| 16.2.82 | Sold as scrap, Harold John & Co |

**XH535**

| | |
|---|---|
| 7.5.60 | First flight |
| 31.5.60 | Accepted off Contract and handed over to MoS Air Fleet. |
| 27.2.61 | To A&AEE, ARI 18146 flight trials. |
| 11.4.61 | To Woodford. Preparation for tests in the USA in preparation for Skybolt installation. |
| 8.6.61 | Despatched to Douglas Aircraft for Electro-Magnetic Compatibility (EMC) tests. |
| 11.7.61 | Arrived at Woodford from the USA |
| 2.11.61 | To A&AEE for EMC tests. |
| 18.9.62 | To Woodford for 'Rapid Blooming Window' installation |
| 18.3.64 | To A&AEE for 'Rapid Blooming Window' trials. |
| 11.5.64 | Crashed at Chute, west of Boscombe Down, after entering uncontrollable spin. Cat.5(s). |
| 20.9.65 | Struck off Charge |

**XH536**

| | |
|---|---|
| 3.5.59 | First flight |
| 17.7.59 | Awaiting Collection. Allotted to MoS Air Fleet. |
| 16.12.59 | A V Roe. CA Release, radio and navigation equipment trials |
| 26.1.60 | Arrived at A&AEE. |
| 30.11.61 | Returned to A V Roe, Woodford. |
| 28.5.62 | Re-allotted for 'Heading Reference System' (HRS) installation. |
| 4.4.63 | To A&AEE. HRS, Decca Mk.4 and roller map trials |
| 23.9.63 | Arrived at Woodford. To modification and retrofit programme. |
| 24.11.65 | 9/12/35 Squadrons |
| 11.2.66 | Cat.5(s) Flying Accident. Flew into Fan Bwlch Clwyth, Brecon Beacons, on low-level exercise. |
| 14.2.66 | Struck off Charge. |

**XH537**

| | |
|---|---|
| 4.8.60 | First flight |
| 31.8.60 | Handed over to MoS Air Fleet. Armament trials |
| 11.10.60 | To RAE Farnborough |
| 31.10.60 | From RAE to A&AEE Boscombe Down, armament trials |
| 30.3.61 | Re-allotted for Skybolt development (flown with dummy missiles) |
| 18.5.63 | Re-allotted for OR360 rapid-processing development. |
| 17.9.63 | Handed over to retrofit programme |
| 31.5.65 | 230 OCU |
| 14.1.72 | HSAL, Bitteswell. Major servicing. |
| -.4.73 | HSAL. Conversion to B.2(MRR) role. |
| 19.6.74 | 27 Squadron. |
| 25.3.82 | Allotted 8749M for display at RAF Abingdon. Re-allotted for Battle Damage Repair training. Sold to B Parkhouse in October 1990 and scrapped, apart from the cockpit section, which survives at the Bournemouth Aviation Museum in 2006. |

**XH538**

| | |
|---|---|
| 4.1.61 | First flight |
| 31.1.61 | To A&AEE. Mk.2 flight re-fuelling clearance |
| 10.3.61 | Returned to A V Roe. Installation of WS-138A Skybolt. |

| | |
|---|---|
| 6.6.63 | Re-allotted for Bristol Olympus 201 development |
| 29.3.65 | To A&AEE. Trials of low-level role equipment, including HRS Mk.2. |
| 7.9.65 | To HSAL Woodford. Installation of ARI 18146, ARI 5792. |
| 28.6.66 | To A&AEE. Trials of X-Band jammer, Red Steer Mk.2 |
| 22.2.67 | To HSAL off CA Charge |
| 14.5.69 | 27/83/617 Squadrons |
| 29.4.70 | 44/50/101 Squadrons |
| 21.4.71 | 230 OCU |
| 11.1.74 | 27 Squadron |
| 23.1.74 | 230 OCU |
| 30.1.74 | 27 Squadron |
| 9.2.76 | Hawker Siddeley Aviation. Mods. |
| 28.7.77 | 35 Squadron |
| 24.5.78 | 9/44/50/101 Squadrons |
| 31.10.78 | 35 Squadron |
| 16.8.79 | 9/44/50/101 Squadrons |
| 23.11.79 | 35 Squadron |
| 11.3.81 | RAF St Athan |
| 31.8.81 | Sold as scrap. W Harold & Co |

**XH539**

| | |
|---|---|
| 10.5.61 | First flight |
| 7.12.61 | Despatched to Edinburgh Field, Australia, for No 4 JSTU. Arrived 12.12.61. First live firing of Blue Steel at Woomera. |
| 7.2.64 | Arrived at HSAL for modification, pending further trials in UK |
| 21.12.64 | High all-up weight and bomb bay tank tests. |
| 16.10.67 | To RAE Bedford. High all-up weight trials, including two-engine take-offs |
| 13.12.67 | To A&AEE. High all-up weight trials. |
| 4.10.68 | HSAL Bitteswell |
| 13.11.69 | Arrived at A&AEE. Trials of conventional armament for low-level role. During its time at A&AEE it was briefly coded 'TM' (for F/Lt Tim Mason). |
| 29.2.72 | Despatched from Boscombe Down to Waddington. Crash rescue training. |

**XH554**

| | |
|---|---|
| 18.2.61 | First flight |
| 10.4.61 | 83 Squadron |
| 1.11.62 | 230 OCU |
| 6.3.63 | A V Roe. Retrofit. |
| 9.11.64 | 230 OCU |
| 13.9.73 | Flying Accident Cat.3R |
| 19.9.73 | Repair on Site, Contractor's Working Party |
| 23.8.74 | 230 OCU |
| 9.6.81 | SoC Cat.5(GI). Allotted 8694M on 14.5.81, RAF Catterick for Fire-fighting School. |

**XH555**

| | |
|---|---|
| 9.6.61 | First flight |
| 17.7.61 | 27 Squadron |
| 21.1.63 | 230 OCU |
| 3.12.63 | HSAL, Bitteswell. Retrofit. |
| 23.4.65 | Handed over to CA Fleet at Bitteswell. ARI 18275 trials. |
| 29.6.65 | 230 OCU |
| 6.11.70 | Allotted to 7 Engineering Squadron, St Athan. |
| 1.10.71 | Struck off Charge Cat.5(s) |

**XH556**

| | |
|---|---|
| 31.8.61 | First flight |
| 21.9.61 | 27 Squadron |
| 5.3.63 | 230 OCU |
| 2.1.64 | HSAL. Retrofit. |
| 21.6.65 | 230 OCU |
| 18.4.66 | Ground accident, Cat.5(c). Undercarriage collapsed on ground at Finningley. |
| 19.4.66 | Struck off Charge |

**XH557**

| | |
|---|---|
| 2.4.60 | First flight |
| 10.5.60 | A V Roe. Handling and performance with enlarged intakes, Olympus 21 installation and fuel heater installation |

**A head-on shot of XH558, taken after it had adopted its display role in 1984.** via Tony Buttler

| | |
|---|---|
| 23.5.60 | Transferred to Handling Squadron at Boscombe Down for 1 month (Pilot's Notes preparation) |
| 21.6.60 | Handed over to CA Fleet. |
| 4.8.60 | Authority to go to A&AEE for parachute streaming tests. |
| 16.9.60 | Damaged in attempted landing at Filton (on delivery flight from Boscombe Down). Landed successfully at St Mawgan, with Cat.3 damage. |
| 4.10.60 | Arrived at Filton. Trial installation (TI) of B.Ol.21 engines. |
| 19.5.61 | Arrived at A V Roe, Woodford for brief handling tests |
| 16.6.61 | Arrived at Filton. Development of Olympus 301 engines. |
| 26.6.64 | To HSAL Woodford. CA Release modifications and retrofit. |
| 6.12.65 | 9/12/35 Squadrons |
| 8.2.66 | 44/50/101 Squadrons |
| 30.12.71 | HSAL |
| 9.5.72 | 44/50/101 Squadrons |
| 19.4.74 | 9/35 Squadrons |
| 15.1.75 | 9/44/50/101 Squadrons |
| 20.3.79 | Bitteswell. Major overhaul. |
| 4.2.80 | 9/44/50/101 Squadrons |
| 10.9.82 | RAF Waddington, Cat.5(c) |
| 8.12.82 | Sold as scrap to Bird Group. |

**XH558**

| | |
|---|---|
| 25.5.60 | First flight |
| 8.7.60 | 230 OCU |
| 11.2.64 | HSAL. Retrofit. |
| 20.2.65 | 230 OCU |
| 26.2.68 | 44/50/101 Squadrons |
| 17.8.73 | HSAL. Conversion to B.2(MRR) role |
| 18.9.74 | 27 Squadron |
| 18.10.76 | 230 OCU |
| 29.11.76 | 27 Squadron |
| 31.3.82 | 9/44/50/101 Squadrons |
| 5.7.82 | British Aerospace, Woodford. Conversion to K.2 version. |
| 12.10.82 | 50 Squadron |
| 25.10.82 | Attached to MoD(PE) Air Fleet at A&AEE Boscombe Down. |
| 30.11.82 | To RAF Waddington, return to 50 Squadron |
| 1.4.84 | Station Flight, RAF Waddington (for Vulcan Display Flight) (Reverted to B.2 configuration). |
| 14.11.84 | Vulcan Display Flight, Waddington |
| 20.9.92 | Last display flight |
| 23.3.93 | Delivered to Bruntingthorpe Registered as G-VLCN 6.2.95. From 7.4.05 registered to the Vulcan to the Sky Trust. As this is written, work is in progress to complete its return to airworthiness for flight in 2007. |

**XH559**

| | |
|---|---|
| 29.6.60 | First flight |
| 24.8.60 | 230 OCU |
| 7.8.63 | A V Roe, Major Servicing and modifications. |
| 11.5.65 | 230 OCU |
| 5.8.68 | HSAL. Mods. |
| 27.2.70 | 230 OCU |
| 27.5.81 | St Athan |
| 29.1.82 | Sold to Harold, John & Co as scrap. |

**XH560**

| | |
|---|---|
| 30.8.60 | First flight |
| 3.10.60 | 230 OCU |
| 23.12.60 | Arrived at Woodford (investigation of 4-engine flame-out) |
| 29.5.61 | Allotted for Skybolt development |
| 16.3.62 | Modification and return to service |
| 26.9.62 | 12 Squadron |
| 29.11.62 | 230 OCU |
| 2.6.64 | HSAL. Retrofit. |

| | |
|---|---|
| 24.8.65 | 9/12/35 Squadrons |
| 10.4.67 | 44/50/101 Squadrons |
| 2.2.68 | 9/12/35 Squadrons |
| 28.6.67 | 9/35 Squadrons |
| 20.11.71 | HSAL, Bitteswell. Storage. |
| 1.2.73 | Conversion to B.2(MRR) role |
| 19.3.74 | 27 Squadron |
| 25.3.82 | 9/44/50/101 Squadrons |
| 5.7.82 | British Aerospace. Conversion to K.2 |
| 24.8.82 | 44/50 Squadrons |
| 1.4.84 | Station Flight, Waddington |
| 29.8.84 | Station Flight, Marham. |
| 5.1.85 | Struck off Charge, Cat.5(c). Nose survives at 'The Cockpit Collection' in Essex, 2006. |

**XH561**

| | |
|---|---|
| 17.9.60 | First flight |
| 4.11.60 | 230 OCU |
| 31.3.66 | HSAL. Retrofit. |
| 8.8.67 | 44/50/101 Squadrons |
| 8.5.68 | 9/35 Squadrons |
| 17.7.74 | HSAL. |
| 10.3.75 | 35 Squadron |
| 14.5.80 | Bitteswell. |
| 6.2.81 | 35 Squadron |
| 4.9.81 | 50 Squadron |
| 4.5.82 | British Aerospace. K.2 conversion |
| 18.6.82 | 50 Squadron |
| 8.4.84 | Station Flight, Waddington. |
| 13.6.84 | Struck off Charge Cat.5 (GI) for fire-fighting at RAF Catterick, allotted 8809M. |

**XH562**

| | |
|---|---|
| 21.10.60 | First flight |
| 9.12.60 | 230 OCU |
| 1.3.63 | 35 Squadron |
| 11.3.63 | 230 OCU |
| 30.4.63 | 35 Squadron |
| 19.9.63 | 230 OCU |
| 2.4.64 | HSAL, Woodford. Retrofit. |
| 1.8.65 | 9/12/35 Squadrons |
| 8.3.66 | 50 Squadron |
| 15.12.66 | Woodford |
| 24.2.67 | 44/50/101 Squadron |
| 24.4.68 | 9/35 Squadrons |
| 16.7.74 | HSAL, mods. |
| 13.5.75 | 9/44/50/101 Squadrons |
| 6.7.77 | St Athan |
| 27.9.77 | 230 OCU |
| 15.2.80 | Bitteswell |
| 1.12.80 | 230 OCU |
| 16.12.80 | 35 Squadron |
| 19.6.81 | 9/44/50/101 Squadrons |
| 19.8.82 | Allotted 8758M for RAF Catterick as Cat.5(GI) for crash-rescue training at the Fire-fighting School. |

**XH563**

| | |
|---|---|
| 1.11.60 | First flight |
| 28.12.60 | 83 Squadron |
| 26.12.62 | 12 Squadron |
| 6.6.63 | A V Roe. Retrofit. |
| 8.3.65 | 230 OCU |

| | |
|---|---|
| 6.8.68 | 44/50/101 Squadrons |
| 18.3.69 | 230 OCU |
| 8.4.69 | To A&AEE. Clearance of SRIM3562 instrument fit (HF radio) |
| 11.6.69 | Despatched from A&AEE to 230 OCU, Finningley. |
| 22.7.69 | To A&AEE for EMC check |
| 2.10.69 | Returned to 230 OCU, Finningley. |
| 3.5.71 | 27/617 Squadrons |
| 7.5.71 | 230 OCU |
| 25.10.71 | HSAL, Bitteswell. Major servicing. |
| 9.2.73 | Conversion to B.2(MRR) role. |
| 11.1.74 | 27 Squadron |
| 31.3.82 | Allotted 8744M for display ('gate guardian' at Operations Centre) at RAF Scampton. |
| 7.11.86 | Sold as scrap to Coopers (Metal) Ltd, Sheffield. Nose rescued and survives with the Cold War Jets Collection at Bruntingthorpe, Leicestershire. |

**XJ780**

| | |
|---|---|
| 28.11.60 | First flight |
| 16.1.61 | 83 Squadron |
| 26.11.62 | 12 Squadron |
| 16.8.62 | 230 OCU |
| 3.3.64 | HSAL. Retrofit. |
| 30.7.65 | 230 OCU |
| 10.10.67 | 44/50/101 Squadrons |
| 16.2.68 | 9/12/35 Squadrons |
| 7.3.69 | 9/35 Squadrons |
| 18.4.69 | 44/50/101 Squadrons |
| 12.1.70 | 9/35 Squadrons |
| 28.7.70 | HSAL. Mods. |
| 8.12.70 | 9/35 Squadrons |
| 17.1.75 | 9/44/50/101 Squadrons |
| 9.7.75 | HSAL. Conversion to B.2(MRR). |
| 31.3.76 | 9/44/50/101 Squadrons |
| 23.11.76 | 27 Squadron |
| 31.3.82 | RAF Scampton |
| -.11.82 | Sold as scrap to Bird Group. |

**XJ781**

| | |
|---|---|
| 10.1.61 | First flight |
| 23.2.61 | 83 Squadron |
| 29.10.62 | 12 Squadron |
| 4.2.64 | 230 OCU |
| 2.3.65 | Woodford. Retrofit. |
| 16.2.66 | 44/50/101 Squadrons |
| 20.4.68 | 9/35 Squadrons |
| 5.12.70 | HSAL. Mods. |
| 20.4.71 | 9/35 Squadrons |
| 23.5.73 | Landing accident at Shiraz, Iran, swung off runway into gulley. Cat.5(c) |
| 27.5.73 | Struck off Charge. |

**XJ782**

| | |
|---|---|
| 16.1.61 | First flight |
| 2.3.61 | 83 Squadron |
| 23.10.62 | 12 Squadron |
| 20.12.63 | 230 OCU |
| 29.3.65 | A V Roe. Retrofit. |
| 29.3.66 | 44/50/101 Squadrons. |
| 9.4.68 | 9/35 Squadrons |
| 11.11.72 | HSAL |
| 17.5.73 | 9/35 Squadrons |
| 8.1.75 | 9/44/50/101 Squadrons |
| 15.2.77 | 27 Squadron |
| 31.3.82 | Cat.5 (spares) at RAF Scampton (but then allotted to Waddington instead). |
| 6.9.82 | Allotted 8766M for display at RAF Finningley. (101 Squadron markings) |
| 3.5.88 | Sold as scrap to Parton, Parton & Allan. |

**XJ783**

| | |
|---|---|
| 3.2.61 | First flight |
| 13.3.61 | 83 Squadron |
| 7.11.62 | 9 Squadron |
| 12.2.64 | 44 Squadron |
| 28.2.64 | 230 OCU |
| 25.9.64 | A V Roe. Retrofit. |
| 3.1.66 | 4/50/101 Squadrons |
| 22.3.68 | 9/35 Squadrons |

| | |
|---|---|
| 21.12.71 | HSAL |
| 28.3.72 | 9/35 Squadrons |
| 16.1.75 | 35 Squadrons |
| 11.8.76 | 230 OCU |
| 23.8.76 | 35 Squadron |
| 7.3.78 | Bitteswell |
| 23.11.78 | 617 Squadron |
| 3.4.81 | 35 Squadron |
| 1.3.82 | Cat.5(c) at RAF Scampton |
| .11.82 | Sold as scrap to Bird Group. |

**XJ784**

| | |
|---|---|
| 9.3.61 | First flight |
| 30.3.61 | From Woodford to Gloster Aircraft, Moreton Valence. TI of Olympus 301. |
| 7.5.61 | To Woodford for contractor's handling trials |
| .7.62 | Re-allotted for trials of rapid take-off equipment and autothrottle installation and development |
| 14.10.64 | Re-allotted for trials of WE177 and conventional stores with long-range tanks in different configurations. |
| 25.11.64 | Despatched to A&AEE for trials |
| 17.8.65 | To HSAL, Woodford. Retrofit. |
| 22.12.66 | 230 OCU |
| 21.7.70 | 9/35 Squadrons |
| 16.12.70 | 44/50/101 Squadrons |
| 18.8.71 | 9/35 Squadrons |
| 15.1.75 | 9/44/50/101 Squadrons |
| 3.7.79 | Bitteswell |
| 14.5.80 | 9/44/50/101 Squadrons |
| 10.9.82 | Cat.5(c) at RAF Waddington. |
| .12.82 | Sold as Scrap to Bird Group. |

**XJ823**

| | |
|---|---|
| 30.3.61 | First flight |
| 21.4.61 | 27 Squadron |
| 8.1.63 | 35 Squadron |
| 11.5.64 | 230 OCU |
| 28.6.65 | HSAL. Retrofit. |
| 1.11.66 | 44/50/101 Squadrons. |
| 4.12.67 | Loaned to A&AEE at Waddington for 1 day, for IFR trial. |
| 19.2.68 | HSAL. Mods. |
| 30.4.68 | 9/35 Squadrons |
| 17.1.75 | 9/44/50/101 Squadrons HSAL. Conversion to B.2(MRR) role. |
| 27.4.77 | 27 Squadron |
| 2.4.81 | 35 Squadron |
| 1.3.82 | 9/44/50/101 Squadrons. |
| 4.1.83 | Holding Flight, Waddington. |
| 21.1.83 | Sold to Mr T Stoddart. |
| 24.1.83 | Flown to Carlisle Airport (Crosby-on-Eden) and preserved there. Still present 2006. |

**XJ824**

| | |
|---|---|
| 24.4.61 | First flight |
| 16.5.61 | 27 Squadron |
| 25.2.63 | 9 Squadron |
| 2.12.63 | 230 OCU |
| 28.5.65 | A V Roe, Woodford. Retrofit. |
| 4.7.66 | 9/12/35 Squadrons |
| 4.10.66 | 44/50/101 Squadrons |
| 19.6.68 | 9/35 Squadrons |
| 24.1.75 | 35 Squadron. |
| 5.6.75 | HSAL. |
| 1.3.76 | 35 Squadron. |
| 15.2.77 | 9/44/50/101 Squadrons |
| 17.9.80 | To HSAL Bitteswell |
| 4.6.81 | 9/44/50/101 Squadrons |
| 15.3.82 | Allotted to the Imperial War Museum at Duxford. Ferried there 13.3.82, still present 2006. |

**XJ825**

| | |
|---|---|
| 7.7.61 | First flight |
| 28.7.61 | 27 Squadron |
| 21.2.63 | 35 Squadron |
| 30.4.64 | 230 OCU |
| 3.9.65 | 9/12/35 Squadrons |
| 3.2.67 | HSAL. Mods. |
| 12.4.67 | 44/50/101 Squadrons |

| | |
|---|---|
| 19.2.68 | 9/12/35 Squadrons |
| 28.10.70 | HSAL |
| 15.3.71 | 9/35 Squadrons |
| 16.1.75 | 35 Squadron |
| 10.3.75 | HSAL. Conversion to B.2(MRR) |
| 13.1.76 | 35 Squadron |
| 15.12.76 | 27 Squadron |
| 6.4.81 | 35 Squadron |
| 1.3.82 | 9/44/50/101 Squadrons |
| 10.5.82 | British Aerospace, Woodford. K.2 conversion. |
| 25.6.82 | 50 Squadron. |
| 5.4.84 | Allotted 8810M for Battle Damage Repair training at Waddington. Scrapped during January 1992. |

**XL317**

| | |
|---|---|
| 24.6.61 | First flight |
| 14.7.61 | Handed over to MoA Air Fleet for Blue Steel trials |
| 15.7.61 | To A&AEE Boscombe Down |
| 5.12.61 | To A V Roe, Woodford. Training missile installation development |
| 7.6.62 | To Scampton for modifications |
| 13.6.62 | 617 Squadron |
| 16.2.65 | A V Roe, retrofit. |
| 3.11.65 | 27/83/617 Squadrons |
| 9.12.70 | 27/617 Squadrons |
| 21.1.71 | HSAL. |
| 28.5.71 | 617 Squadron |
| 1.12.81 | Allotted 8725M for battle-damage repair training at RAF Akrotiri. Cat.5(GI). Scrapped December 1986. |

**XL318**

| | |
|---|---|
| 11.8.61 | First flight |
| 4.9.61 | 617 Squadron |
| 2.4.64 | A V Roe, Woodford. Retrofit. |
| 21.4.65 | 27/83/617 Squadrons |
| 19.11.69 | 617 Squadron |
| 22.5.72 | 230 OCU |
| 18.10.72 | HSAL. Mods. |
| 4.4.73 | 230 OCU |
| 5.3.74 | 617 Squadron |
| 18.6.75 | 9/44/50/101 Squadrons |
| 5.8.75 | 230 OCU |
| 1.7.81 | 617 Squadron |
| 17.12.81 | Allotted as 8733M for the RAF Museum. Displayed at Hendon in 2006. |

**XL319**

| | |
|---|---|
| 1.10.61 | First flight. |
| 23.10.61 | 617 Squadron |
| 28.4.64 | 27/83/617 Squadrons |
| 5.5.64 | A V Roe, Woodford. Retrofit. |
| 22.7.65 | 27/83/617 Squadrons |
| 30.4.70 | 27/617 Squadrons |
| 14.5.70 | 230 OCU |
| 22.4.71 | 617 Squadron |
| 8.5.72 | HSAL. |
| 21.9.72 | 230 OCU |
| 16.10.78 | 35 Squadron |
| 22.5.79 | Bitteswell |
| 25.3.80 | 35 Squadron |
| 1.3.82 | 9/44/50/101 Squadrons |
| 20.1.83 | Allotted to the North East Air Museum at Usworth for display. |
| 21.1.83 | Flown to Sunderland Airport, Usworth. On display in 2006. |

**XL320**

| | |
|---|---|
| 9.11.61 | First flight |
| 4.12.61 | 617 Squadron |
| 21.8.64 | A V Roe, Woodford. Retrofit. |
| 30.9.65 | 27/83/617 Squadrons |
| 30.9.69 | HSAL for conversion. |
| 27.11.69 | 27/617 Squadrons |
| 29.3.72 | 230 OCU |
| 20.10.72 | HSAL |
| 26.2.73 | 230 OCU |
| 2.6.81 | St Athan. Cat.5(s). |
| 31.8.81 | Sold as scrap. W Harold & Co. |

**XL321**

| | |
|---|---|
| 12.61 | First flight |
| 1.1.62 | 617 Squadron |
| 2.3.65 | Woodford. Retrofit. |
| 1.12.65 | 27/83/617 Squadrons |
| .7.70 | 27/617 Squadrons |
| .4.71 | HSAL. Mods. |
| 3.8.71 | 27/617 Squadron. |
| 9.3.72 | 230 OCU |
| 5.9.72 | 617 Squadron |
| .6.76 | 9/44/50/101 Squadrons |
| 11.76 | 230 OCU |
| .7.81 | 35 Squadron |
| 4.9.81 | 617 Squadron |
| .10.81 | 35 Squadron |
| 1.1.82 | 50 Squadron |
| 9.8.82 | Allotted as 8759M for RAF Catterick for Fire-Fighting School. Cat.5(GI). |

**XL359**

| | |
|---|---|
| 0.1.62 | First flight |
| .2.62 | 617 Squadron |
| 12.64 | A V Roe. Retrofit. |
| .9.65 | 27/83/617 Squadrons |
| 3.9.70 | 27/617 Squadrons |
| 1.10.71 | 230 OCU |
| 7.81 | 35 Squadron |
| .3.82 | Allotted for gate guard duty at RAF Scampton (provisionally 8744M). Not taken up (replaced by XH563) |
| 1.82 | Sold as scrap to Bird Group. |

**XL360**

| | |
|---|---|
| 1.1.62 | First flight |
| 3.62 | 617 Squadron |
| 2.65 | A V Roe. Retrofit. |
| 7.10.65 | 27/83/617 Squadrons |
| 4.9.70 | 27/617 Squadrons |
| 1.70 | HSAL |
| 4.5.71 | 27/617 Squadrons |
| 3.7.71 | 230 OCU |
| 5.8.75 | 9/44/50/101 Squadrons |
| 1.10.75 | 230 OCU |
| 4.2.77 | HSAL |
| 12.77 | 617 Squadron |
| 1.5.78 | 35 Squadron |
| 1.82 | 101 Squadron |
| 5.1.83 | To Midland Air Museum, Baginton. |
| 2.83 | Flown to Coventry Airport. On display in 2006. |

**XL361**

| | |
|---|---|
| 1.2.62 | First flight |
| 5.3.62 | 617 Squadron |
| 7.63 | Arrived at Woodford from Scampton. Missile separation trials |
| 5.7.63 | To Scampton |
| 9.8.63 | To Woodford. Blue Steel low-level systems trials |
| .4.64 | 27/83/617 Squadrons |
| 5.3.65 | Woodford. Retrofit. |
| 3.1.66 | 27/83/617 Squadrons |
| 12.69 | 27/617 Squadrons |
| 10.70 | 230 OCU |
| .4.71 | 617 Squadron |
| 2.5.71 | 230 OCU |
| 3.8.71 | HSAL. |
| 1.12.71 | 230 OCU |
| 6.12.74 | To A&AEE. SRIM 3898 trials |
| 0.1.75 | 230 OCU |
| 4.1.75 | 617 Squadron |
| 8.75 | To A&AEE. Static pressure error check |
| 9.75 | 617 Squadron |
| 8.77 | 35 Squadron |
| 9.78 | Bitteswell |
| 7.79 | 35 Squadron |
| 3.6.81 | 9/44/50/101 Squadrons |
| 1.12.81 | To CFB Goose Bay, Labrador, for display. |

**XL384**

| | |
|---|---|
| 6.3.62 | First flight |
| 4.62 | 230 OCU |
| 7.8.63 | A V Roe. Retrofit |
| 5.8.64 | 27/83/617 Squadrons |
| 10.4.69 | 27/617 Squadrons |
| 2.2.70 | HSAL. Mods. |
| 11.6.70 | 27/617 Squadrons |
| 23.7.70 | 44/50/101 Squadrons |
| 27.11.70 | 27/617 Squadrons |
| 19.4.71 | 230 OCU |
| 19.5.71 | 27/617 Squadrons |
| 12.8.71 | Flying Accident. Allotted for repair by Contractor's Working Party. Work suspended. |
| 14.1.75 | Struck off Charge as Cat.5 (components) Allotted 8505M for weapon loading training at Scampton on 30.9.76. Re-allotted as 8670M for RAF Scampton on 29.1.81, crash rescue training. SoC 23.5.85 |

**XL385**

| | |
|---|---|
| 30.3.62 | First flight |
| 18.4.62 | 9 Squadron |
| 1.10.63 | HSAL. Retrofit. |
| 12.10.64 | 27/83/617 Squadrons |
| 6.4.67 | Crashed on take-off at Scampton after two engines exploded. Destroyed by fire. Cat.5(s). |

**XL386**

| | |
|---|---|
| 2.5.62 | First flight |
| 14.5.62 | 9 Squadron |
| 4.11.63 | HSAL. Retrofit |
| 16.8.64 | 27/83/617 Squadrons |
| 1.4.70 | 230 OCU |
| 6.3.74 | HSAL |
| 22.10.74 | 230 OCU |
| 30.9.77 | 9/44/50/101 Squadrons |
| 26.8.82 | Allotted 8760M for crash-rescue training at RAF Manston. Cat.5(GI). Blown-up September 1992. |

**XL387**

| | |
|---|---|
| 16.5.62 | First flight |
| 4.6.62 | 230 OCU |
| 2.12.63 | HSAL. Retrofit. |
| 5.2.65 | 27/83/617 Squadrons |
| 5.2.68 | 27/617 Squadrons |
| 13.5.71 | HSAL |
| 24.9.71 | 617 Squadron/230 OCU share |
| 10.1.73 | 44/50/101 Squadrons |
| 26.1.78 | Bitteswell |
| 3.11.78 | 9/44/50/101 Squadrons |
| 28.1.82 | St Athan, Cat.5 (spares). Allotted 8748M 17.3.82 for crash rescue training at RAF St Athan. |
| 2.6.83 | Sold as scrap, T Bradbury & Co |

**XL388**

| | |
|---|---|
| 25.5.62 | First flight |
| 14.6.62 | 9 Squadron |
| 3.1.64 | HSAL. Retrofit. |
| 22.2.65 | 27/83/617 Squadrons |
| 29.7.70 | 27/617 Squadrons |
| 19.4.71 | 230 OCU |
| 10.5.71 | 27/617 Squadrons |
| 28.1.72 | HSAL |
| 24.5.72 | 230 OCU |
| 15.9.72 | 617 Squadron |
| 29.9.72 | 230 OCU |
| 2.2.73 | 617 Squadron |
| 14.5.72 | 230 OCU |
| 1.11.73 | 617 Squadron |
| 1.4.74 | 44/50/101 Squadrons |
| 29.10.74 | 9/44/50/101 Squadrons |
| 19.11.76 | Bitteswell |
| 7.9.77 | 9/44/50/101 Squadrons |
| 2.4.82 | Allotted 8750M for crash rescue training at RAF Honington. |
| 13.6.85 | Sold to Swefeling Engineering Co. Cockpit section to Blyth Valley Aviation Collection. In 2006 the nose of this Vulcan was on display at 'AeroVenture', Doncaster. |

**XL389**

| | |
|---|---|
| 13.6.62 | First flight |
| 13.7.62 | 230 OCU |
| 4.2.64 | HSAL. Retrofit. |
| 20.5.65 | 27/83/617 Squadrons |
| 19.5.70 | 27/617 Squadrons |
| 11.11.70 | 230 OCU |
| 1.1.71 | 617 Squadron |
| 7.4.72 | 230 OCU |
| 30.6.72 | 617 Squadron/230 OCU |
| 26.6.74 | 44/50/101 Squadrons |
| 7.5.75 | HSAL. Mods. |
| 28.1.76 | 9/44/50/101 Squadrons |
| 31.8.81 | Sold as scrap, W Harold & Co. |

**XL390**

| | |
|---|---|
| 3.7.62 | First flight |
| 20.7.62 | 9 Squadron |
| 3.3.64 | HSAL. Retrofit. |
| 27.5.65 | 27/83/617 Squadrons |
| 22.4.70 | 27/617 Squadrons |
| 30.4.71 | 230 OCU |
| 3.6.71 | 617 Squadron |
| 31.5.74 | 230 OCU |
| 4.6.74 | 617 Squadron |
| 6.2.75 | HSAL. Mods. |
| 3.10.75 | 617 Squadron |
| 11.8.78 | Crashed at Glenview NAS, Illinois, USA, during practice for display. |
| 21.8.78 | Struck off Charge. Cat.5(s) |

**XL391**

| | |
|---|---|
| ? | First flight |
| 22.5.63 | Handed over to MoA Air Fleet |
| 28.5.63 | To A&AEE. Parachute streaming tests. |
| 30.5.63 | Returned to A V Roe, Woodford |
| 6.6.63 | Allotted for Olympus 301 development in low-level role. |
| 10.2.64 | To A&AEE for trials |
| 25.11.64 | To HSAL, Woodford. 'Rapid Blooming Window' and ODM trials |
| 29.4.65 | To A&AEE for RBW and ODM trials |
| 25.5.65 | Returned to Woodford |
| 14.7.65 | To BCDU, Finningley |
| 6.1.66 | Arrived at A&AEE, ODM trials |
| 21.2.66 | Arrived at HSAL. TI of long-range Drum tanks |
| 19.10.66 | To A&AEE. Trials |
| 1.5.67 | HSAL. Mods. |
| 31.7.68 | 9/35 Squadrons |
| 17.1.75 | 9/44/50/101 Squadrons |
| 2.11.78 | Bitteswell. Mods. |
| 31.7.79 | 9/44/50/101 Squadrons. 44 Sqn Markings. |
| 11.2.83 | Sold to 'Manchester Vulcan Bomber Society', Blackpool. |
| 16.2.83 | Flown to Blackpool Airport. Scrapped at Blackpool on 12th January 2006 after abortive resale. |

**XL392**

| | |
|---|---|
| 19.7.62 | First flight |
| 2.8.62 | 83 Squadron |
| 15.9.64 | 27/83/617 Squadrons |
| 21.4.65 | HSAL. Retrofit. |
| 23.2.66 | 27/83/617 Squadrons |
| 26.6.70 | HSAL. Mods. |
| 17.11.70 | 27/617 Squadrons |
| 21.5.76 | HSAL. Mods. |
| 25.2.77 | 617 Squadron |
| 4.1.82 | 35 Squadron. |
| 1.3.82 | Allotted 8745M for crash rescue training at RAF Valley. Cat.5(GI). Scrapped August 1993. |

**XL425**

| | |
|---|---|
| 6.8.62 | First flight |
| 31.8.62 | 83 Squadron |
| 20.5.65 | HSAL. Retrofit. |
| 2.3.66 | 27/83/617 Squadrons |
| 25.3.70 | 27/617 Squadrons |
| 18.5.72 | HSAL. Mods. |
| 1.11.71 | 27 Squadron |
| 30.11.72 | 617 Squadron |
| 4.1.82 | Assessed as Cat.5(scrap) at Scampton. |
| .4.82 | Sold as scrap, Bird Group. |

A photo of B.2 XM570 of No 27 Squadron, carrying Blue Steel after the transfer to the low-level role, at a Battle of Britain Open Day.
via Phil Butler

**XL446**

| | |
|---|---|
| 16.11.62 | First flight |
| 30.11.62 | 27 Squadron |
| 20.10.65 | HSAL. Retrofit. |
| 16.9.66 | 44/50/101 Squadrons |
| 28.12.67 | 230 OCU |
| 18.4.72 | Scampton |
| 31.7.72 | 9/35 Squadrons |
| 17.1.75 | 35 Squadron |
| 7.9.77 | HSAL Bitteswell. Mods. |
| 10.5.78 | 35 Squadron |
| 24.5.78 | 9/44/50/101 Squadrons |
| 31.10.78 | 617 Squadron |
| 4.1.82 | 35 Squadron |
| 1.3.82 | Scampton. Cat.5(c) |
| .11.82 | Sold as scrap, Bird Group. |

**XM569**

| | |
|---|---|
| 11.12.62 | First flight |
| 1.2.63 | 27 Squadron |
| 16.12.65 | HSAL, Woodford. Mods. |
| 22.11.66 | 44/50/101 Squadrons |
| 22.1.68 | 9/12/35 Squadrons |
| 3.4.73 | HSAL. Mods. |
| 24.10.73 | 9/35 Squadrons |
| 4.7.74 | 27 Squadron |
| 23.11.76 | 9/44/50/101 Squadrons. 44 Sqn markings. |
| 21.1.83 | Wales Aircraft Museum at Cardiff Airport (Rhoose) |
| 2.2.83 | Flown to Cardiff. The main airframe later scrapped after the failure of the Wales Aircraft Museum, but the nose was later displayed at the Jet Age Museum, Staverton. Although the Jet Age Museum is no longer open, the nose is still on loan to the Museum and is in store at another site. |

**XM570**

| | |
|---|---|
| 31.1.63 | First flight |
| 27.2.63 | 27 Squadron |
| 13.1.66 | HSAL. Retrofit. |
| 2.1.67 | 44/50/101 Squadrons |
| 29.1.68 | 9/12/35 Squadrons |
| 10.6.68 | 9/35 Squadrons |
| 8.3.74 | 27 Squadron |
| 8.12.76 | 35 Squadron |
| 4.9.78 | 617 Squadron |
| 31.10.78 | 35 Squadron |
| 11.3.81 | Assigned as Cat.5 (scrap) at St Athan. |
| 29.1.82 | Sold as scrap, Harold John & Co. |

**XM571**

| | |
|---|---|
| 31.1.63 | First flight |
| 22.2.63 | 83 Squadron |
| 22.3.66 | HSAL. Retrofit. |
| 21.1.67 | 9/12/35 Squadrons |
| 8.7.67 | 44/50/101 Squadrons. |
| 13.9.67 | 9/12/35 Squadrons |
| 5.12.67 | 44/50/101 Squadrons |
| 4.3.68 | 9/35 Squadrons |
| 24.8.72 | HSAL. Mods. |
| 28.12.72 | 9/35 Squadrons |
| 14.1.75 | 27 Squadron |
| 9.4.75 | 35 Squadron |
| 16.6.75 | 9/44/50/101 Squadrons |
| 3.11.75 | 35 Squadron |
| 15.6.76 | 9/44/50/101 Squadrons |
| 15.11.76 | 35 Squadron |
| 28.3.77 | HSAL Bitteswell. Mods. |
| 17.6.78 | 35 Squadron |
| 9.1.79 | St Athan. |
| 27.3.79 | 617 Squadron |
| 20.8.79 | 9/44/50/101 Squadrons |
| 4.12.79 | 617 Squadron |
| 8.1.82 | 101 Squadron |
| 5.7.82 | British Aerospace, Woodford. K.2 conversion. |
| 14.7.82 | A&AEE. CA Release for Tanker role |

**XL426**

| | |
|---|---|
| 13.08.62 | First flight |
| 07.09.62 | Awaiting collection |
| 13.09.62 | 83 Sqn |
| 21.06.65 | HSA, refit |
| 14.03.66 | 27/83/617 Sqns |
| 19.07.66 | HSAL, Bitteswell, mods |
| 21.10.66 | 27/83/617 Sqns |
| 28.10.69 | HSAL, Bitteswell, mods |
| 22.12.69 | 27/83/617 Sqns |
| 29.03.72 | 230 OCU |
| 07.04.72 | 617 Sqn |
| 28.06.72 | 230 OCU |
| 04.07.72 | 617 Sqn |
| 11.07.72 | 230 OCU |
| 01.08.72 | 617 Sqn |
| 13.04.73 | 230 OCU |
| 16.04.73 | 617 Sqn |
| 30.07.73 | HSAL, Bitteswell, mods |
| 21.02.74 | 27 Sqn ) |
| 21.02.74 | 617 Sqn ) |
| 17.11.77 | HSA, Bitteswell, mods. |
| 21.06.78 | 617 Sqn |
| 13.02.81 | St Athan, Major Inspection |
| 28.05.81 | 617 Sqn, Scampton |
| 05.01.82 | 50 Sqn, Waddington |
| 01.04.84 | Station Flight Waddington (for Vulcan Display Flight) |
| 22.12.86 | Sold to Mr R Jacobson, Southend Airport. Registered as G-VJET 7.7.87. Latest registered owner is Richard John Clarkson, as Trustee of the Vulcan Restoration Trust, from 11.7.94. At Southend Airport 2006. |

**XL427**

| | |
|---|---|
| 14.9.62 | First flight |
| 2.10.62 | 83 Squadron |
| 16.8.65 | HSAL. Mods. |
| 18.4.66 | 27/83/617 Squadrons |
| 17.6.71 | HSAL. Mods. |
| 12.11.71 | 27/617 Squadrons |
| 5.7.72 | 617 Squadron |
| 25.9.72 | 230 OCU |
| 4.1.74 | 27 Squadron |
| 11.8.76 | 230 OCU |
| 27.8.76 | 27 Squadron |
| 2.5.77 | 9/44/50/101 Squadrons |
| 25.1.80 | St Athan |
| 17.4.80 | 9/44/50/101 Squadrons |
| 13.8.82 | Allotted 8756M for crash rescue training at RAF Macrihanish. Cat.5(GI). Scrapped by June 1995. |

**XL443**

| | |
|---|---|
| 18.9.62 | First flight |

| | |
|---|---|
| 8.10.62 | 83 Squadron |
| 7.9.65 | HSAL. Retrofit. |
| 18.5.66 | 27/83/617 Squadrons |
| 6.3.70 | 27/617 Squadrons |
| 12.4.72 | 9/35 Squadrons |
| 24.6.75 | 35 Squadron |
| 9.5.78 | Bitteswell. Mods. |
| 5.2.79 | 35 Squadron |
| 4.1.82 | Assigned Cat.5(s) at Scampton, allotted for RAF Museum but not taken up. |
| .4.83 | Sold as scrap to Bird Group. |

**XL444**

| | |
|---|---|
| 12.10.61 | First flight |
| 1.11.62 | 27 Squadron |
| 18.9.65 | HSAL. Retrofit. |
| 2.6.65 | 27/83/617 Squadrons |
| 18.6.66 | 230 OCU |
| 19.6.67 | 27/83/617 Squadrons |
| 31.12.70 | 27/617 Squadrons |
| 5.4.71 | 230 OCU |
| 11.5.71 | 617 Squadron |
| 25.1.77 | Bitteswell. Mods. |
| 17.11.77 | 617 Squadron |
| 31.5.78 | 35 Squadron |
| 5.1.81 | St Athan. Major Inspection. |
| 8.4.81 | 9/44/50/101 Squadrons |
| 10.9.82 | Assigned Cat.5(c) at Waddington. |
| 8.12.82 | Sold as scrap to Bird Group. |

**XL445**

| | |
|---|---|
| 30.10.62 | First flight |
| 26.11.62 | 27 Squadron |
| 23.11.65 | HSAL. Retrofit. |
| 3.10.66 | 44/50/101 Squadrons |
| 18.4.68 | 9/35 Squadrons |
| 1.2.72 | HSAL. Mods. |
| 19.6.72 | 9/35 Squadrons |
| 16.1.75 | 35 Squadron |
| 16.6.77 | 9/44/50/101 Squadrons |
| 1.10.77 | 35 Squadron |
| 16.10.78 | 230 OCU |
| 2.3.79 | Bitteswell. Mods. |
| 21.12.79 | 230 OCU |
| 19.3.80 | St Athan. Major inspection. |
| 1.7.81 | 35 Squadron |
| 18.11.81 | 44 Squadron |
| 5.7.82 | British Aerospace. K.2 conversion. |
| 23.7.82 | 44/50 Squadrons |
| | 50 Squadron. |
| 8.4.84 | Allotted 8811M for Battle Damage Repair and Crash Rescue training at Lyneham. Up for disposal in October 1990. In 2006 the nose of this aircraft was on display at the Norfolk & Suffolk Aviation Museum at Flixton, Bungay, Suffolk. |

5.10.82 44/50 Squadrons
       50 Squadron
.4.84 Station Flight Waddington. Allotted 8812M for RAF Gibraltar as Cat.5(Gl) 22.3.84.
Flown to Gibraltar but later scrapped (by 1990).

**XM572**
2.63 First flight
.3.63 83 Squadron
8.2.66 HSAL. Retrofit.
.1.67 44/50/101 Squadrons
5.2.68 HSAL. Mods.
9.3.68 9/35 Squadrons
6.11.68 HSAL. Mods.
.1.69 9/35 Squadrons
4.1.75 35 Squadron
7.10.76 HSAL. Mods.
3.8.77 35 Squadron
.5.78 St Athan. Major Inspection.
1.7.78 35 Squadron
.9.81 9 Squadron
0.9.82 Waddington. Assigned Cat.5(c).
.1.82 Sold as scrap to Bird Group.

**XM573**
.7.2.63 First flight
8.3.63 83 Squadron
4.3.66 HSAL. Retrofit.
6.4.67 44/50/101 Squadrons
9.2.68 230 OCU
6.6.70 9/35 Squadrons
8.4.74 27 Squadron
3.77 9/44/50/101 Squadrons
0.6.78 St Athan. Major Inspection.
.9.78 9/44/50/101 Squadrons
8.12.78 230 OCU
.4.81 9/44/50/101 Squadrons. 50 Squadron markings.
2.5.81 Scampton
.82 To Strategic Air & Space Museum at Offutt AFB, Omaha, Nebraska, for display. Still on display in 2006.

**XM574**
8.3.63 First flight
1.6.63 27 Squadron
1.1.66 HSAL. Mods.
.6.66 27/83/617 Squadrons
0.1.70 27/617 Squadrons
.11.71 44/50/101 Squadrons
3.12.72 HSAL. Mods.
2.6.73 44/50/101 Squadrons
8.8.73 9/35 Squadrons
4.1.75 35 Squadron.
4.8.75 617 Squadron
1.7.79 St Athan. Major Inspection.
.10.79 617 Squadron
4.9.81 Assigned to Cat.5(c) at St Athan, for display.
9.1.82 Sold as scrap to Harold John & Co.

**XM575**
9.4.63 First flight
2.5.63 617 Squadron
0.11.64 HSAL. Mods.
2.3.65 27/83/617 Squadrons
8.7.70 44/50/101 Squadrons
7.11.70 27/617 Squadrons
2.12.72 HSAL. Mods.
8.6.73 617 Squadron
5.3.74 9/44/50/101 Squadrons
.10.80 St Athan. Major inspection.
.1.81 9/44/50/101 Squadrons (44 Sqn markings)

25.1.83 Sold to Loughborough & Leicestershire Air Museum and Preservation Society (LLAMPS) for display at East Midlands Airport.
28.1.83 Flown to East Midlands. On display in 2006 at the Nottingham East Midlands Airport Aeropark. The registration G-BLMC was reserved in August 1984 for a possible ferry flight to Bruntingthorpe, but was never taken up.

**XM576**
16.5.63 First flight
21.6.63 27/83/617 Squadrons
4.1.65 HSAL. Mods.
31.3.65 27/83/617 Squadrons
25.5.65 Crashed at Scampton. Wing hit ground on overshoot, aircraft swung and hit building. Assessed as Cat.4R for repair.
6.12.65 Re-assessed as Cat.5(c).
7.12.65 Struck off Charge.

**XM594**
4.6.63 First flight
19.7.63 27 Squadron
3012.65 HSAL. Mods.
16.5.66 27/83/617 Squadrons
17.7.70 27/617 Squadrons
29.3.72 HSAL. Mods.
24.8.72 44/50/101 Squadrons
19.1.73 9/44/50/101 Squadrons
9.7.76 Bitteswell. Mods.
31.3.77 9/44/50/101 Squadrons
24.1.78 St Athan. Major Inspection
26.5.78 9/44/50/101 Squadrons. 44 Sqn marks.
19.1.83 Sold to Newark Air Museum.
7.2.83 Flown to Winthorpe. On display in 2006.

**XM595**
4.7.63 First flight
21.8.63 617 Squadron
8.10.64 HSAL. Mods.
8.2.65 27/83/617 Squadrons
19.1.70 27/617 Squadrons
1.1.71 617 Squadron
12.2.74 HSAL. Mods.
19.8.74 617 Squadron
5.5.79 St Athan. Major Inspection.
9.10.79 617 Squadron
20.12.79 9/44/50/101 Squadrons
25.4.80 617 Squadron
4.1.82 35 Squadron
1.3.82 Assigned Cat.5(c) at Scampton.
11.82 Sold as scrap to Bird Group.

**XM596**
Not flown. Airframe used for structural and fatigue testing relating to the low-level role to which Vulcans were to be transferred.

**XM597**
12.7.63 First flight
28.8.63 12 Squadron
4.9.64 HSAL. Mods.
21.12.64 9/12/35 Squadrons
18.4.67 44/50/101 Squadrons
29.11.71 HSAL Woodford. TI of ARI 18228/1 radar warning receiver.
4.10.72 To A&AEE for trials
12.2.73 44/50/101 Squadrons
22.10.73 HSAL. Mods.
26.4.74 44/50/101 Squadrons
8.6.78 Bitteswell. Mods.
6.3.79 9/44/50/101 Squadrons
30.7.79 St Athan. Major inspection
5.11.79 9/44/50/101 Squadrons
       50 Squadron
12.4.84 Ferried to East Fortune following transfer as a gift to the Museum of Flight. On display in 2006.

**XM598**
15.8.63 First flight
4.9.62 12 Squadron
1.12.64 HSAL. Mods.
6.1.65 9/12/35 Squadrons
31.1.66 HSAL. Mods.
2.3.66 9/12/35 Squadrons
29.12.66 HSAL. Mods.
13.3.67 9/12/35 Squadrons
9.4.68 44/50/101 Squadrons
20.5.71 HSAL. Mods.
13.10.71 9/44/50/101 Squadrons
29.9.75 HSAL. Mods.
9.7.76 9/44/50/101 Squadrons
23.11.77 St Athan. Major inspection.
26.2.79 9/44/50/101 Squadrons. 44 Squadron markings.
19.1.83 Allotted 8778M for ground instruction at No 2 SoTT, RAF Cosford.
20.1.83 Flown to Cosford on transfer to the Cosford Aerospace Museum, and is included in the Cold War Exhibition Hall opened at the Museum in 2007.

**XM599**
30.8.63 First flight
1.10.63 35 Squadron
1.12.64 HSAL. Mods.
18.1.65 9/12/35 Squadrons
11.1.66 HSAL. Mods.
1.2.66 9/12/35 Squadrons
18.8.66 HSAL. Mods.
31.1.67 9/12/35 Squadrons
9.1.68 44/50/101 Squadrons
24.4.68 Bitteswell. Mods.
31.5.68 44/50/101 Squadrons
4.11.71 HSAL. Mods.

This photograph shows the erstwhile XM596 after it had been withdrawn from the production line and installed in the test rig which was to simulate the arduous life of its fellows, flying through turbulent air at high speed and very low level. The airframe never wore its allotted serial number. British Aerospace via Phil Spencer

**B.2 XM597 taxying at Waddington.** via Phil Butler

| | |
|---|---|
| 7.3.72 | 44/50/101 Squadrons |
| 3.12.74 | HSAL. Mods. |
| 1.9.75 | 9/44/50/101 Squadrons |
| 5.11.79 | Bitteswell. Mods. |
| 15.8.80 | 9/44/50/101 Squadrons |
| 27.5.81 | Assigned Cat.5(s) at St Athan. |
| 29.1.82 | Sold as scrap, Harold John & Co. |

**XM600**

| | |
|---|---|
| 6.9.63 | First flight |
| 3.10.63 | 35 Squadron |
| 23.6.65 | HSAL. Mods. |
| 16.9.65 | 9/12/35 Squadrons |
| 1.8.66 | HSAL. Mods. |
| 20.1.67 | 9/12/35 Squadrons |
| 2.5.68 | 9/35 Squadrons |
| 30.5.68 | 44/50/101 Squadrons |
| 28.1.74 | HSAL. Mods. |
| 4.12.74 | 44/50/101 Squadrons. (9 Sqn added in 1.75). |
| 18.1.77 | Caught fire in the air and abandoned near Spilsby, Lincs. Cat.5(s) |

**XM601**

| | |
|---|---|
| 21.10.63 | First flight |
| 5.11.63 | 9 Squadron |
| 7.10.64 | Crashed on landing at Coningsby and destroyed by fire. |
| 8.10.64 | Struck off Charge as Cat.5(s). |

**XM602**

| | |
|---|---|
| 28.10.63 | First flight |
| 13.11.63 | 12 Squadron. |
| 29.3.65 | HSAL. Mods. |
| 10.6.65 | 9/12/35 Squadrons |
| 17.3.67 | HSAL. Mods. |
| 1.6.67 | 9/12/35 Squadrons |
| 24.4.68 | 44/50/101 Squadrons |
| 26.5.70 | HSAL. Mods. |
| 9.10.70 | 44/50/101 Squadrons |
| 13.3.75 | 9/44/50/101 Squadrons |
| 26.3.75 | HSAL. Mods. |
| 5.12.75 | 9/44/50/101 Squadrons |
| 17.8.78 | St Athan. Major inspection |
| 4.11.78 | 9/44/50/101 Squadrons |
| 3.7.80 | Bitteswell. Mods. |
| 31.3.81 | 9/44/50/101 Squadrons. 101 Squadron markings. |
| 4.1.82 | Assigned Cat.5 (spares recovery) at St Athan. |
| 16.3.82 | Allotted 8771M for display at RAF St Athan Historic Aircraft Museum. Airframe scrapped after the museum closed. In 1989 a proposed private sale fell through and the aircraft was scrapped in 1992. Cockpit section went to the Avro Heritage Centre at Woodford; it is now at Bruntingthorpe with the Vulcan to the Sky Trust (VTST), in use as a crew procedures trainer for XH558 (2006). |

**XM603**

| | |
|---|---|
| 15.11.63 | First flight |
| 4.12.63 | 9 Squadron |
| 12.7.65 | HSAL. Mods. |
| 6.10.65 | 9/12/35 Squadrons |
| 18.1.68 | 44/50/101 Squadrons |
| 19.8.74 | HSAL. Mods. |
| 5.6.75 | 9/44/50/101 Squadrons |
| 15.8.77 | St Athan. Major inspection. |
| 3.11.77 | 9/44/50/101 Squadrons |
| 20.12.79 | Bitteswell. Mods. |
| 18.9.80 | 9/44/50/101 Squadrons. 44 Squadron markings. |
| 12.3.82 | To British Aerospace, Woodford, for preservation. (5,733 F/H). The aircraft remains at Woodford in 2006, but 'Health & Safety considerations' now prevent volunteers from carrying out maintenance work on it, so its future must be in doubt. |

**XM604**

| | |
|---|---|
| 15.11.64 | First flight |
| 4.12.63 | 35 Squadron |
| 9.8.65 | Bitteswell. Mods. |
| 11.11.65 | 9/12/35 Squadrons |
| 30.1.68 | Flew into ground, Burley, Rutland (on approach to Cottesmore) after an engine shed compressor blades which severed the flying controls. Cat.5(s). |

**XM605**

| | |
|---|---|
| 22.11.63 | First flight |
| 30.12.63 | 9 Squadron |
| 8.9.65 | HSAL. Mods. |
| 14.12.65 | 9/12/35 Squadrons |
| 16.2.68 | 44/50/101 Squadrons |
| 2.7.71 | HSAL. Mods. |
| 7.12.71 | 44/50/101 Squadrons. (9 Sqn added in 1.75) |
| 23.12.75 | HSAL. Mods. |
| 30.9.76 | 9/44/50/101 Squadrons |
| 30.11.79 | St Athan. Major inspection. |
| 21.2.80 | 9/44/50/101 Squadrons. 50 Squadron markings. |
| 2.9.81 | Allotted to Castle AFB, California, USA, for display. |
| 8.9.81 | Flown to Castle AFB. In 2006 it remains on display at the Castle Air Museum at Castle Airport, (the former Air Force Base, which closed in 1994). (5,378 F/H) |

**XM606**

| | |
|---|---|
| 28.11.63 | First flight |
| 30.12.63 | 12 Squadron |
| 30.10.63 | HSAL. Mods. |
| 18.2.65 | 9/12/35 Squadrons |
| 14.6.65 | HSAL, Woodford. TI of GD Terrain-Following Radar (ARI 5959) and LR tank installation |
| 24.2.66 | To A&AEE for trials |
| 2.5.67 | HSAL. Mods. |
| 8.4.68 | 9/35 Squadrons |
| 13.5.68 | 44/50/101 Squadrons |
| 13.4.72 | HSAL. Mods. |
| 25.8.72 | 44/50/101 Squadrons. 9 Sqn added in 1.75. |

| | |
|---|---|
| 6.10.77 | Bitteswell. Mods. |
| 27.7.78 | 9/44/50/101 Squadrons |
| 14.6.82 | Allotted to Barksdale AFB, Louisiana, USA, for display at the 'Eighth Air Force Museum'. Still on display in 2006. |

**XM607**

| | |
|---|---|
| 29.11.63 | First flight |
| 1.1.64 | 35 Squadron |
| 21.12.64 | HSAL. Mods. |
| 30.3.65 | 9/12/35 Squadron |
| 22.3.68 | 9/35 Squadron |
| 24.5.68 | 44/50/101 Squadron |
| 21.12.70 | HSAL. Mods. |
| 23.4.71 | 44/50/101 Squadrons |
| 17.6.74 | HSAL. Mods. |
| 27.3.75 | 9/44/50/101 Squadrons |
| 31.1.79 | St Athan. Major inspection |
| 18.4.79 | 9/44/50/101 Squadrons |
| 25.3.80 | Bitteswell. Mods. |
| 18.12.79 | 9/44/50/101 Squadrons. 44 Sqn markings. |
| 19.1.83 | Allotted 8779M for display at RAF Waddington. Still present in 2006. |

**XM608**

| | |
|---|---|
| 24.12.63 | First flight |
| 29.1.64 | 9 Squadron |
| 16.1.65 | HSAL. Mods. |
| 9.4.65 | 9/12/35 Squadrons |
| 23.2.68 | 44/50/101 Squadrons. (9 Sqn added 1.75) |
| 6.4.81 | Assigned Cat.5(c) at St Athan. |
| 2.12.82 | Sold as scrap to Bird Group. |

**XM609**

| | |
|---|---|
| 2.1.64 | First flight |
| 29.1.64 | 12 Squadron |
| 30.10.64 | HSAL. Mods. |
| 4.3.65 | 9/12/35 Squadrons |
| 7.8.67 | 230 OCU |
| 1.11.67 | 9/12/35 Squadrons |
| 30.3.68 | 44/50/101 Squadrons |
| 7.4.74 | HSAL. Mods. |
| 7.2.75 | 9/44/50/101 Squadrons |
| 30.7.79 | Bitteswell. Mods. |
| 7.7.80 | 9/44/50/101 Squadrons |
| 12.3.81 | Assigned Cat.5(s) at St Athan. |
| 31.8.81 | Sold as scrap to W Harold & Co. |

**XM610**

| | |
|---|---|
| 22.1.64 | First flight |
| 12.2.64 | 9 Squadron |
| 18.10.65 | HSAL. Mods. |
| 3.2.66 | 9/12/35 Squadrons |
| 24.5.67 | Bitteswell. Mods. |
| 9.8.67 | 9/12/35 Squadrons |
| 5.2.68 | 44/50/101 Squadrons |
| 8.1.71 | Caught fire in the air and abandoned at Wingate, County Durham. |
| 11.1.71 | Struck off Charge, Cat.5(s). |

**XM611**

| | |
|---|---|
| 23.1.64 | First flight |
| 4.2.64 | 9 Squadron |
| 18.3.66 | HSAL. Mods. |
| 8.7.66 | 9/12/35 Squadrons |
| 9.8.66 | HSAL. Mods. |
| 2.10.67 | 9/12/35 Squadrons |
| 28.5.68 | 44/50/101 Squadrons |
| 28.9.76 | HSAL Bitteswell. Mods. |
| 24.6.77 | 9/44/50/101 Squadrons |
| 12.12.78 | St Athan. Major inspection |
| 6.3.79 | 9/44/50/101 Squadrons |
| 27.1.82 | Assigned Cat.5(c) at St Athan. |
| 6.83 | Sold as scrap to T Bradbury & Co. |

**XM612**

| | |
|---|---|
| 3.2.64 | First flight |
| .3.64 | 9/12/35 Squadrons |
| .9.65 | HSAL. Mods. |
| 10.11.65 | 9/12/35 Squadrons |
| 9.1.68 | 44/50/101 Squadrons |
| .3.68 | A&AEE. Trials of air stream direction detector comparator unit. |
| 4.68 | 44/50/101 Squadrons |
| .3.72 | HSAL. Mods. |
| 1.7.72 | 44/50/101 Squadrons. 9 Sqn added 1.75. |
| 4.1.77 | HSAL Bitteswell. Mods. |
| 10.10.77 | 9/44/50/101 Squadrons |
| 18.7.78 | St Athan. Major Inspection |
| 18.10.78 | 9/44/50/101 Squadrons |
| 15.8.80 | Bitteswell. Repair in Works. |
| .5.81 | 9/44/50/101 Squadrons |
| 19.1.83 | Sold to Norwich Aviation Museum. |
| 30.1.83 | Flown to Norwich Airport for City of Norwich Aviation Museum. Still present 2006. |

**XM645**

| | |
|---|---|
| 5.2.64 | First flight |
| 2.3.64 | 9/12/35 Squadrons |
| .12.65 | HSAL. Mods. |
| 1.2.66 | 9/12/35 Squadrons. |
| .4.67 | HSAL. Mods. |
| .6.67 | 9/12/35 Squadrons |
| 15.12.67 | 44/50/101 Squadrons |
| 8.68 | 230 OCU |
| 2.4.71 | 44/50/101 Squadrons |
| 10.8.73 | HSAL. Mods. |
| 8.2.74 | 44/50/101 Squadrons |
| 2.3.74 | 9/35 Squadrons. |
| 15.1.75 | 9/44/50/101 Squadrons. |
| 14.10.75 | Crashed at Zabar, Malta. Undershot runway at Luqa and blew up while attempting to climb away. |
| 15.10.75 | Struck off Charge as Cat.5(s). |

**XM646**

| | |
|---|---|
| 6.3.64 | First flight |
| .4.64 | 9/12/35 Squadrons |
| .2.65 | HSAL. Mods. |
| 1.4.65 | 9/12/35 Squadrons |
| .3.66 | HSAL. Mods. |
| .7.66 | 9/12/35 Squadrons |
| 2.10.68 | HSAL. Mods. |
| 9.12.67 | 9/12/35 Squadrons |
| 6.3.68 | HSAL. Mods. |
| 15.5.68 | 9/12/35 Squadrons |
| 1.8.73 | HSAL. Mods. |
| 2.3.74 | 9/35 Squadrons |
| 7.1.75 | 9/44/50/101 Squadrons |
| 7.9.77 | St Athan. Major inspection |
| 2.12.77 | 9/44/50/101 Squadrons |
| 1.82 | Assigned Cat.5(c) at St Athan for spares recovery. |
| 9.6.83 | Sold as scrap to T Bradbury & Co. |

**XM647**

| | |
|---|---|
| 2.4.64 | First flight |
| 16.4.64 | 9/12/35 Squadrons |
| 6.10.65 | HSAL. Mods. |
| 12.1.66 | 9/12/35 Squadrons |
| 17.5.66 | HSAL. Mods. |
| 5.9.66 | 9/12/35 Squadrons |
| 22.9.67 | HSAL. Mods. |
| 29.11.67 | 9/12/35 Squadrons |
| 28.6.68 | HSAL. Mods. |
| 6.8.68 | 9/35 Squadrons |
| 21.8.72 | HSAL. Mods. |
| 23.1.73 | 9/35 Squadrons |
| 21.7.78 | Bitteswell. Mods. |
| 31.5.79 | 9/44/50/101 Squadrons. 50 Squadron markings. |
| 17.8.82 | Allotted 8765M for ground instruction at RAF Laarbruch, found 'unsuitable' after arrival there. |
| 25.2.85 | Sold as scrap, Solair UK Ltd. |

**XM648**

| | |
|---|---|
| 17.4.64 | First flight |
| 6.5.64 | 9/12/35 Squadrons |
| 17.12.65 | HSAL. Mods. |
| 18.2.66 | 9/12/35 Squadrons |
| 6.7.67 | HSAL. Mods. |
| 22.9.67 | 9/12/35 Squadrons |
| 25.1.68 | 44/50/101 Squadrons |
| 30.4.69 | HSAL. Mods. |
| 6.6.69 | 44/50/101 Squadrons |
| 26.2.71 | HSAL. Mods. |
| 5.7.71 | 44/50/101 Squadrons |
| 22.3.76 | HSAL Bitteswell. Mods. |
| 11.1.77 | 9/44/50/101 Squadrons |
| 6.6.80 | St Athan. Major Inspection. |
| 11.9.80 | 9/44/50/101 Squadrons |
| 10.9.82 | Assigned Cat.5(c) at Waddington. |
| 12.82 | Sold as scrap to Bird Group. |

**XM649**

| | |
|---|---|
| 28.4.64 | First flight |
| 14.5.63 | 9/12/35 Squadrons |
| 12.4.65 | HSAL. Mods. |
| 23.6.65 | 9/12/35 Squadrons |
| 11.5.66 | HSAL Bitteswell. Mods. |
| 19.8.66 | 9/12/35 Squadrons |
| 30.8.67 | HSAL. Mods. |
| 31.10.67 | 9/12/35 Squadrons |
| 18.1.68 | 44/50/101 Squadrons |
| 29.5.69 | HSAL. Mods. |
| 2.12.69 | A&AEE. Installation and flight trials of Decca Doppler 72 equipment. |
| 11.1.70 | 44/50/101 Squadrons |
| 23.2.70 | To A&AEE. Further trials |
| 6.3.70 | 44/50/101 Squadrons |
| 24.1.73 | HSAL. Mods. |

**XM650** (continued)

| | |
|---|---|
| 27.7.73 | 44/50/101 Squadrons. Also 9 Sqn from 1.75. |
| 26.3.79 | St Athan. Major inspection. |
| 21.6.79 | 9/44/50/101 Squadrons |
| 2.9.81 | Assigned Cat.5(c) at St Athan. |
| 2.12.82 | Sold as scrap, Bird Group. |

**XM650**

| | |
|---|---|
| 12.5.64 | First flight |
| 5.6.64 | 9/12/35 Squadrons |
| 3.3.65 | HSAL. Retrofit. |
| 18.5.65 | 9/12/35 Squadrons |
| 14.4.66 | HSAL. Mods. |
| 22.7.66 | 9/12/35 Squadrons |
| 2.10.67 | HSAL. Mods. |
| 20.12.67 | 44/50/101 Squadrons |
| 27.4.71 | HSAL. Mods. |
| 6.9.71 | 44/50/101 Squadrons. Also 9 Sqn from 1.75. |
| 27.1.76 | HSAL. Mods. |
| 16.11.76 | 9/44/50/101 Squadrons |
| 27.9.78 | St Athan. Major inspection. |
| 12.12.78 | 9/44/50/101 Squadrons |
| 5.1.82 | Assigned Cat.5(s) at St Athan. |
| 16.3.83 | Allotted 8748M as Cat.5(GI), but replaced by XL387. |
| 22.3.84 | Sold as scrap, Bournewood Aviation. |

**XM651**

| | |
|---|---|
| 1.6.64 | First flight |
| 22.6.64 | 9/12/35 Squadrons |
| 11.6.65 | HSAL. Mods. |
| 2.9.65 | 9/12/35 Squadrons |
| 25.7.66 | HSAL. Mods. |
| 30.12.66 | 9/12/35 Squadrons |
| 8.4.68 | 9/35 Squadrons |
| 24.4.68 | 44/50/101 Squadrons |
| 9.9.71 | HSAL. Mods. |
| 27.1.72 | 44/50/101 Squadrons |
| 7.8.75 | HSAL. Mods. |
| 21.5.76 | 9/44/50/101 Squadrons |
| 10.9.81 | Assigned Cat.5(c) at Waddington. |
| .11.82 | Sold as scrap, Bird Group. |

**XM652**

| | |
|---|---|
| 16.7.64 | First flight |
| 17.8.64 | 9/12/35 Squadrons |
| 22.4.65 | HSAL. Mods. |
| 12.7.65 | 9/12/35 Squadrons |
| 15.6.67 | HSAL. Mods. |
| 13.9.67 | 9/12/35 Squadrons |
| 24.12.67 | 44/50/101 Squadrons |
| 22.6.73 | HSAL. Mods. |
| 18.12.73 | 44/50/101 Squadrons. Also 9 Sqn from 1.75. |
| 3.12.77 | Bitteswell. Mods. |
| 5.9.78 | 9/44/50/101 Squadrons |
| 6.12.78 | British Aerospace. Mods. |

**.2 XM648 at its dispersal at RAF Luqa, Malta in 1969.** via Phil Butler

28.2.79  9/44/50/101 Squadrons
21.6.79  St Athan. Major inspection.
24.9.79  9/44/50/101 Squadrons
         50 Squadron.
20.2.84  Sold as scrap Boulding Industrial Supplies Ltd.
         In 2006 its nose is an exhibit at the Military Aircraft
         Cockpit Collection at Welshpool

## XM653

14.8.64  First flight
4.9.64   9/12/35 Squadrons
3.5.65   HSAL. Mods.
19.7.65  9/12/35 Squadrons
17.2.67  HSAL. Mods.
14.4.67  9/12/35 Squadrons
24.1.68  44/50/101 Squadrons
31.5.72  HSAL. Mods.
23.10.72  44/50/101 Squadrons. Also 9 Sqn from 1.75.
21.6.77  Bitteswell. Mods.
27.1.77  9/44/50/101 Squadrons
10.8.79  St Athan. Cat.3 Repair
19.9.80  Re-categorised Cat.5(c).
28.7.81  Sold as scrap.

## XM654

2.10.64  First flight
26.10.64  9/12/35 Squadrons
21.7.65  HSAL. Mods.
18.10.65  9/12/35 Squadrons
3.4.68   9/35 Squadrons
30.4.68  44/50/101 Squadrons
17.12.73  HSAL. Mods.
6.6.74   44/50/101 Squadrons. Also 9 Sqn from 1.75.
5.2.79   Bitteswell. Mods.
6.11.79  9/44/50/101 Squadrons
29.10.82  Assigned Cat.5(c) at Waddington
2.12.82  Sold as scrap, Bird Group.

## XM655

2.11.64  First flight
23.11.64  9/12/35 Squadrons
25.11.65  HSAL. Mods.
9.2.66   9/12/35 Squadrons
8.9.66   HSAL. Mods.
27.2.67  9/12/35 Squadrons
12.1.68  44/50/101 Squadrons
2.7.73   Bitteswell. Mods.
24.1.74  44/50/101 Squadrons. Also 9 Sqn from 1.75.
23.6.78  Bitteswell. Mods.
26.3.79  9/44/50/101 Squadrons
7.4.79   St Athan. Major inspection.
12.7.79  9/44/50/101 Squadrons. 50 Squadron markings

11.2.84  Ferried to Wellesbourne Mountford. Sold to R
         Jacobson.
         Registered as G-VULC on 27.2.84. (Registration
         N655AV reserved in the USA during 1985, but not
         taken up). G-VULC last registered on 21.1.93 to
         Radarmoor Ltd at Wellesbourne Mountford.
         Registration cancelled 25.3.02. This Vulcan was
         still present in 2006; it is owned by the operators
         of Wellesbourne Mountford airfield and is
         occasionally ground-run.

## XM656

25.11.64  First flight
15.12.64  9/12/35 Squadrons
19.5.65  HSAL. Mods.
1.9.65   9/12/35 Squadrons
5.5.66   Bitteswell. Mods.
1.8.66   9/12/35 Squadrons
13.9.67  HSAL. Mods.
22.11.67  9/12/35 Squadrons
2.2.68   44/50/101 Squadrons
24.3.69  HSAL. Mods.
9.5.69   44/50/101 Squadrons
3.9.70   HSAL. Mods.
19.1.71  44/50/101 Squadrons
22.10.74  HSAL. Mods
2.7.75   9/44/50/101 Squadrons
29.3.78  St Athan. Major Inspection.
20.6.78  9/44/50/101 Squadrons
1.2.80   Bitteswell. Mods.
13.10.80  9/44/50/101 Squadrons. 9 Squadron markings.
9.8.82   Allotted 8757M for crash-rescue training at RAF
         Cottesmore. Cat.5(GI).
.3.83    Sold as scrap.

## XM657

21.12.64  First flight
15.1.65  9/12/35 Squadrons
22.9.65  HSAL. Mods.
29.12.65  9/12/35 Squadrons
27.4.67  HSAL. Mods.
4.7.67   9/12/35 Squadrons
19.3.68  44/50/101 Squadrons
1.10.71  HSAL. Mods.
10.2.72  9/44/50/101 Squadrons
21.4.76  HSAL. Mods.
24.1.77  9/44/50/101 Squadrons
25.10.79  St Athan. Major Inspection.
21.12.79  9/44/50/101 Squadrons. 44 Squadron markings.
5.1.82   Allotted 8734M 18.12.81 for Crash rescue/fire-
         fighting training at RAF Manston and arrived there
         on 12.1.82. Burned by November 1992.

## GROUND INSTRUCTIONAL VULCANS

At the end of their lives, many Vulcans became instructional airframes at Schools of Technical Training, or were expended as crash-rescue trainers at Fire-Fighting schools (or for the fire crews at various active RAF airfields). For many years, such instructional airframes received new serial numbers consisting of numerals suffixed by the latter 'M'. The series of numbers was begun at a time when serial numbers beginning with the letter 'N' (and later letters in the alphabet) were allotted to Fleet Air Arm aircraft, and it was assumed that RAF aircraft (once numbers up to M9999 were used up) would then adopt numbers from 1A onwards so that 'grounded' airframes were given numbers from '1M', at the opposite end of the series reserved for RAF aircraft. The numbers are often (incorrectly) called 'Maintenance' numbers because of the use of the letter 'M' and a presumption (again, incorrect) that RAF Maintenance Command allotted the numbers. This was never the case, and the series of numbers started eighteen or so years before Maintenance Command itself came into existence. The Ground Instructional serial numbers were always allotted by personnel within the RAF's technical training functions, serving within several different chains of command over the years, but never 'Maintenance'). The list of 'M'-numbered Vulcans appears below:

| | | | | | |
|---|---|---|---|---|---|
| 7738M | XA904 | 8505M | XL384 | 8758M | XH562 |
| 7746M | XA892 | 8591M | XA893 | 8759M | XL321 |
| 7812M | XA899 | 8670M | XL384 | 8760M | XL386 |
| 7856M | XA898 | 8694M | XH554 | 8765M | XM64? |
| 7857M | XA905 | 8725M | XL317 | 8766M | XJ782 |
| 7896M | XA900 | 8733M | XL318 | 8771M | XM60? |
| 7897M | XA901 | 8734M | XM657 | 8778M | XM59? |
| 7974M | XH479 | 8744M | XH563 | 8779M | XM60? |
| 7993M | XH498 | 8745M | XL392 | 8809M | XH56? |
| 7994M | XH500 | 8748M | XL387 | 8810M | XJ825 |
| 7995M | XA910 | 8749M | XH537 | 8811M | XL445 |
| 7996M | XH475 | 8750M | XL388 | 8812M | XM57? |
| 8047M | XH478 | 8756M | XL427 | | |
| 8048M | XH533 | 8757M | XM656 | | |

Notes: XH481, XH483, XH502, XH504 and XH505 were allotted as Instructional [Cat.5(GI)] airframes in 1967/68 but no 'M' numbers were allotted to these aircraft, probably due to administrative error. 8748M is believed to be the former XL387, but it should be noted that the record for XM650 gives it as becoming 8748M.

**B.2 XM651 taxying at Waddington.** via Phil Butler

# Vulcan Flying Units

**A B.2 of No 50 Squadron landing at RAE Bedford.**

## TRIALS UNITS

This section covers organisations wholly or partly operated by the Ministry of Supply and its various successors – most recently the Ministry of Defence (Procurement Executive).

### Royal Aircraft Establishment

Formerly the Royal Aircraft Factory at Farnborough, having its origins in the Balloon Factory established in the 19th Century. It became the RAE on 1st April 1918 and was the main Government establishment for aeronautical research until finally closed down in 1994. Its Headquarters was always at Farnborough, but after the Second World War a separate organisation (the National Aeronautical Establishment, NAE) was set up at Thurleigh airfield, near Bedford. The Thurleigh organisation became part of the RAE in 1957. Experimental flying with the Vulcan took place at both the Farnborough and Bedford sites, with armament trials being a main activity at Farnborough, and the development of 'automatic landing' and other aerodynamic work at Bedford.

### Royal Radar Establishment

Originally formed at the Telecommunications Research Establishment during the Second World War, with its 'Air Department' located at Malvern and related Telecommunications Flying Unit being based close by, at Defford in Worcestershire. The unit began to move to the larger nearby airfield of Pershore during 1955, resulting in the closure of Defford later. The RRE was concerned with the development of radio and radar equipment for all three armed services. Although the RRE flew very many aircraft of a wide variety of types, the only Vulcan operated by the RRE was the B.1 XA895, during the development of the Red Steer Mk.2 tail-warning radar for the Vulcan B.1A, for which this machine was the Trials Installation aircraft in 1965. The RRE Flying Unit later moved to Bedford (Thurleigh) and its work was subsequently absorbed by the RAE.

### Aeroplane and Armament Experimental Establishment

Boscombe Down was the main centre for evaluation of aircraft, armament and equipment for use by the RAF and Fleet Air Arm. Its work continues today, although in 1992 it was renamed the Aircraft and Armament Evaluation Establishment. Formed from the earlier 'Aeroplane Experimental Establishment' at Martlesham Heath in 1924, the A&AEE remained there until moving to Boscombe Down on the outbreak of the Second World War. The Empire Test Pilots' School (ETPS), which did operate one of the Avro 707s, was formed from a section of the A&AEE in 1943, and – although a separate entity that was based at Farnborough during the 707 period – has since returned to Boscombe Down, where it shares the facilities and, on occasion, aircraft with the A&AEE. The Handling Squadron, an RAF unit which prepared 'Pilot's Notes' and other aircraft documentation was amalgamated into the A&AEE in 1954.

### Blind Landing Experimental Unit

A Ministry of Supply organisation, initially based at Martlesham Heath in Suffolk (although much of its early flying was conducted at nearby Woodbridge, which had a 3,000 yard-long runway built as an emergency strip during the Second World War). It conducted experiments on airborne and ground-based radio and radar guidance systems and airfield lighting systems to enable more reliable operation of both civilian and military aircraft in bad visibility. Originally formed immediately post-war, the BLEU later (in 1949) amalgamated with the Bomb Ballistics Unit at the same airfield and was shortly renamed the Armament and Instrument Experimental Unit (AIEU) at the same location. In 1957

the AIEU became the Blind Landing Experimental Unit once more and moved to the RAE site at Bedford (Thurleigh). The AIEU flew one of the Avro 707A models, and after the move to Bedford the BLEU operated the 707A and, later, Vulcan B.1 XA899 during its 'autoland' development trials (1959-1962). Eventually, the BLEU was absorbed into the RAE per se and ceased to be an independent unit.

### RAF BOMBER COMMAND

Bomber Command (from 1968 Strike Command, following the amalgamation of Bomber and Fighter Commands), via No 1 Group, controlled the Vulcan Squadrons, together with the Vulcan and Canberra OCUs, the Bomber Command Development Unit, the Valiant-equipped Electronic Warfare Squadron and the Thor missile Squadrons. The Valiant and Victor bomber Squadrons and their OCU came under the control of No 3 Group.

No 1 Group had its Headquarters at RAF Bawtry, near to the airfield at Finningley, which was one of its flying bases. The only Vulcan units ever to come under another chain of command were the two Squadrons of the Near East Air Force Bomber Wing when they were transferred to Cyprus between 1969 and 1975.

For much of the life of the Vulcan in the V-Bomber Force the individual Squadrons were grouped into Wings centred on their base airfield. This arose from the centralised servicing arrangements for the base's aircraft, such that maintenance was organised centrally, without each Squadron having separate servicing capability. In theory this meant that aircraft could be readily exchanged within squadrons, and certainly led to crews from one squadron

sometimes flying aircraft bearing the markings of another unit. The compositions of the various Wings are summarised below.

### Akrotiri Wing

(otherwise the NEAF Bomber Wing)
As mentioned above, the NEAF was not part of Bomber Command or No 1 Group, being part of a completely separate Command structure, the Near East Air Force.

This Wing controlled the Akrotiri-based Vulcan squadrons that were tasked to support the now-defunct Central Treaty Organisation. Thus Nos 9 and 35 Squadrons and their aircraft are sometimes recorded under the heading of 'NEAF Bomber Wing', which had also previously operated with Canberra squadrons before the arrival of the Vulcans. The unit flew the Vulcan from February 1969 until January 1975, when the Near East Air Force was disbanded and the Squadrons returned to the UK. Although the NEAF was tasked to support CENTO, the Bomber Wing also had NATO tasks as well as supporting roles relating to British interests in the Near and Middle East.

| | |
|---|---|
| 9 Sqn | Feb 1969 to Jan 1975 (to Waddington) |
| 35 Sqn | Jan 1969 to Jan 1975 (to Scampton) |

### Coningsby Wing

Badge: Red/Brown Castle modelled on Tattershall Castle.

| | |
|---|---|
| 9 Sqn | Mar 1962 - Nov 1964 |
| 12 Sqn | Jul 1962 - Nov 1964 |
| 35 Sqn | Dec 1962 - Nov 1964 |

The Wing squadrons moved to Cottesmore in November 1964.

**XM597 of the Waddington Wing, seen at Leuchars on 15th September 1973.** Phil Butler

## Cottesmore Wing

| Sqn | Nov 1964 - Feb 1969 (to Akrotiri) |
| 12 Sqn | Nov 1964 - Dec 1967 (Disbanded) |
| 35 Sqn | Nov 1964 - Jan 1969 (to Akrotiri) |

## Finningley Wing

Badge: White Rose of Yorkshire on Blue Shield.

| 101 Sqn | Oct 1957 - Jun 1961 (to Waddington) |
| BCDU/SCDU | Mar 1960 - Dec 1968 |
| | (Vulcans not used after Nov 1966) |
| 230 OCU | Jun 1961 - Dec 1969 (to Scampton) |

## Scampton Wing

The Scampton Wing squadrons (27, 83 and 617) operated Vulcans modified to carry the Blue Steel stand-off missile during the service of this weapon from 1962 to 1969.

| 27 Sqn | Apr 1961 - Mar 1972. |
| | (Disbanded, reformed later) |
| 27 Sqn | Nov 1973 - Mar 1982 (Disbanded) |
| 35 Sqn | Jan 1975 - Feb 1982 (Disbanded) |
| 83 Sqn | Oct 1960 - Aug 1969 (Disbanded) |
| 617 Sqn | May 1958 - Jan 1982 (Disbanded) |
| 230 OCU | Dec 1969 - Aug 1981 (Disbanded) |

## Waddington Wing

Badge: Red Cross of St George on Shield (from the City of Lincoln coat of arms). Often worn in addition to Squadron marking.

| 9 Sqn | Jan 1975 - Apr 1982 (Disbanded) |
| 44 Sqn | Aug 1960 - Dec 1982 (Disbanded) |
| 50 Sqn | Aug 1961 - Mar 1984 (Disbanded) |
| 83 Sqn | May 1957 - Oct 1960 (to Scampton) |
| 101 Sqn | Jun 1961 - Aug 1982 (Disbanded) |
| 230 OCU | May 1956 - Jun 1961 (to Finningley) |

Individual squadron details are as follows:

## No 9 Squadron

Unit markings: Green Bat, or Grey Bat, with number 'IX' on yellow background, or grey 'Batman' motif on yellow background.

Formed 1st February 1962 at Coningsby with Vulcan B.2s (having operated EEC Canberras up to July 1961). The unit moved to Cottesmore in November 1964 and then to Akrotiri in Cyprus in February 1969. In January 1975, 9 Squadron returned to the UK to be based at Waddington, where it remained until disbanded on 29th April 1982. (Squadron reformed June 1982 with Panavia Tornado GR.1.)

## No 12 Squadron

Unit marking: Fox's Mask (that is, a front view of the head).

Formed 1st July 1962 at Coningsby with Vulcan B.2s (having operated EEC Canberras until July 1961.) The Squadron moved to Cottesmore in November 1964 and remained there until it was disbanded on 31st December 1967. (Squadron reformed October 1969 with Blackburn Buccaneer S.2.)

## No 27 Squadron

Unit markings: Grey Elephant, or Grey or Blue 'Dumbo' character (after 1973).

Formed 1st April 1961 at Scampton with Vulcan B.2s. The unit had previously flown Canberras from 1953 to 1956. No 27 was disbanded on 29th March 1972, but was reformed on 1st November 1973 at Waddington with the Vulcan B.2(MRR) for the 'Maritime Reconnaissance Role'. This version of the Vulcan is sometimes recorded as the SR.2 (SR for Strategic Reconnaissance). The Squadron was disbanded on 31st March 1982. (Squadron reformed August 1983 with Panavia Tornado GR.1.)

## No 35 Squadron

Unit markings: A black or grey winged horse's head with yellow mane and wings, or stylised number '35' in yellow on grey background.

Formed 1st December 1962 at Coningsby with Vulcan B.2s. It had previously flown Canberras until 1961. The unit moved to Cottesmore in November 1964, and then to Akrotiri in Cyprus in January 1969. No 35 then returned to Scampton in January 1975 with the rundown of the Near East Air Force. The Squadron disbanded on 28th February 1982.

**XM575 of No 44 Squadron.** via Tony Buttler

## No 44 Squadron

Unit marking: Stylised number '44' in grey on white background.

Formed 10th August 1960 at Waddington with Vulcan B.1s. As with most other Vulcan units, No 44 had earlier flown Canberras in Bomber Command. The B.1/B.1A Vulcans gave way to the B.2 version in November 1967. No 44 remained at Waddington until disbanded on 31st December 1982.

## No 50 Squadron

Unit markings: Two red running dingoes.

Formed 1st August 1961 at Waddington with its Vulcan B.1s mainly coming from No 617 Squadron when the latter received the B.2 version. No 50 started to re-equip with the B.2 in December 1965. During the Falklands War in 1982, the unit converted to the tanker role, with its aircraft being modified to K.2 standard. The Squadron disbanded on 31st March 1984, the last Squadron to fly the Vulcan.

## No 83 Squadron

Unit marking: Brown deer's antler with six tines.

Formed 21st May 1957 at Waddington with Vulcan B.1s. It had previously flown the Lincoln B.2 in Bomber Command, until 1955. In August 1960 its B.1 Vulcans were handed over to the re-forming No 44 Squadron and No 83 moved to RAF Scampton where it received new Vulcan B.2s in December. No 83 disbanded on 19th July 1969 although it remained nominally in existence until 31st August 1969.

## No 101 Squadron

Unit marking: Stylised number '101' in red, with a rampant lion on battlements within the zero of '101'.

Formed 15th October 1957 at Finningley with Vulcan B.1s, having been a Canberra unit until the previous year. Moved to Waddington in June 1961 and received B.2 Vulcans there in January 1968. No 101 disbanded on 4th August 1982. (Reformed May 1984 with Vickers VC.10 K.2/K.3.)

## No 617 Squadron

Unit markings: Three red lightning flashes, or within a diamond surround, three red lightning flashes striking a yellow wall and releasing water.

Formed 1st May 1958 at Scampton with Vulcan B.1s, having earlier flown the Canberra. The B.1 Vulcans were replaced by the B.2 version in September 1961. No 617 disbanded on 31st December 1981 (reformed January 1983 with Panavia Tornado GR.1).

Other units operating the Vulcan at various times were:

## Bomber Command Development Unit

The Bomber Command Development Unit was a solely Royal Air Force unit, first formed in 1954 at RAF Wittering, although for several years it had no established aircraft strength, 'borrowing' aircraft from operational squadrons as and when any were required for particular trials. On 1st June 1959 a Trials Flight was formed, receiving three Vickers Valiants, and soon afterwards a number of English Electric Canberras. During February 1960 the BCDU moved from Wittering to Finningley. The BCDU operated examples of the Vulcan B.1 and B.1A (XA895, XA907, XA911) between June 1961 to November 1966, and a Vulcan B.2 (XL391) from July 1965 to January 1966. No unit markings were worn, although one aircraft wore the unit's title on its fin. On the amalgamation of Fighter and Bomber Commands as Strike Command on 1st April 1968, the Unit became the Strike Command Development Unit and was disbanded on 31st December 1968. Sub-

sequently, all operational equipment trials were conducted by the A&AEE.

## No 4 Joint Services Trial Unit

During much of the post-war period, operational trials and experiments with British guided missiles and other weapons systems were often carried out at the Long Range Weapons Establishment (otherwise titled the Weapons Research Establishment, WRE) at Woomera in Australia. This was an Establishment run jointly by the British and Australian Governments. The Headquarters of the Establishment was at a former explosives factory near Salisbury in South Australia, but the associated bombing ranges and other facilities were spread over a wide area in several Australian states. The Royal Australian Air Force provided maintenance facilities for trials aircraft at Edinburgh Field, although many of the aircraft remained 'on charge' with the Royal Air Force or 'Ministry' establishments such as RAE or A&AEE. If 'target' aircraft such as pilotless Meteors, Canberras or Jindiviks were needed, these were provided by No 1 or No 2 Air Trials Units of the RAAF, while the weapons systems would be operated by numbered 'Joint Services Trials Units' (JSTUs) composed of military personnel from the services involved with the equipment, often supported by civilian staff drawn from contractors and experimental establishments. The Vulcan was involved as one of the 'carriers' of the Avro Blue Steel missile, the trials of which were the responsibility of No 4 JSTU. No 4 JSTU was formed at A V Roe's Woodford site on 1st September 1956 and left for Edinburgh Field in December 1959. Trial launches of Blue Steel from Valiant, Victor and Vulcan aircraft continued from 1960 to 1964 in Australia. Further trials were conducted in the UK by No 18 JSTU based at Scampton, with a small number of missiles being launched by aircraft from various Victor and Vulcan squadrons. No 18 JSTU (which was formed from the UK-based element of No 4 JSTU when the main group of No 4 moved to Australia) did not have any specific aircraft attached, being concerned primarily with the missiles, although it could call on aircraft from No 617 Squadron when trials

required aircraft to be used. The Vulcan B.2 attached to No 4 JSTU was XH539. Although many of the 'JSTUs' were literally 'Joint Service' with involvement of other British and Australian armed services, Nos 4 and 18 were composed of RAF personnel only, although they worked closely with representatives of A V Roe and Elliott Brothers (London) Ltd of Rochester (the latter company made the Blue Steel's Inertial Navigation System).

## No 230 Operational Conversion Unit

Badge: Upright Yellow sword on blue/white 'wave' background.

This unit was first formed at Lindholme in 1947 as the 'Heavy Bomber' conversion unit for the Avro Lincoln, although it was equipped with Lancasters at the time of its formation, these aircraft being taken over from the former No 1653 Conversion Unit at Lindholme. After being disbanded in 1955, No 230 OCU reformed on 31st May 1956 at Waddington as the Vulcan training unit. The first Vulcan B.1 (XA895) was delivered to the unit in August 1956, and the first B.2 (XH558) in July 1960. The OCU moved to Finningley on 18th June 1961 and then to Scampton on 8th December 1969. It was disbanded on 31st August 1981. The OCU flew more examples of the Vulcan than any other unit. (Vulcan operations actually finished in June 1981.)

## Vulcan Display Flight

The Vulcan Display Flight was formed at Waddington on 1st April 1984, having previously operated as the 'Vulcan Display Team' within No 55 Squadron (a Handley Page Victor unit based at Marham). The sole purpose of the Flight was to display one of the surviving Vulcan B.2s at air displays and other events. The Vulcans flown were XL426 and XH558. The unit disbanded in 1992 following the retirement and sale of XH558.

Individual Squadron markings are shown in a separate section. These were normally painted on the vertical fin of the aircraft, although occasionally also on the crew entry door below the fuselage. Unit badges were also sometimes painted on aircraft noses aft of the roundel or on the crew entry door. In addition to Squadron markings, Finningley and Waddington-based aircraft often wore a 'Wing' marking denoting their parent station, as did Coningsby aircraft for a brief period. Another variation was used on aircraft participating in USAF Strategic Air Command bombing and navigation competitions in the USA, where the 'Panther' marking of No 1 Group was painted on fins. This arose because all Vulcan units belonged to No 1 Group, and the crews in the competition might be drawn from any of the No 1 Group units. At least two of the Vulcan aircraft now preserved in the USA wear this marking.

# Survivors

The list below identifies the surviving Vulcan complete airframes and cockpit sections still in existence as we go to press, although at least one example (XM603) is under threat of being scrapped. (Locations shown in brackets are not publicly accessible)

**Avro 707A**
WD280    RAAF Museum, Point Cook, Victoria, Australia
WZ736    Museum of Science & Industry, Manchester

**Avro 707C**
WZ744    Cosford Aerospace Museum, Shropshire

**Avro Vulcan B.1** (cockpits)
XA893    Cosford Aerospace Museum, Shropshire
XA903    Wellesbourne Wartime Museum, Wellesbourne Mountford Airfield, near Stratford on Avon, Warwickshire

**Avro Vulcan B.2** (cockpits)
XH537    Bournemouth Aviation Museum, Hurn Airport, Dorset
XH560    (The Cockpit Collection, Rayleigh, Essex)

XH563    Cold War Jets Collection, Bruntingthorpe, Leicestershire
XL388    Aeroventure Museum, Doncaster, South Yorkshire
XL445    Norfolk and Suffolk Aviation Museum, Flixton, near Bungay. Suffolk
XM569    (Jet Age Museum, Gloucester)
XM602    Vulcan to the Sky Trust, Bruntingthorpe
XM652    Military Aircraft Cockpit Collection, Welshpool, Montgomeryshire.

**Avro Vulcan B.2** (complete)
XH558    Vulcan to the Sky Trust, Bruntingthorpe, Leicestershire, as G-VLCN. To fly 2007.
XJ823    Solway Aviation Museum, Carlisle Airport, Cumbria
XJ824    Imperial War Museum, Duxford, Cambridgeshire
XL318    Royal Air Force Museum, Hendon, London
XL319    North East Aircraft Museum, Usworth, Sunderland
XL360    Midland Air Museum, Coventry Airport, Warwicks.

XL426    Vulcan Restoration Trust, Southend Airport, Essex
XM573    Offutt AFB, Omaha, Nebraska, USA
XM575    Aeropark, East Midlands Airport, Leicestershire.
XM594    Newark Air Museum, Winthorpe Showground, Nottinghamshire.
XM597    Museum of Flight, East Fortune Airfield, near East Linton, to the East of Edinburgh.
XM598    National Cold War Exhibition, Cosford Aerospace Museum, Shropshire
XM603    (Avro Heritage Centre, Woodford Airfield)
XM605    Castle Air Museum, California, USA
XM606    Barksdale AFB, Louisiana, USA
XM607    8779M, displayed at RAF Waddington, Lincs.
XM612    City of Norwich Aviation Museum, Norwich Airport, Norfolk
XM655    XM655 Preservation Society, Wellesbourne Mountford Airfield, near Stratford on Avon, Warwicks.

**XH558 on take-off showing the heat haze behind the engines, at a RIAT display.** Eric Morgan

# Vulcans in Colour

No original colour pictures of Avro 707B VX790 are known to the authors. However Russell Adams, the famous photographer who worked with Gloster Aircraft in the 1950s, did photograph this aeroplane in colour, but his transparencies appear no longer to exist. This scan, made from a printed advertisement for A V Roe & Company, almost certainly shows one of his images.

The first Avro 707A, WD280, seen here in the RAAF Museum at Point Cook, near Melbourne, on 16th February 2003. This 707 was used for trials in Australia before being sold as surplus and eventually making its way to the Museum. Gerry Manning

The second 707A, WZ736, at Finningley on 14th September 1968, where it was in storage on behalf of the RAF Museum and was statically displayed on 'Battle of Britain' open days. This aircraft is now in the Manchester Museum of Science and Industry. Phil Butler C11610

The two-seat Avro 707C, WZ744, also at Finningley on 14th September 1968. This example was also held on behalf of the RAF Museum, and later went to the Cosford Aerospace Museum, where it remains on display. Phil Butler C11612

The Conway-powered VX777, landing at the SBAC Show at Farnborough in September 1957. Peter Berry

VX777, the second Avro 698 prototype, photographed at Farnborough during the SBAC Show on 7th September 1962. The prototype had by then been retired and was used for ground-based resonance testing. Tony Griffiths

The second production Vulcan B.1, XA890, photographed during the 1955 SBAC Show at Farnborough. The marking on the fin is the 'Avro' logo. Peter Berry

Vulcan B.1 XA890 at RAF Abingdon on 14th September 1963. This aircraft was flown by the Royal Aircraft Establishment at Farnborough for armament and equipment trials and remained in its silver colours throughout its life.
via Terry Panopalis

XA892, shown marked as 7746M at Halton after becoming an instructional airframe. It remained in the silver colour scheme, never having served with an operational squadron. The code '16' is another Halton-applied identity code.
via Terry Panopalis

XA898 was photographed during a visit to Westover Air Force Base in Massachusetts during May 1961. At the time it belonged to No 230 OCU and wears the Waddington station badge. via Terry Panopalis

XA898 is seen again here at RAF Finningley on 14th September 1963, still with No 230 OCU which in the meantime had moved to Finningley. via Terry Panopalis

A final shot of XA898 shows it at Halton as 7856M of No 1 School of Technical Training, after becoming a Ground Instructional Airframe. The code number '30' was applied at Halton. via Terry Panopalis

The Vulcan XA903, modified as a flying test-bed for the Bristol Olympus 593 engine for the BAC/Aérospatiale Concorde, flying past at Farnborough on 21st September 1968.
Phil Butler C11718

Another flying shot of XA903, also at Farnborough on 21st September 1968.
Gerry Manning

A shot of XA903 in its RB.199 test-bed configuration, making its last landing at RAE Farnborough on 1st March 1979.
RAE via Terry Panopalis

Vulcan B.1 XA903 in the white overall scheme, but showing the style used before the introduction of 'toned-down' anti-flash national markings on operational aircraft. via Phil Butler

Vulcan B.1A XA907 of the BCDU at Finningley on 19th September 1964, by now camouflaged and fitted with a flight-refuelling probe on its nose. Tony Griffiths

This air-to-air shot shows Vulcan B.1s XA896, XH503 and XH504 of No 230 OCU in September 1959, all in the original white colour scheme. All three carry the Waddington station badge. MoD T1191 via Tony Buttler

This take-off shot shows a Waddington Vulcan, with two others visible.
MoD T1908/1 via Tony Buttler

XH476, another B.1A, photographed at its home base of Waddington on 19th September 1964, also camouflaged. The enlarged tailcone of the B.1A is well shown in this view. No squadron or station markings are worn, but XH476 belonged to the Waddington Wing at the time, and was probably with No 44 Squadron. Tony Griffiths

XH481 of No 101 Squadron is seen here at the RAF Church Fenton Battle of Britain Display on 20th September 1958. via Terry Panopalis

An air-to-air shot of B.1 XH497 in the white colour scheme with no unit markings. via Terry Panopalis

A view of Vulcan B.1A XH503, at Waddington on 9th September 1964. Note that both this aircraft and XH476 wore their serial numbers repeated on the inner main undercarriage doors. No unit markings are shown, but this one was probably with No 44 Squadron at the time. Gerry Manning

Another view of a Vulcan B.1A shows XH505 at Finningley on 14th September 1963, wearing the Waddington Wing marking. via Terry Panopalis

This shot shows Vulcan B.2(MRR) XH534 at Finningley on 30th July 1977, wearing camouflage and one of the later-style 'Dumbo' markings of No 27 Squadron. Gerry Manning

Vulcan B.2 XH535 is shown over Edwards Air Force Base in the Mojave Desert, California, in formation with Boeing B-52H 60-0006 during the Vulcan's visit to the USA for Electro-Magnetic Compatibility testing in connection with the Skybolt project in June/July 1961.
via Terry Panopalis

This shot shows B.2 XH539 of the A&AEE at Boscombe Down during an Open Day on 18th March 1971. It had earlier been the first Vulcan to fire a Blue Steel missile during trials at Woomera, but was by now engaged in conventional armament trials at Boscombe. It wears the toned-down national markings on its white finish, and a USAF Systems Command badge (a 'zap' from a visit to the USA) on its fin. It never served with a squadron, but ended its days at Waddington as a crash-rescue training item. Gerry Manning

B.2 XH554 is shown here making a slow flypast at Valley on 13th August 1977. The unit marking of No 230 OCU appears on its fin. Gerry Manning

B.2 XH558, the 'Vulcan to the Sky' survivor, seen here at the International Air Tattoo at Greenham Common on 22nd July 1983 in the markings of No 50 Squadron (two running dingoes in red), with the Waddington station badge. Gerry Manning

This view shows B.2 XH559 at Finningley on 30th July 1977, wearing the markings of No 35 Squadron. Gerry Manning

**XH560 is shown here as a B.2[MRR] of No 27 Squadron, at McClellan AFB, Sacramento, California in December 1975. It is carrying its atmospheric-sampling pods.** Terry Panopalis

**This photograph shows XH560 after conversion to a K.2 tanker, during its trials at A&AEE Boscombe Down. The red-and-white markings are to guide potential receivers of fuel.** via Terry Panopalis

**A shot of B.2 XH562 at Leuchars on 2nd September 1978, dwarfing the Scottish Aviation Bulldog of East Lowlands University Air Squadron alongside it. It wears the unit marking of No 230 OCU.** Gerry Manning

Something a little different – this shows XH562 of No 9 Squadron at Ohakea in New Zealand during March 1972, after being 'zapped' by the RNZAF. The Vulcan returned to the UK before the kiwi marks were removed. via Terry Panopalis

Vulcan B.2 XJ823, photographed landing at Finningley on 4th September 1982. It wears No 50 Squadron's markings. Gerry Manning

This photo shows the B.2[MRR] XH563 of No 27 Squadron at Leuchars on 20th September 1975. The 27 Squadron marking is the 'old style' outline of an Indian elephant, later to be superseded by the more colourful 'Dumbo' versions. The aircraft also shows the under-wing atmosphere sampling pods sometimes used by the MRR version. Gerry Manning

Another B.2(MRR) of No 27 Squadron, XJ825, is pictured at Brawdy on 29th May 1980, showing the 27 Squadron 'Dumbo', but no underwing pods, which were only carried when required for particular tasks. Gerry Manning

This photograph shows Vulcan B.2A XL317 of No 617 Squadron in the anti-flash colour scheme (white with toned-down national and Squadron markings), and also carrying a Blue Steel missile. The blue panel below the starboard wing carries defensive electronic equipment, the Red Shrimp jammer. via Tony Buttler

This picture of B.2 XL320 was taken at Wattisham on 16th September 1972. The aircraft wears the badge of No 230 OCU. Also visible in this shot is the flight-refuelling probe and the small nose radome (terrain-following radar) below the probe, both of these being fitted during upgrades after the initial entry into service. Phil Butler C52002

This image of B.2 XL361 at Finningley on 30th July 1977 shows the later markings of No 617 Squadron, based on their official squadron badge. Gerry Manning

The air-to-air shot shown here is of camouflaged XL-serialled B.2A carrying a Blue Steel missile. via Terry Panopalis

A photo taken at Toronto in August 1968 shows XL386 and XL389 of the Scampton Wing, in identical camouflage schemes. via Terry Panopalis

Opposite page:

This view shows XL387, XH557 (of 9 Squadron) and XM606 (of 50 Squadron) at Offutt AFB in Nebraska during the Strategic Air Command Bombing Competition in April 1980. Note that the furthest aircraft has the 'wraparound' camouflage that was applied to many low-level-role aircraft after experience during Red Flag exercises in the USA. via Terry Panopalis

This photo of XL387 shows the 'toned-down' white anti-flash scheme worn earlier by the Vulcan. It also shows the Finningley station badge worn by this No 230 OCU aircraft, when photographed at Gaydon in September 1963. Tony Griffiths

Shown in this shot is Vulcan B.2 XL388 of No 44 Squadron, taken flying past with its air brakes extended at Leuchars during the Battle of Britain Display on 4th September 1976. Gerry Manning

This page:

XL389 of No 9 Squadron is shown at Finningley on 30th July 1977, carrying the Waddington badge in addition to the 'bat' of 9 Squadron. Gerry Manning

XL390 was photographed at RAF St Athan on 18th September 1971 and wears no unit markings, although it was with No 617 Squadron at the time. Phil Butler C41707

This photo shows an example of a Vulcan B.2 (XL425) camouflaged all over and bearing No 617 Squadron markings. During steep turns at low-altitude the former grey undersides stood out, so the camouflage was extended also to the lower surfaces for those units operating at low-level. Photo taken at Mildenhall, 24th August 1980. Gerry Manning

This photo shows the Vulcan Demonstration Flight B.2, XL426, during a show at Liverpool Airport on 19th August 1984, very shortly after the VDF was formed. Phil Butler C110819

XL427 is seen here at Finningley on 2nd September 1978, wearing the Waddington station badge and those of No 9 Squadron. Phil Butler C100604

This view shows B.2 XL445 of the Cottesmore Wing in July 1968, wearing no unit markings. via Terry Panopalis

XL446, seen here at Wethersfield on 1st July 1967 is from the Waddington Wing, but wears no unit markings. via Terry Panopalis

very clean looking XM570 seen at Waddington on 19th September 1964. Although with No 27 Squadron it carries no unit markings. Tony Griffiths

view of K.2 tanker XM571, trailing its refuelling drogue. It still wears No 101 Squadron markings, relic of its pre-tanker service. Joe L'Estrange

Vulcan B.2 XM572 landing at Akrotiri during the time that Nos 9 and 35 Squadrons constituted the Near East Air Force Bomber Wing. Rolls-Royce E176570 via Tony Buttler

XM572 is pictured at McClellan AFB in March 1978, wearing 35 Squadron markings. via Terry Panopalis

XM595 appeared at the SBAC Show at Farnborough and was photographed on 12th September 1964. Again it carried no unit markings, although allotted to No 617 Squadron at the time. Tony Griffiths

XM595 appeared seven years later at the display at Alconbury on 14th August 1971, this time wearing the markings of 27 Squadron, although it is recorded with 617 Squadron again by this date. The unit markings may be a throwback to previous service (recorded as '27/617 Squadrons') from the previous year. Phil Butler C41404

XM597 was photographed at Waddington in July 1974 and wears the Wing markings. It has the ARI 18228/1 radar warning receiver at the top of its fin. via Terry Panopalis

XM597 was photographed at Finningley on 4th September 1982, wearing the Waddington station badge but no Squadron markings. It is believed to have been on the strength of No 44 Squadron at the time. Gerry Manning

A view of XM602 landing at London, Ontario, on 7th June 1981, streaming its landing parachute. It wears the markings of No 101 Squadron and the Waddington Wing. Terry Panopalis

Another view of XM602 during its flying display at London on 7th June 1981. Terry Panopalis

This photo of XM605 was taken at Finningley on 30th July 1977 and shows the markings of No 101 Squadron in addition to the Waddington badge.
Phil Butler C92502

XM606 flying in the USA during the 1974 'Giant Voice' competition (won by the Vulcans on that occasion). via Terry Panopalis

XM607 is also shown at Finningley on 30th July 1977, wearing the markings of No 44 Squadron.
Gerry Manning

XM609 completes the trio of Vulcans photographed at Finningley on 30th July 1977, a good day for looking at Vulcans! This one is also wearing the markings of No 44 Squadron. Gerry Manning

XM609 is seen again here, making a flypast at a display at Booker (Wycombe Air Park) on 29th July 1973. It wears the Waddington Wing marking without a Squadron badge and also a Union Flag on its fin. Phil Butler C62117

XM646 was another participant in the Review at Finningley on 30th July 1977, this time wearing the markings of No 9 Squadron. Gerry Manning

This page:

**This flying shot of XM650 was taken at Leuchars on 20th September 1975 and shows the aircraft wearing No 44 Squadron markings.** Gerry Manning

**A later Leuchars display included XM651, seen here on 2nd September 1978 with No 50 Squadron markings.** Gerry Manning

**XM652 was photographed at Finningley on 21st September 1974 wearing its Waddington Wing markings.** via Terry Panopalis

Opposite page:

**XM653 of the Waddington Wing was photographed at Barksdale AFB in November 1974. It wears the Union Flag on its fin and also has the Panther of No 1 Group aft of the roundel.** via Terry Panopalis

**A typical scene on a V-Bomber airfield during the Force's existence would be four Vulcans on their Operational Readiness Platform, ready to go – as seen here at Finningley for a demonstration on 19th September 1981. They include one example from each Squadron of the Waddington Wing (XM575 of No 44), XL359 (of No 35), XL444 (of No 9), and XM646 (of No 101).** Gerry Manning

**Preserved examples have included XM603, repainted in the white colour scheme. Sadly, given politically-correct attitudes to 'Health & Safety', volunteers were banned from working on the airframe and as this is written this valuable aircraft is about to be scrapped.** via Phil Butler

Top: **XM573 is still preserved at Offutt AFB, Omaha, Nebraska, in the USA. Note the No 1 Group 'Panther' badge on its fin. Photo dated 28th July 1986.** Gerry Manning

Above: **XM605 is also preserved at Castle Air Museum at the former Castle AFB in California. Photo dated 2nd October 1984. It also wears the No 1 Group badge.** Gerry Manning

Left: **This photograph, taken at RAF Gan in the Maldive Islands, shows the style of markings painted on the crew access door – here the markings of Nos 9, 12 and 35 Squadrons (the Coningsby Wing) are displayed.** Joe L'Estrange

Opposite page:

**The badges shown here are representative of those worn by Vulcans during their long years of service.** Illustrations by David Howley

1 Group

1 Group

Waddington Wing

Waddington Wing

Finningley Wing

230 OCU

9 Squadron

9 Squadron

12 Squadron

27 Squadron

27 Squadron

35 Squadron

35 Squadron

44 Squadron

50 Squadron

83 Squadron

101 Squadron

617 Squadron

617 Squadron

617 Squadron

## GLOSTER METEOR
Britain's Celebrated First-Generation Jet

Phil Butler and Tony Buttler

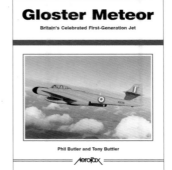

This is a celebration of one of the most successful British aircraft of all time. The Gloster Meteor first flew during World War Two and served with 16 overseas air forces as well as the RAF.

The book has a strong emphasis on the design and development of the aircraft and its initial flight testing. There are numerous data tables and details of the serials carried by the aircraft, plus many previously unpublished or relatively unknown photographs, including some rare early colour shots.

Softback, 280 x 215 mm, 144 pages
181 b/w, 71 colour photographs
978 1 85780 230 6  **£19.99**

## VICKERS VALIANT
The First V-Bomber

Eric B Morgan

The Valiant was the shortest-lived of the post-war V-bombers, first flying in 1951 and with production of 104 aircraft ending in 1957, and official withdrawal in January 1965 after investigation had shown that the main wing spars were suffering from metal fatigue. Valiants participated in British atomic bomb tests and made noteworthy long-distance flights, principally operating from Marham and Gaydon. Includes a full listing of each aircraft's history.

Softback, 280 x 215 mm, 128 pages,
155 b/w and colour photographs
978 1 85780 134 7  **£14.99**

## FARNBOROUGH
100 Years of British Aviation

Peter J Cooper

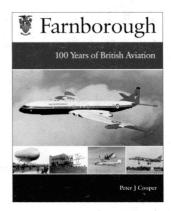

Home to the famous biennial Farnborough Air Show, this Hampshire town has had a pivotal role in the history of British aviation from 1905 when flying first commenced there.

This fully illustrated history portrays in words and nearly 400 mono and colour illustrations the airfield and the many and varied aircraft associated with it. In the course of his research, the author has unearthed a large number of previously unpublished images which appear in the book.

Hardback, 282 x 213 mm, 208 pages
173 colour, 200 b/w photographs
978 1 85780 239 9  **£24.99**

## BRITISH SECRET PROJECTS
Jet Fighters Since 1950

Tony Buttler

A huge number of fighter projects have been drawn by British companies over the last 50 years, in particular prior to the 1957 White Paper, but with few turned into hardware, little has been published about these fascinating 'might-have-beens'. Emphasis is placed on some of the events which led to certain aircraft either being cancelled or produced. Some of the varied types included are the Hawker P.1103/P.1136/ P.1121 series, and the Fairey 'Delta III'

Hbk, 282 x 213 mm, 176 pages
90 b/w photos, 8 pages of colour,
plus 140 three-view drawings
978 1 85780 095 1  **£24.95**

## BRITISH SECRET PROJECTS
Jet Bombers Since 1949

Tony Buttler

This long-awaited title forms a natural successor to the author's successful volume on fighters. The design and development of the British bomber since World War II is covered in similar depth and again the emphasis is placed on the tender design competitions between projects from different companies. The design backgrounds to the V-Bomber programme, Canberra, Buccaneer, Avro 730, TSR.2, Harrier, Jaguar and Tornado are revealed.

Hbk, 282 x 213 mm, 224 pages
160 b/w photos, 9 pages of colour,
plus line drawings
978 1 85780 130 9  **£24.99**

## BRITISH SECRET PROJECTS
Fighters & Bombers 1935-1950

Tony Buttler

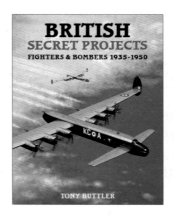

This volume again places the emphasis on unbuilt designs that competed with those that flew, and covers aircraft influenced by World War Two – projects that were prepared from the mid-1930s in the knowledge that war was coming through to some which appeared after the war was over. The latter includes early jets such as the Attacker, Sea Hawk and Venom which all flew post-war but to wartime or just post-war requirements.

Hbk, 282 x 213 mm, 240 pages
205 b/w, 16 colour photos,
plus line drawings
978 1 85780 179 8  **£29.99**

## BRITISH SECRET PROJECTS
Hypersonics, Ramjets & Missiles

Chris Gibson and Tony Buttler

Deals with the advanced projects through which the aviation industry sought to further high-speed flight, to prolong the effectiveness of the V-bomber force in defending the country against nuclear attack, or to develop increasingly sophisticated missiles to counter the latest threat. The book includes a detailed rundown of colour codes such as Blue Danube, Green Satin and Red Beard, used when Cold War deception was at its height.

Hbk, 282 x 213 mm, c192 pages
c300 b/w and colour illustrations,
plus drawings
978 1 85780 258 0  July  **£24.99**

# QUALITY AVIATION MAGAZINES

## Aircraft ILLUSTRATED Monthly

- Unbeatable coverage of the complete aviation scene - military, civil, both past and present by leading journalists
- Unrivalled coverage of the airshow scene - news, previews, interviews, 'in cockpit' reports and much more
- Stunning images from the world's top aviation photographers, including many exclusives from John Dibbs
- Special supplements
- Major competitions and much more

### THE AVIATION MAGAZINE WITH EVERYTHING!

## Combat AIRCRAFT Bi-monthly

- Enjoy unmatched analysis of the world's military aircraft and the forces that fly them
- Over 100 fabulous action photographs every issue, taken by some of the best photographers on the planet
- Magnificent colour artwork, plus detailed cutaways
- Simply the best coverage of men, the machines and the missions that make up today's world of military aviation

### THE WORLD'S LEADING MILITARY AVIATION MAGAZINE!

Available from all leading newsagents and hobby stores, or order direct from:

Subscription Dept, Ian Allan Publishing Ltd, Riverdene Business Park, Molesey Road, Hersham, Surrey  KT12 4RG  UK

**Tel:** +44(0) 1932 266622  **Fax:** +44(0) 1932 266633  **e-mail:** subs@ianallanpub.co.uk

Top: **An anonymous Vulcan B.2 flying past at a display at Sleap airfield in May 1969.** Phil Butler

Above: **A landing shot of XH558 at an air display while with the Vulcan Display Team.** via Phil Butler

Front cover illustration:
**This view shows a fly-past by XH558 during its days with the Vulcan Display Flight.**
via Phil Butler

An imprint of
Ian Allan Publishing

**www.ianallanpublishing.com**

ISBN 978-1-85780-256-6

9 781857 802566

USA $35.95  UK £19.99

Printed in England